BELOVED
COUNTRY

BELOVED COUNTRY

SOUTH AFRICA'S
SILENT WARS

DANIEL REED

BBC BOOKS

This book is published to accompany the
television series entitled Beloved Country
which was first broadcast in Spring 1994

Published by BBC Books,
a division of BBC Enterprises Limited,
Woodlands, 80 Wood Lane, London W12 0TT

First published 1994

ISBN 0 563 36963 9

Map by Technical Art Services

Set in Monophoto Ehrhardt by Ace Filmsetting Ltd, Frome
Printed in England by Clays Ltd, St Ives plc
Jacket printed by Belmont Press Ltd, Northampton

Contents

Acknowledgements

Hundreds of South Africans took the time to talk to me, despite the pressures of the conflict around them and the considerable hazard posed by speaking candidly to a journalist. Many did so in the belief that if the world at large were able to glimpse beyond the political circus of high-level negotiations at the underlying civil strife in South Africa, then something might be done to alleviate it. The fear shared by most contributors, sadly, was that even a general election would not bring peace to the 'beloved country'. May they be proved wrong.

South African journalists Enoch Mthembu and Wally Mbhele shared the dangers and the excitement of several research trips, providing invaluable local knowledge; Irwin 'Che' Kinnes of the ANC, whose quick wits and savvy in the Cape Flats ganglands averted disaster on at least one occasion, shared memorable take-away coffees outside Vinoos' in Gatesville. Sources in Phola Park, Tokoza and Katlehong, who must unfortunately remain nameless, spent long hours sifting through unpleasant memories of the recent past. Lauren Segal graciously gave me access to research material which she gathered in 1991 while writing a paper for the Centre for the Study of Violence and Reconciliation at Wits University. Jacob and Mary, and Rashied, Rashad and the HLs tolerated my frequent intrusions into their private worlds.

The opportunity to write this book was, of course, provided by the BBC. Paul Hamann, Head of Documentaries, launched the timely and ambitious television series which sent our team to South Africa for the best part of a year. Chris Terrill, the Series Producer, was supportive and understanding in the weeks when the demands of writing conflicted with those of film-making. Kelly Davis, who edited the text, was always sensitive and encouraging. My thanks to them all, and to everyone at BBC Books, especially Sheila Ableman and Martha Caute, for their support while I was writing the book.

Daniel Reed, Cape Town, South Africa
November 1993

Note: In a few instances names have been changed or omitted in order not to place individuals at risk.

To B.S

Hard life in South Africa
what a waste of strength and power
in our fatherland
with talks of all kinds
shadowed by massacres and township carnage

O! what a delay to our dreams of freedom
and permanent liberation of the
human race
with all multi-talks undermined
and worthless

Yet back to Africa and the world
I must return
to revise the struggle
that teaches me
not to relax too long
around the table of reforms
but bullet must conclude
to pave the way to freedom
in defence of our people against the wicked partner

TURNIER CEBA, ANC YOUTH LEAGUE, PHOLA PARK

We lack the natural cohesion of a single culture and language that frequently forms the cornerstone of nationhood. Consequently, we shall have to rely heavily on the other cornerstone - that of common values and ideals.

STATE PRESIDENT F. W. DE KLERK, 'MANIFESTO FOR THE NEW SOUTH AFRICA', FEBRUARY 1991

The only shared culture in South Africa is the culture of killing.

BREYTEN BREYTENBACH, AFRIKANER POET

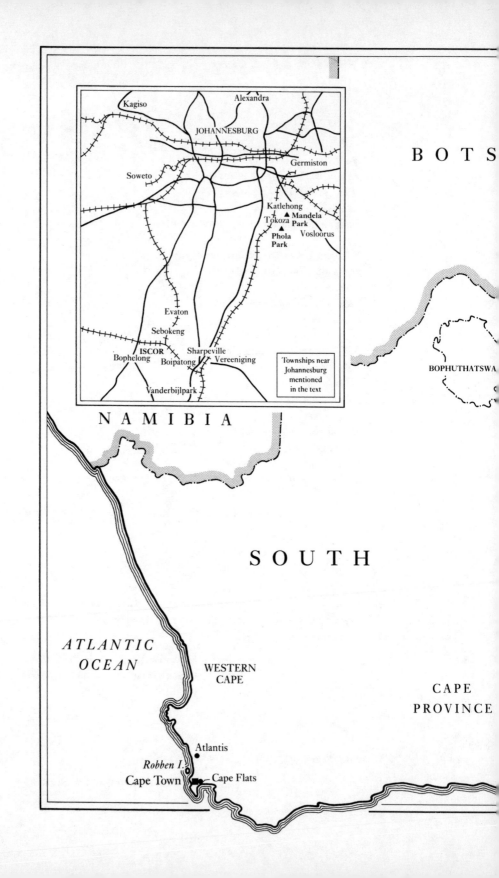

Kagiso

Alexandra

JOHANNESBURG

Germiston

Soweto

Katlehong
Tokoza ▲ Mandela
Park
▲
Phola Vosloorus
Park

Evaton

Sebokeng

ISCOR Sharpeville
Bophelong Boipatong Vereeniging

Vanderbijlpark

Townships near
Johannesburg
mentioned
in the text

B O T S

BOPHUTHATSWA

N A M I B I A

S O U T H

ATLANTIC
OCEAN

WESTERN
CAPE

CAPE
PROVINCE

Atlantis

Robben I.
Cape Town Cape Flats

ZIMBABWE

WANA

VENDA

EASTERN
TRANSVAAL

T R A N S V A A L

MOZAMBIQUE

BOPHUTHATSWANA

BOPHUTHATSWANA

BOPHUTHATSWANA

■ Pretoria

■ Johannesburg

SWAZILAND

OPHUTHATSWANA

Volksrust
Charlestown

ZULU
LAND

O R A N G E   F R E E   S T A T E

NATAL

Ulundi

MSINGA   Nkandla   Enseleni

■ Kimberley

Tugela R.

Esikawini

Bloemfontein

MIDLANDS

Pietermaritzburg

LESOTHO

Edendale ●■

KwaMashu

Durban ■

F R I C A

TRANSKEI

TRANSKEI

N

TRANSKEI

Umtata ■

INDIAN OCEAN

EASTERN
CAPE

CISKEI

Grahamstown ■

East London

KwaZulu

East Rand

Vaal Triangle

■
Port Elizabeth

The Sunday War

South Africa is in the grip of a bitter civil war, but only on Sundays. That's the way it often seems in this schizophrenic country, for the factional violence in the Black townships becomes newsworthy only if two dozen or more people are slaughtered in a single incident. By some bizarre coincidence these massacres usually take place on a Sunday. For the rest of the week South Africa clings to a deceptive normality, displaying an apparent indifference to the suffering of its Black citizens. Yet this unacknowledged civil war is shaping the new South Africa just as irrevocably as the much-publicized political negotiations.

Since 1990 South Africa has been experiencing the most violent years in its history, a chaotic interregnum euphemistically known as 'a period of transition to a new, democratic South Africa'. So far the transition period, characterized by lengthy negotiations between the White government and its former foes in the newly unbanned African National Congress (ANC), has lasted four years, during which more people have died violently than in the Boer War. Most of these 60 000 deaths, according to the South African Police, have been the result of crime. A mere 14 000 have been classified as 'unrest-related' (attributable to political motives). In practice, however, it is difficult to distinguish between the two, as political and criminal violence in South Africa's townships go hand in hand. When a charred body is found in the street, the police seldom bother to investigate. When the newspapers publish their laconic summary of the previous day's slaughter, the refrain 'the motives for the attack were unknown' appears in every paragraph. In any case, apart from the problems of distinguishing political corpses from non-political ones, the police estimate of the death toll is itself unreliable. A great many killings, both political and criminal, go unreported.

The phrase 'civil war' is controversial in South Africa. The business community knows that talk of civil war frightens off foreign investors. Meanwhile the ANC contends, somewhat disingenuously, that there is no real civil war, and that the violence is being orchestrated exclusively by the regime and its puppets. As long as it is winning the territorial contest on the ground, however, there is no reason for the ANC to acknowledge the crisis and risk postponing its rise to power in the general election. The government, for its part, having initiated the transition to a new South Africa, is anxious to promote the impression that the process is taking place in a controlled and orderly manner. The powers-that-be have effectively combined to hush up the slaughter of Black South Africans in the townships.

Unlike the conflicts in Angola and Bosnia, the South African civil war involves no spectacular displays of artillery, tanks or jets. Instead of standing armies in the field it involves bands of urban guerillas, well-trained hit squads and, in the early stages of the war, massed regiments of several thousand spear-toting warriors. Instead of ranging over open battlefields this war is being fought street by street, village by village, leaving thousands of abandoned homes and bullet-riddled cars. The tens of thousands of casualties and refugees, the many millions of lives poisoned by grief, fear and hatred are no less real than in Somalia or Azerbaijan.

The last four years has seen the militarization of South Africa's Black townships increase to such an extent that the state security forces are now powerless to curb the influx of illegal weapons or the activities of local guerilla units. Tactics have grown more sophisticated, the fighters more disciplined and hardened, the strategies more ruthless, including the 'ethnic cleansing' of civilians from occupied areas.

War has spawned a flourishing economy of gun-runners, professional looters, hired assassins, collectors of war levies and purveyors of battle-medicine, tapping a market worth many millions of rand. South Africa is awash with cheap illegal firearms, from hand guns to assault rifles and grenade-launchers. Violent crime has soared. Fighting has become a way of life, accompanied by a generalized war psychosis. In the East Rand townships (the main war zone in the Transvaal), where two million people are caught up in a fierce territorial war, the average ten-year-old boy can strip down an AK-47 and put it back together again in less time than it takes to build a Lego house. Young children have become inured to the sound of gunfire and the smell of burning human flesh.

Strange though it may seem, the average White South African knows little of all this. The reasons are twofold. Firstly, the civil war takes place exclusively within the confines of Black South Africa. Black South Africa is a place where, as a rule, Whites never set foot. Apartheid's city planners took the precaution of building the Black townships a safe distance from White residential areas, separating them with a security buffer zone at least 20 kilometres wide, referred to by the town planning fraternity as 'a machine-gun belt'. The townships were designed with a small number of exit roads, easily sealed off in the event of a crisis, so all hell can break loose in the Black townships without ruffling the tranquillity of the White suburbs.

Secondly, the (White) South African media has failed to keep the public informed. White journalists seldom enter the townships for more than a few hours at a time, and then only fearfully and when absolutely necessary. For most Whites, therefore, Black South Africa remains a dark, uncharted continent. Editorial indifference, according to a leading White reporter on the Johannesburg *Sunday Times*, is largely to blame.

'There is a low level of interest,' he shrugs. 'People couldn't care less because it's Black people who are dying.'

He attributes the shallow reporting of so-called 'Black on Black violence' to the fact that journalists are bewildered by a changing South Africa. 'It used to be easy . . . You either agreed with the system or you didn't. We could sit around at dinner parties and say how much we hated apartheid. Now we don't know what we feel. We're not used to there being several sides to each story. There are no easy answers any more. Everything is so much more complex.'

The internecine violence in Black South Africa is reported in the form of a body count on the inside pages of South Africa's dailies: 'East Rand killings bring toll to 1200', '544 found dead in East Rand since July 3', '23 die in new Reef attacks', 'Another 17 killed on East Rand' . . . There is seldom any analysis, at best a couple of paragraphs quoting police spokesmen. No attempt is made to put the violence in context, to try to explain or raise questions, let alone write balanced, well-informed stories. The indifference of the South African media means that the events of the civil war (which, while reprehensible, are motivated by military logic) are portrayed as irrational, insane acts of barbarism. This reinforces the prejudice amongst Whites that Blacks are wont to slaughter one another for no apparent reason.

The spilling of White blood, by contrast, calls forth an orgy of reportage, a frantic search for heroes, tear-jerking interviews with relatives, a national outcry. The deaths become meaningful, significant, endowed with a greater logic: 'They did not die in vain'. 'They died for a new South Africa' . . .

A case in point was the Sunday massacre in St James's Church, Cape Town in July 1993, in which Black gunmen opened fire on a White congregation at evening prayer. In the previous two months there had been a number of even more horrifying and bloody massacres on the East Rand. More than 500 Black South Africans had died there in the first three weeks of July alone. The South African Broadcasting Corporation and the national print press (including the left-liberal newspapers) had remained silent on the details of all these killings, reporting only the body counts. When eleven Whites were gunned down in St James' church, the media went berserk. TV audiences were bombarded with dramatic reconstructions of the massacre and soul-searching fireside homilies by leading White churchmen. The St James's Church massacre assumed the proportions of a national tragedy which traumatized White South Africa for a week. That same weekend the toll on the East Rand was fifty-three dead and a couple of hundred seriously wounded. A brief TV bulletin showed bullet-riddled windows and a burning police vehicle. The moving interviews with victims and witnesses, which had characterized the TV coverage of the St James's story, were obviously judged to be inappropriate. This was, after all, just another weekend of 'Black on Black violence'.

Unable to make sense of the carnage, Whites have developed acute violence fatigue. 'Ring-fence the whole bloody lot of them and let them get on with it,' exploded one Johannesburg White over breakfast as news of the latest township massacre came over the radio.

'My mother says the only solution is to drop a bomb on the townships,' said one suburban White woman. Her neighbour nodded: 'I would be very happy if God never created them. Only give me a machine or something to clean the house.'

Many Whites actually believe that people with a darker shade of skin are naturally more violent. ('The darker the skin the more violent the race,' explains one White lady.) Others are genuinely upset and baffled by the relentless killing. An anonymous White caller to Tim Modise's talk show on Radio Metro, an upmarket Black radio station, was incredulous at the drive-by murder of a young mother and her baby at a township taxi rank. He could not comprehend how a man could bring himself to gun down defenceless civilians in cold blood. He asked Tim Modise to explain. The mere fact of being Black did not, of course, give the talk-show host any special insights into violence, which was probably as remote from his own middle-class existence in Johannesburg as it was from his White caller's. Modise struggled valiantly, but no vague sociological platitudes ('scarce resources', lack of education, poor employment opportunities) would satisfy the caller. He rang off sounding baffled.

This book sets out to shed some light on the civil war in South Africa and its social origins. South Africa is moving beyond the simple truths of the struggle against apartheid towards a more fragmented, complicated existence. 'It's helluva complex, hey?' South Africans who have had first-hand experience of the conflict are fond of saying. Are Zulus and Xhosas, the two largest ethnic groups in South Africa, pursuing an age-old tribal vendetta? Or is the fighting the result of a power struggle between the African National Congress (ANC) and the Inkatha Freedom Party (IFP)? Who is fighting whom and why? There are no easy answers to these questions, only 'yes, buts' followed by endless qualifications.

Beloved Country endeavours to piece together a few insights into the violence by placing the war in the context of a massive social upheaval caused by the end of apartheid. It aims to give a sense of how the violence appears to people on the ground, rather than trying to squeeze current events into the familiar (but obsolete) terms of reference of the struggle against apartheid, as most writers still attempt to do. The material in this book comes from the testimony of ordinary victims, eyewitnesses and participants, as well as the author's first-hand experience. Most of these events have never been described before in any detail.

Because the violence in South Africa is so widespread, this book does not claim to offer a comprehensive account of the township wars. Much work remains to be done on the causes of the conflict, including a proper investigation into the activities of government-sponsored *agents provocateurs*, the so-called 'third force' which has undoubtedly helped to inflame township violence, though to what extent is unclear.

Neither can this book claim to be a portrait of South Africa as a whole. In some areas of the country a semblance of peace prevails. That said, outside the White enclaves, where the privileged few live in comfort and tranquillity, South Africa is an extremely troubled and violent land. This book will have achieved its purpose if it introduces the reader to the complex, ambiguous realities of this uncivil war, a world far removed from that of the men in suits who sit around the negotiating table debating South Africa's political future.

Beloved Country focuses on the two geographical areas worst affected by the civil war: the crowded industrial heartland of the southern Transvaal, in the vicinity of the commercial capital Johannesburg; and rural, Zulu-speaking Natal, where lush hills and sugar cane plantations undulate down to the Indian Ocean. The civil war has inflamed numerous other areas, but fighting has been fiercest in these two regions, which have a combined population of some seventeen million people.

Particular attention is devoted to the townships of Katlehong, Tokoza and Phola Park on the East Rand, an industrial zone south-east of Johannesburg. These townships, with a combined population of nearly two million, are South Africa's most deadly killing fields. Phola Park, a largely Xhosa-speaking squatter camp, exemplifies many of the problems and trends found in South Africa's other giant shanty towns, where up to a third of the population lives. The feud between the East Rand townships and the workers' hostels has close parallels in a number of the other townships in the vicinity of Johannesburg, from Soweto in the south to Kagiso in the west and Alexandra in the north of the city.

A brief sketch of the historical background to today's civil war might begin in 1652, when a mob of Dutchmen stumbled ashore and stole a few hectares of land from the local inhabitants to establish a supply station for a Dutch trading company. In the 1830s a few thousand 'Afrikaners', the descendants of those same Dutchmen, took their slaves and trekked north to purloin more land from the Africans. In 1899 the Boer War drove these Afrikaner peasants off their land, turning them into resentful White trash and forcing them to rub shoulders with poor Blacks in the cities. In 1913, after Britain had created South Africa by uniting two of her colonies, the Cape and

Natal, with two conquered Afrikaner republics, the Transvaal and the Orange Free State, the new Afrikaner-led union government passed laws which forced Black South African farmers off the land and into crowded reservations, creating a supply of cheap labour for White farms and mines. In 1948 the newly-elected apartheid government took the policy a step further, envisaging a new South Africa where Blacks would be systematically turned into aliens in their own country. Up to four million Black South Africans were forcibly removed.

Then, in 1960, apartheid began to falter. More than a dozen African countries achieved independence from colonial rule. Harold Macmillan, the British Prime Minister, announced to South African parliamentarians in Cape Town that 'the wind of change' was 'blowing through the continent'. Black political activism in the country intensified before being banned by the government in mid-1960, in the wake of the Sharpeville massacre. In 1976 a move to introduce Afrikaans as the only official medium of instruction in Black schools triggered an uprising of schoolchildren in Soweto. Several rioters were shot dead by police, and a wave of arrests followed. Thousands of angry youths left the country to join the ANC's guerilla army in exile and Black politics suddenly took on a more militant character. A new, dynamic and mercurial Black South African force was born: 'the youth', otherwise known as 'the comrades'.

By the late seventies it became clear that the flow of Black South Africans into the cities and the tide of militancy amongst Black youth could no longer be effectively controlled by the state. Prime Minister Botha's government reached the conclusion that the 'grand apartheid' of the sixties and seventies was in crisis. And Botha warned White South Africans to 'Adapt or die.' Apartheid was revamped, boosting the security apparatus on the one hand while wooing 'moderate' Blacks on the other. One of the tactics adopted was WHAM – Winning Hearts and Minds. WHAM said that the government should let Blacks climb a little way up the social ladder, while keeping them off the top rungs. Blacks were thus allowed to own their own houses, open small businesses and participate in local government. Those who took advantage of these concessions were, however, seen as traitors and victimized by the township youth. In a sense, WHAM worked, polarizing the townships into pro- and anti-government factions.

WHAM was part of the Botha regime's so-called Total Strategy, devised as a response to the Total Onslaught, an imagined Communist conspiracy to take over the world, beginning with South Africa. The Total Strategy called for the militarization of White South Africa under the supervision of the State Security Council, a politburo-style clique of politicians and generals. The ordinary channels of government were bypassed by a National Security Management System, creating a secretive, parallel state in which civilian and military powers were intertwined. A counter-insurgency campaign was launched to weaken anti-government organizations such as the United Democratic Front (UDF). Government death squads assassinated several UDF leaders and other outspoken critics of apartheid. During the uprisings of the eighties tens of thousands of activists were detained and thousands tortured in custody. In 1986, at the height of the insurrection, 500 Blacks were shot dead by the South African Police, more than in any year before or since.

Between 1948 and 1990 South Africa lived under 'ethnic Communism', with nationalized industries and towering bureaucracies which Stalin might well have envied. Like Soviet Communism, however, apartheid was clumsy and expensive. By 1990 the South African economy, starved of foreign investment by sanctions, was deep in recession. In February 1990 the new State President, F.W. de Klerk, unexpectedly announced the unbanning of Black political organizations and the release of jailed ANC leader Nelson Mandela. South Africa was to turn over a fresh leaf and become, in de Klerk's phrase, a 'New South Africa'. Shortly before Mandela's release, de Klerk (later dubbed 'the laas baas', the last White boss) addressed the opening session of parliament with the words: 'The season of violence is over. The time for reconstruction and reconciliation has arrived.' Within six months, however, a civil war was raging in the Black townships of the Transvaal.

PART ONE

The Roots of the Conflict

1 Oklova!

There is one Zulu word which sums up South Africa's longest-running 'low intensity' civil war: *oklova*. *Oklova* is a term of abuse which translates roughly as 'moron', 'monkey' or 'yokel' (interpretations vary). The vowels echo the sucking sound of someone trying to extract his foot from a cowpat. *Oklova* is the most offensive jibe in the repertoire of insults which the young Zulu comrades like to direct at their Inkatha-supporting elders from the peasant villages of KwaZulu.

Zulu society is at odds with itself: country bumpkins versus petty bourgeoisie; unschooled versus schooled; traditional power versus economic power; Inkatha Freedom Party (IFP) versus African National Congress (ANC). Each side has carved out its territory, its zones of control. There are no longer any neutral spaces. The whole of Natal has been divided up.

Inkatha's turf is the dirt-poor villages of Zululand, with their subservient, beleaguered peasant populations. Inkatha secured its power in the rural areas by hijacking Zulu institutions, mobilizing the authority of king, chief and headman for political purposes. 'Inkatha' became a compulsory subject in KwaZulu schools. The IFP has installed itself as the defender of Zulu values and culture while exploiting those same institutions, initially for expansion, now increasingly for mere survival.

Opposing the IFP are schoolchildren, teachers, office and factory workers living in or near the cities of Natal, who clashed with Inkatha during the anti-government uprisings of the eighties. The urban petty bourgeoisie, who saw money rather than tradition as the source of their power, began to view Inkatha as an obstacle to their aspirations, and as an ally of the White government. Between them the two factions have carved up Natal and consolidated their territories by throwing out anyone who doesn't carry the right membership card (smart people carry both). Preparations are afoot for the final phase of the war.

Inkatha is led by old-fashioned strongmen with little or no education. The 'comrades' (ANC, Communist Party) are led by learned feudal barons who like to talk about poetry, European history, or their pet theories on civil service reform. The Zulu civil war is a class war as much as anything, between the yokels and the yuppies. The White government backed the yokels (they knew their place). Zululand went up in flames. Now both sides are locked in an arms race, barricaded inside their strongholds, preparing for the showdown. 'There's a stalemate,' says one observer. 'They're watching each other with hawk eyes.'

Zulu identity has become a taboo issue in progressive circles. ANC Zulus reject the 'postcard Zulu image' of smiling warriors, bare-breasted maidens and the obsession with King Shaka, the Zulu Napoleon who created a military state out of a cluster of small, benign clans. IFP Zulus constantly refer to the great Zulu nation and its glorious history.

Zulu men on both sides of the political and class divide brag about their fighting prowess. King Shaka, who used to have people clubbed to death for sneezing in his presence, transformed Zulu manhood into a military institution. 'Fighting is not a bitches' game,' says Humphrey Ndhlovu, an IFP leader in the Transvaal. 'It's a nice game. We enjoy fighting. It's like eating breakfast,' he adds cryptically.

White boys who grew up on farms in Natal sometimes become obsessed with Zulu machismo. A number of these so-called *Zulu mshlope* (White Zulus) are to be found in senior positions within the IFP. Some are prone to dressing up in skins and fighting with sticks, while others go in for Zulu mysticism and talk about being suckled by a Zulu woman, about the circles of companionship round the fire. ('The second ring of warmth is as close as the White man can get,' says a White farmer who sits on the IFP National Executive.)

Natal–KwaZulu is the South African government's biggest headache. If peace can't be achieved in Natal there can be no conclusive peace in the Johannesburg area because of the large numbers of Zulu migrant workers there. The two military campaigns are interlinked, with both the IFP and the ANC sending men and guns in taxis up to the East Rand when the need arises. Some Zulu-speakers doubt whether there will ever be peace.

'The killers here in South Africa are the Zulus. Wherever there are Zulus there is fighting,' says a young Zulu journalist. 'Zulu culture is violent, every man must carry a stick. It's easy to die in Natal.'

Natal–KwaZulu consists of two distinct but overlapping areas, where most of South Africa's eight and a half million Zulu-speakers reside, the largest ethnic group in the country. KwaZulu, a self-governing 'homeland', was cobbled together from forty-four chunks of non-arable land. This archipelago of scraps of land was declared to be the natural home of all Zulus. Like the other ethnic homelands, KwaZulu was conceived as a reservoir of migrant labour for industries and farms in the adjoining White areas of Natal. In parts of KwaZulu which are poor and far away from local industries, most of the men migrate to the workers' hostels of Johannesburg. Males from other areas work in factories closer to home. Natal, home to 800 000 Indians and 600 000 Whites, contains all the industry, mineral wealth and arable land in the area.

North of the Tugela River, which runs down to the Indian Ocean and divides Natal in two, is the Zulu heartland and the capital of KwaZulu, Ulundi. Ulundi has its own parliament, the KwaZulu Legislative Assembly, and its own police force. The KwaZulu budget is heavily subsidized by the South African government. Ulundi is the seat of the KwaZulu government and the location of the Zulu king's household, as well as the innermost stronghold of the Inkatha Freedom Party. The IFP is unopposed in the KwaZulu Legislative Assembly, and IFP membership in KwaZulu is often less a matter of choice than of necessity.

Inkatha was founded in 1975 by Chief Buthelezi, the leader of the KwaZulu homeland government, at a time of rising labour unrest. In 1973 Durban had been gripped by a wave of strikes. Inkatha started life as a 'National Cultural Liberation Movement' where 'national' meant the Zulu nation and membership was reserved for Zulus. 'The business of Black liberation is our business,' declared Buthelezi at the launch.

The organization took its name from the unifying symbol of the Zulu nation, a sacred coil made of grass smeared with dirt from the king's body. The *inkatha* was 2 feet wide, the thickness of an arm. After drinking *intelezi* (battle-medicine) troops on their way to war made themselves vomit into a pit filled with grass from the royal *kraal* (homestead). The grass was fished out and added to the *inkatha*, which grew in size with every battle. The *inkatha* was destroyed in 1879 when British troops burned the royal *kraal*.

Although Buthelezi and Inkatha appeared initially to identify with the African National Congress, adopting the ANC's black, yellow and green colours, by 1979 the two organizations were at loggerheads. Buthelezi was promoted, particularly outside South Africa, as a moderate critic of apartheid and a possible future candidate for the national leadership.

During the township unrest of the eighties, hundreds died in 'Black on Black violence' in Natal as Inkatha forces clashed violently with the comrades. Inkatha, which was viewed by the state security forces as a pro-government organization, collaborated openly with the South African Police against the ANC-aligned United Democratic Front. By 1987 the disagreements between Inkatha and the ANC had turned into open warfare.

In 1990, in an attempt to rid Inkatha of its exclusively Zulu image and compete nationally against the ANC, Buthelezi relaunched his organization as the Inkatha Freedom Party, 'an all South-African political party' whose membership was now open to all comers, including Whites.

A year later the IFP was severely embarrassed when it emerged that the party had received secret funding from the South African Police. Shortly afterwards the Minister for Law and Order admitted that the police were also funding an IFP-aligned labour union. The 'Inkathagate' scandal dented Buthelezi's already fragile credibility as a national leader, bolstering the ANC's claims that he was a puppet of the South African government.

2 Little Hendrik the Dike-Builder

For centuries the Dutch have lived with the fear of floods. Large parts of the Netherlands lie below sea level. The Dutch supposedly have an inborn respect for dikes. Little Hendrik Verwoerd was no exception, despite the fact that he left Amsterdam for Africa at the age of two. Little Hendrik grew up to become the most notorious dike-builder of the century.

As Minister of Native Affairs, one of a clique of fascist Afrikaners in the new government of 1948, Hendrik set out to safeguard the future security and prosperity of White South Africans from the twin evils of the *swart gevaar* (Black peril) and the *oorstrooming* (swamping) of the cities. This he did, naturally enough for a born Dutchman, by building a complex system of legislative dikes and sluice gates. He called the system *apartheid*, meaning 'separateness'.

The purpose of the dikes was to halt the tide of Black migration to the cities. The number of Black people in South Africa's cities had doubled in the decade spanning the Second World War. The war had created new openings for Black South Africans in the factories of the Transvaal. Apartheid was designed, first of all, to drain the surplus Black population out of the cities, while ensuring that the flow of Blacks into the cities was tightly regulated. Hendrik's apartheid system was the basis for the new South Africa of 1948. It was the government's Big Idea. But in many ways it was no more than a modernized, dusted-off version of a previous Big Idea, dreamed up by an English post office clerk in 1905.

In 1905 Sir Godfrey Lagden, the colonial Native Affairs Commissioner did some fresh thinking on 'native policy' for South Africa. He was a former post office clerk who had spent some time in the rural areas of South Africa. On his return he had promoted himself to the colonial government as an expert on native affairs.

The problem of the day was how to forge a united country in which Afrikaans and English-speaking Whites could live together once more after the devastation of the Boer War and the bitterness aroused by the deaths of 22000 Boer women and children in British concentration camps. The first task was to rebuild the economy. Lagden, a pipe-smoking, one-man think-tank, pointed out that African men would have to be moved off the land and into the factories of the Transvaal, for without cheap, plentiful labour a new South Africa, in which Boer and Briton were united, could not be built.

Lagden's master plan involved institutionalizing a system of African reserves, creating a dumping ground for African families, while the economically useful males could live in labour compounds near the cities. 'A man cannot go with his wife and children onto the labour market,' wrote Lagden. 'He must have a dumping ground. Every rabbit must have a warren where he can live and burrow and breed, and every native must have a warren too.' The key to forcing men off the land and into the labour market, Lagden stressed, was to create a land shortage in the reserves.

Lagden's blueprint for the new South Africa inspired a set of laws which laid the foundations for total segregation. Native reserves were created on 7 per cent of the land area of South Africa. Africans were moved to the reserves in large numbers and forbidden to buy land outside. The Natives' Land Act of 1913 destroyed Black society in South Africa. Sol Plaatje, a young Black journalist at the time, wrote: 'Awakening on Friday morning, June 20, 1913, the South African native found himself, not actually a slave, but a pariah in the land of his birth.'

Black families who had previously made a good living farming on land leased from White farmers had a choice – they could either hand over their cattle to the farmer and become low-paid labourers, or be evicted at short notice. The roads of South Africa filled with Black families trekking to the reserves with their cattle.

Plaatje told the story of a typical family, the Kgobadis. Kgobadi had been making more than £100 a year farming on leased land, sharing the profits with the White farmer who owned the land. That winter Kgobadi received an ultimatum. If he was not willing to put himself, his oxen and his family at the farmer's service for 30 shillings a month, he should 'betake himself from the farm of the undersigned by sunset of the same day, failing which his stock would be seized and impounded and himself handed over to the authorities for trespassing on the farm.'

Kgobadi took to the road with his pregnant goats and his sick child. The goats fell by the roadside, one by one. On the second day of their wandering the child died. As they had no right to set foot anywhere except on the road, on pain of arrest, the family dug a grave under cover of darkness. 'Even criminals dropping straight from the gallows,' wrote Plaatje angrily, 'have an undisputed claim to six feet of ground on which to rest their criminal remains, but under the cruel operation of the Natives' Land Act little children, whose only crime is that God did not make them White, are sometimes denied that right in their ancestral home.'

On the heels of the Land Act came a long series of oppressive laws, expanded and refined by successive governments, which regulated literally every aspect of Black South Africans' existence. There was relative freedom in the reserves, but no way to make a living and nowhere near enough land to farm. Lagden's master plan worked like a dream. The men came off the land in their tens of thousands and into the cities looking for work, desperate for cash to send home to hungry families in the reserves.

Hendrik, always one for tinkering, took Lagden's idea one step further. After he became Prime Minister in 1958, he gave the reserve system a cruel new twist. The *Bantustans* (Native Reserves), he said, should become self-governing African 'homelands', implying that Black South Africans did not belong in South Africa at all. Hendrik was consolidating and extending his dikes. Parliament was told to vote for the Promotion of Bantu Self-Government Act of 1959, which it duly did.

The new act didn't find favour with Black South Africans, who rioted at Sharpeville and were machine-gunned for their trouble. A few days after the Sharpeville massacre, in the nearby Vaal town of Meyerton, Hendrik reassured a crowd of cheering Whites that the Black masses were orderly and peace-loving. A month later one of Hendrik's ungrateful White subjects, an anti-apartheid campaigner by the name of David Pratt, shot him twice in the face. But Hendrik had work to do, dikes to build, and this gave him the will to survive.

Between 1960 and 1983 more than three and a half million orderly, peace-loving Black South Africans were uprooted from their homes and forcibly expelled to homelands which many of them had never set eyes on before. It was the world's most grandiose feat of social engineering since Joseph Stalin's collectivization of Soviet agriculture in the 1930s. Adolf Hitler, one of Hendrik's heroes, would have doffed his hat. Little Hendrik from Holland, with his clever system of dikes, had secured his place in the pantheon of the world's most notorious social engineers.

When it came to the nitty gritty of keeping Blacks out of the cities, Hendrik's talent lay in improving and fine-tuning the existing apparatus of segregation and control. In 1922 the Transvaal Local Government Commission had proposed a remedy for the growing problem of Africans in the cities. 'It should be a recognised principle,' read the Commission's report, 'that natives – men, women and children – should only be permitted within municipal areas in so far as and for as long as their presence is demanded by the wants of the White population . . . The masterless native in urban areas is a source of danger and a cause of degradation of both Black and White.' The Commission's proposals became the Urban Areas Act of 1923.

Thirty years later Hendrik took a fresh look at the Urban Areas Act and decided to modernize and improve. The carrying of a new-style, ninety-six-page pass book, the *dompas* (dumb pass), complete with fingerprint records, was made compulsory for every Black person in South Africa. The associated act of parliament was called, in Hendrik's zany apartheid doublespeak, the Abolition of Passes Act. But, much as Hendrik would have liked to have gone down in history as the originator of the pass system, the British had beaten him to it by some eighty years. A crude pass system for Black males had been in operation since the British first invaded South Africa in 1795.

Hendrik's Native Laws Amendment Act of 1952 was the crowning achievement of his first five years as Minister of Native Affairs: it laid down the laws of influx control, a system of sluice gates which allowed just the right amount of Black labour into White areas. Black women were now forced to carry passes, as well as men. If you were Black you had no business being in the cities unless you could prove you had a job. You had seventy-two hours to find employment, after which you would be arrested and deported to a Black reserve or 'homeland'. From the reserve, the only way you could get back to the city was by signing a six- or twelve-month migrant labour contract.

If, however, you had worked for ten years for the same employer, or had lived in an urban area continuously for fifteen years, or had been born there of parents who fulfilled these last two conditions, you were entitled to live in a tribally segregated dormitory location (township), at a safe distance from the city. If you lost your job you had seventy-two hours to find another one, or be deported to a reserve. If your wife satisfied the influx control criteria but you didn't, you were deported nevertheless.

In 1958, when Hendrik was elected Prime Minister, he cast an approving eye over his new, improved system of dikes. Now it's only a matter of time, he thought. All he had to do was sit back and wait. By 1978, Hendrik believed, the Black tide would turn and the White lowlands of South Africa would be saved from the flood. Hendrik was jolly pleased with himself, and thought God was jolly pleased too. He said as much in his inaugural speech to parliament. 'In accordance with His will,' he said in his nasal whine, making little chopping movements with his left hand, 'it was determined who should assume the leadership of the Government in this new period of the life of South Africa.'

But there was a glitch, which showed that Hendrik's God, even if he didn't care about Black South Africans, at least had a wicked sense of humour. At the same time that Hendrik was designing bigger and better dikes to save the cities of South Africa from being *oorstroomed*, God made the economy boom. Masses of cheap Black labour was needed in the new factories. The dikes began to leak.

Hendrik tried to stem the flow by bribing and cajoling industrialists to build their new factories in the areas bordering the reserves or homelands. He made a law which said that Blacks couldn't do certain skilled jobs except in those border areas. But try as he might, even with all five fingers plugging the hole in the dike, Hendrik could not stem the flow of Black Africans to the cities. 'If South Africa has to choose,' he piped petulantly, 'between being poor and White or rich and multiracial, then it must rather choose to be White.'

In 1966 Hendrik was stabbed to death by a demented Greek parliamentary messenger. Ironically, 1978, the year in which he predicted that the tide would turn and the number of Black people leaving the country for the homelands would exceed the number coming in, was the first year in which the number of Whites leaving the country exceeded the number coming in. The politicians of the day realized that Hendrik's system of dikes was not working. They sat down and put their heads together. The Minister of Co-operation and Development (nouveau apartheidspeak for Native Affairs) came up with an 'Orderly Movement and Settlement of Black Persons Bill'. The others shook their heads sceptically, said no, it wouldn't work.

In 1985 a government commission of enquiry finally acknowledged that the battle to keep Blacks out of the country by what was termed the 'prevent-and-control technique' had been lost. The following year the influx control system was dismantled and the pass laws abolished. The twenty millionth Black South African to be arrested for pass law offences since 1916 was released. The flood gates were opened. Hendrik turned in his grave.

3 From Toyi-Toyi to Cobold

On the fourteenth floor of Shell House, the high-rise corporate headquarters of the African National Congress in downtown Johannesburg, Shaheed Rajie, guerilla-commander-turned-bureaucrat and head of the ANC's Projects Department, reflects on the changes in the ANC since its unbanning.

'1990 came. Mandela was released. Suddenly it was a new ball game. We needed offices, computers, fax machines, cars.' Clad in a stripy shirt and tie, with round horn-rimmed glasses, Rajie, who commanded an ANC guerilla base on the Western front during the Angolan war, looks more like an official of the World Bank than a Havana-educated cadre. 'It was easy in the past to criticize,' he explains, in the staccato manner of a man who has too much to do. 'Now we had to devise things that worked. People wanted to know our policies on a whole range of issues. Suddenly, for instance, we had to have a desk of mineral and energy affairs. We had to graduate from illegal stuff, from dancing the toyi-toyi and making the country ungovernable to mastering information technology, to computer languages such as Cobold,' he says, waving at the Apple-Mac on his desk.

Within four years of being unbanned in February 1990, the African National Congress had to be ready not only to fight a general election but to provide the nucleus of a new civil service and government, drafting policy on everything from health-care to nuclear power. Since 1960 the ANC had been illegal in South Africa, with membership punishable by arrest and imprisonment, its leadership in jail or in exile. When the ANC returned to the country thirty years later the rank and file had considerable expertise in how to mobilize thousands of supporters, evade the authorities, and hold secret meetings but had few office skills.

Shaheed remembers the frenzy of training:

> We ran courses on answering the phone, what to say when you pick up the receiver. Those courses still go on every day. We had to explain to people who had never worked in offices what time to come to work in the morning, what time lunch was, tea-breaks and so on. No underground stuff any more, we said. It is not enough to toyi-toyi and hide AK-47s. You have to become a professional political party.

After working from cramped premises in central Johannesburg for nearly two years, the ANC moved to Shell House, the former home of Shell Oil. 'When we first started,' says Shaheed, 'we had to line up for a computer. We didn't have cars, so people had to share lifts. It was a nightmare operation.' By 1993, however, the ANC had equipped itself with office furniture, word-processors, security systems, a fleet of cars and 850 full-time staff nationwide.

Revolutionary symbols were incorporated into the new office culture. Callers on hold to the Youth League at Shell House found themselves listening to an electronic rendition of 'Nkosi Sikelel' i-Afrika', the ANC's melancholy anthem. Plastic filing trays appeared in ANC colours. Next to xeroxed portraits of Fidel Castro and stirring denunciations of capitalism appeared smart posters featuring reassuringly sober ANC leaders in well-cut suits, counselling peace and democracy.

A new breed of civil servant emerged within the ANC, a tiny elite of capable, educated, sharply dressed men and women who took on the day-to-day managerial tasks and gradually accumulated real power behind the scenes. More administrators are being trained by the Civil Service Unit. But there are still not enough to fill government posts in the new South Africa. 'We're looking at the whole democratic movement, what we call the democratic organs of civil society,' explains Shaheed, lapsing into the academic jargon which has become the ANC's house style, 'plus those from the old establishment prepared to make the transition. Some of them are being retrained.'

One of the rewards of turning professional was a decent wage. Before 1990 no one in the ANC received a salary, everyone was a volunteer in the struggle. After unbanning, all ANC employees, from Nelson Mandela to the tea-lady, were paid the same wage: 2000 rand a month (about £400). 'Real post-communism stuff,' chuckles Shaheed. 'But it didn't work.' Finally, in 1992, a ten-grade wage-scale was introduced for the ANC's full-time employees, reflecting differences in status within the organization, from members of the National Executive Committee, through heads of departments, down to secretarial staff. 'Senior leadership figures are still shocked by having money. They can't get used to the idea of a regular wage going into their bank account,' smiles Shaheed.

Most of the ANC's money comes from Scandinavia. The largest regular contribution to the ANC's annual budget is a direct grant from the Swedish government. The next biggest donor is the Norwegian government, followed by Danish and Australian non-governmental organizations. The Non-Aligned Movement, the Organization of African Unity and the US Congress have all made sporadic donations. But Sweden remains the ANC's major financier, paying for everything from the security system at Shell House to the negotiating team at the new South Africa talks. Every so often ANC officials quietly report back to a certain Lina Johanssen at the Swedish Embassy to justify the expenditure and explain any changes in the agreed budget. 'Without the Swedish money we might have had to resort to the South American system of raising funds,' quips Shaheed, only half in jest. 'Hitting banks.'

Although the managerial elite at ANC headquarters may now prize computer literacy above the ability to toyi-toyi, it was this jubilant, high-stepping dance which symbolized the ANC's return to popularity in the 1980s after a decade in the cold. When 100 000 people do the toyi-toyi at an ANC rally, the ground trembles. The toyi-toyi is an exuberant wardance, accompanied by deep-throated yells and a chant of 'toyi-toyi-toyi-toyi-toyi-tooooyi!', which injects courage and determination into the ranks of the 'comrades' while causing their enemies to quake. Each knee in turn is punched high in the air in a syncopated rhythm, hopping on one leg in between.

'The toyi-toyi has developed into a show of strength,' explains Mthuthuzeli Matshoba of the ANC's Department of Arts and Culture. 'It says we exist, we are here, you cannot easily forget about us!'

Apparently the toyi-toyi came to South Africa from the Zimbabwean guerilla training camps, where it was used as a warm-up exercise by the Zimbabwean People's Revolutionary Army to boost fitness and morale. The toyi-toyi was, it seems, invented by the warriors of Mzilikazi, a renegade Zulu general who fled from the Zulu king Shaka, taking his regiments all the way to modern-day Zimbabwe. Legend has it that they started off from Zululand 'at a trot', hence the warlike, trotting rhythm of the toyi-toyi. The dance came into vogue when ANC cadres (guerilla officers), who were arrested while trying to infiltrate back into South

Africa, taught it to their fellow detainees, who in turn spread it through the townships on their release.

The toyi-toyi became de rigueur at gatherings of the United Democratic Front (UDF), a broad alliance of anti-apartheid organizations founded in Cape Town in 1983, which became the ANC's internal wing. The UDF rallied resistance against the South African government's new constitution of 1983, which extended voting rights to Coloureds and Indians but stopped short of enfranchising Black South Africans. A year after its launch, the UDF could claim the support of some 600 organizations and three million people.

That year the UDF comrades launched a rebellion against 'sell-out' Black local authorities, a rebellion which turned into the most violent anti-government uprising in South African history. The UDF had caught the mood of the township youth, reflected in the slogan 'Make the country ungovernable' which was the message of Oliver Tambo's New Year's Day broadcast on Radio Freedom from exile in 1985. The government responded by imposing successive 'states of emergency' from 1985 to 1990, during which time thousands of Blacks were killed and maimed by the South African security forces and tens of thousands detained.

Although the government succeeded in quelling the rebellion by the massive use of force, it soon became apparent that the lid could not be kept on township youth for ever. The stage was set for the resurrection of the African National Congress in the guise of the government's principal negotiating partner in the transition to a new South Africa. After twenty-seven years of incarceration as public enemy number one, Nelson Mandela was suddenly referred to by President F.W. de Klerk as 'a friendly man, an interesting man . . .'

The African National Congress had finally arrived, nearly eighty years after its establishment in 1912 by members of a tiny group of Black South African professionals drawn from diverse ethnic groups. The ANC's first executive committee consisted of three attorneys, four churchmen, a newspaper editor and three businessmen.

'We have discovered that in the land of our birth,' announced Dr Pixley Seme, an Oxford-educated Zulu lawyer, 'Africans are treated as hewers of wood and drawers of water.' More to the point, they had discovered that in the new Union of South Africa, (founded two years previously) the prospects for educated, professional Black men such as themselves looked very poor. One of the Congress's first actions was to send a delegation to London to point out to the British colonial authorities that Blacks were being treated unfairly by the Afrikaner-led South African government. The envoys were sent packing, and the ANC lapsed into obscurity until the early fifties, when a new generation of young activists introduced a more vigorous style of protest against White rule.

In 1949, the year after apartheid ('separateness') was inaugurated by the ruling National Party, the ANC Youth League ousted the organization's ageing leadership, whose brand of polite protest seemed hopelessly inadequate in the face of harsh new racist legislation. At the Congress's annual conference a militant 'Programme of Action' was adopted, calling for 'immediate and active boycott, strike, civil disobedience, non-cooperation and such other means as may bring about the realization of our aspirations.' Three Youth Leaguers in particular rose to prominence during the fifties, a triumvirate which was to dominate the ANC for the next forty years: Nelson Mandela, Walter Sisulu and Oliver Tambo. Tambo and Mandela were lawyers, Sisulu a former miner.

The new post-war militancy led to the Defiance Campaign of 1952, the biggest organized demonstration of peaceful resistance by Black South Africans up to that time. ANC supporters defied the government's pass laws, entering White areas without permits and using Whites-only entrances to public buildings, challenging the authorities to arrest them. Within six months 8500 arrests had been made, including twenty ANC leaders. The South African Police crushed the Defiance Campaign, but the ANC had the last word: its paid-up membership increased from 7000 to more than 100000 over the same six months.

Two years after the Defiance Campaign the African National Congress reached another important milestone. Representatives of the ANC, together with Indian and Coloured politicians and trade unionists, met on an athletics field near Soweto to discuss a proposed Freedom Charter, a document voicing the political aspirations of all South Africans 'for the democratic South Africa of the future'. To this day the 1955 Freedom Charter remains the bedrock ANC policy document. The first line reads: 'South Africa belongs to all who live in it, Black and White . . . ' It represented an unequivocal commitment to non-racialism: the idea that not all Whites were bad; that the ANC's quarrel was with White rule, not with Whites as such. As the Freedom Charter was being discussed, the 3000 delegates to the Congress were surrounded by police, body-searched and placed under arrest on suspicion of treason.

A minority of 'Africanists' within the ANC, however, believed that Whites had no place in the liberation movement. In 1959 the Africanists split from the ANC to form the Pan-Africanist Congress (PAC), which attained notoriety in the 1980s with its slogan of 'One settler, one bullet!' (abbreviated for convenience to 'Settler, settler! Bullet, bullet!'). It was the PAC's anti-pass-law protest in Sharpeville in March 1960 (upstaging the ANC's campaign, due to begin ten days later) which ended in the famous massacre of sixty-nine protesters by the South African Police.

The Sharpeville crisis provoked the government to ban the ANC, the PAC and other extra-parliamentary political organizations. Black defiance was crushed by a massive show of force and 18000 arrests were made.

Afterwards Black South Africans queued submissively for hours to replace the passes they had burned in defiance during the protests. The ANC finally abandoned its strategy of non-violent resistance and resorted to guerilla warfare.

Nelson Mandela, by now deputy president of the ANC, quit his law practice and went into hiding, becoming commander-in-chief of the organization's new guerilla wing, uMkhonto we Sizwe ('Spear of the Nation', or 'MK' for short). After a few months' guerilla training in Algeria, Mandela slipped back into the country, was promptly arrested and eventually sentenced to life imprisonment, together with Sisulu and six others. They were flown to Robben Island, a former leper colony off the coast of Cape Town, where rebel Xhosa chiefs had been incarcerated by the British colonial authorities during the border wars of the nineteenth century.

The choice of Robben Island was a neat irony, since Mandela was himself the son of a Xhosa chief. He, Sisulu and Tambo all came from the villages of Transkei, the Xhosa 'native reserve', which, together with the Eastern Cape, makes up the Xhosa-speaking area of South Africa. Before the organization was banned, the bulk of the ANC's membership came from the Eastern Cape. Of the 8500 activists arrested during the Defiance Campaign, 6000 were Xhosas. Three decades later the predominance of Xhosas in the ANC would lead to the accusation by the Zulu nationalists of Inkatha that the ANC was pro-Xhosa and anti-Zulu.

While this is far from the truth, the fact remains that the ANC's biggest power base is amongst the Xhosa ethnic group, the second largest in South Africa after the Zulus. The ANC has also acquired a massive following in Zulu-speaking Natal province, with estimates placing ANC support as high as half of the total Zulu-speaking population. But the ANC's key leaders in recent years (Mandela, Tambo, Sisulu, Thabo Mbeki and Chris Hani) have all been Xhosa-speakers, and it is undeniable that Xhosas constitute the largest single ethnic group within the organization.

The explanation for this may partly lie in the fact that the Xhosas, whose territory was invaded by the British and annexed to the Cape Colony, were the first Black people in southern Africa to be systematically exposed to mission schooling. The first major educational institutions in Africa open to Blacks were established in the (Xhosa-speaking) Eastern Cape: Fort Hare, Lovedale College and Healdtown. The Xhosa educated elite thus became Westernized, literate and politically-conscious half a century earlier than other Blacks in southern Africa.

In addition to the influence of missionary education, a relatively large number of Black people in the Cape Colony were qualified to vote in parliamentary elections, compared with a handful in the neighbouring British colony of Natal and none at all in the Afrikaner republics of the Transvaal and Orange Free State. It was perhaps hardly surprising that the leadership of the ANC, founded on modern liberal principles, should include a disproportionate number of Xhosas.

The ANC's 'special relationship' with the Xhosa-speakers of South Africa and the corresponding paucity of Zulus at senior level is, however, never openly discussed within the organization. The ANC was founded precisely in order to overcome such divisions in the fight against White domination, and is extremely sensitive to charges of tribalism. 'The aberrations of the Xhosa-Fingo feud, the animosity that exists between the Zulus and the Tongas, between the Basuto and every other native must be buried and forgotten,' wrote the Zulu lawyer Dr Pixley Geme, the founder of the ANC, in a letter to the Xhosa-language newspaper *Imvo*.

Nowadays, thanks to the ANC's consistent abhorrence of tribalism, the ANC-led Alliance (a three-way partnership between the ANC, the Congress of South African Trade Unions and the Communist Party) is the closest South Africa has to a national, non-ethnic political movement. The preponderance of Xhosas in the ANC seems to matter only to the more jingoistic Inkatha supporters and to those Whites who view South Africa's current troubles as merely another episode in a long history of tribal warfare.

The divisions which threaten to undermine the ANC in the nineties are not ethnic in nature, but reflect emerging class divisions in Black South Africa. As the ANC embraces power and privilege, becoming absorbed into the ruling class, there is a danger that the organization will drift back to its distant roots and become merely a vehicle for the upwardly mobile Black educated classes.

There is already massive disenchantment amongst the ANC's constituency in the squatter camps and the poorer townships. The young Black comrades, locked in bitter wars with the police and rival Black political organizations, view the negotiations with the governing National Party as a betrayal of the many sacrifices made in the course of the struggle. While the moral authority of Mandela and the ANC is still unassailable, the cat-calls, bored silences and massive walk-outs which greet Nelson Mandela's speeches at ANC rallies could well translate into lost votes in the next general election. An entire generation of Black South African youth has little vested interest in an orderly transition to a new status quo in which Whites will undoubtedly retain their hold on the economy and on the country's key civil and military institutions, while a new Black elite claims its share of those privileges and shuts out the masses.

The frustrations of the ANC's grass-roots supporters have been expressed most eloquently by Winnie Mandela, the ANC leader's estranged wife. (The couple separated after it was revealed that Winnie was involved in the kidnapping and assault of a fourteen-year-old activist, who was accused of being an informer and tortured to death by her bodyguards.)

'I am not opposed to negotiations,' she said in her first interview on

South African TV. 'Even if there is a war, at the end we have to sit down and talk. What I am opposed to is selling the masses. The answer does not lie with those who drink tea and eat biscuits in the corridors of the World Trade Centre [the Johannesburg venue for multi-party talks]. The answer lies with the people of Boipatong, Phola Park, KwaMashu and Crossroads.'

Winnie's pronouncements, like those of many demagogues, contain a core of truth beneath the rhetoric. If the ANC continues to neglect the popular touch in favour of the grey suits and bland phrases necessary to win the confidence of White South Africans and foreign investors, there is every chance that the one political movement capable of building a united South Africa will itself become divided, or lose its support to more militant rivals. The ANC rode to power on the back of a massive uprising by Black urban youth in the townships during the 1980s. The real test of the movement's first years in power will be whether it can satisfy the aspirations and retain the loyalty of millions of unschooled youngsters. If it fails, these young people may well take to the township streets once more, to remind the ANC leadership that 'we exist, we are here, you cannot easily forget about us!' When that time comes, the ANC's guerilla commanders may have to forsake their computer consoles and learn how to toyi-toyi all over again.

PART TWO

The Vaal Triangle and the East Rand

4 The Most Hated Place in the Vaal Triangle

The first outbreak of civil war in the Transvaal occurred in the Vaal Triangle. The Vaal Triangle rustbelt contains most of South Africa's heavy industry. 'Satanic mills' is the phrase which springs to mind on the sinister eastern approach to the Iron and Steel Corporation (ISCOR) Vanderbijlpark steel plant. The stark wastelands next to the works are scorched black by winter grass-fires. Areas which are not charred are so dry that the grass has turned a dirty shade of khaki. Black and khaki are the colours which dominate the Vaal Triangle. Waste piled 50 feet high in a flat-topped heap a kilometre long forms a vast black rampart in front of the steelworks, which takes up the entire horizon with lines of smoke-stacks and blast furnaces. The air is foul with heavy, sulphurous vapours. The usually clear Transvaal winter sky is smudged with dark blotches and rust-coloured clouds. The roads are straight and deserted. The only sound is the occasional moan of a locomotive shunting materials within the plant.

Politically the Vaal Triangle has always been combustible. In the fifties, workers in the Triangle's steel, chemical and fertilizer plants were strongly unionized. Unemployment was high. The Vaal had a history of rebellion against the government. In 1960, 20000 people assembled outside the police station at Sharpeville one lunchtime to protest against the government's pass laws. The protest was led by the Pan Africanist Congress, upstaging the African National Congress, which was due to launch its anti-pass-law campaign ten days later. A total of 300 policemen, many of whom had never seen a crowd before, stood inside the wire fence. The government sent jets to buzz the protesters, who waved cheerfully at the planes and threw their hats in the air.

Later that afternoon there was some pushing and shoving at the front of the crowd and a section of the perimeter fence collapsed. The policemen opened fire with machine-guns, shooting people down as they tried to run away. When the guns finally stopped 69 people lay dead and 180 were wounded. Three policemen had been slightly injured by stones. Sharpeville was the twelve-year-old apartheid regime's first public massacre. It signalled the beginning of a new reign of terror by the White government, and the abandonment of passive protest in favour of armed resistance by the Black liberation movements.

In the springtime of 1984 the fuse of a national explosion was lit once again in the Vaal Triangle when residents started burning newly installed Black municipal councillors. The so-called Vaal Uprising spread to the East Rand, then to the whole of the Transvaal. Khuzwayo 'Sam' Dhlamini, the Deputy Mayor of the small Vaal Triangle township of Bophelong, was the first to die. He was hacked to death one morning as he opened his front door to an angry mob. His body was placed on top of his car and burned. The new township councils had increased rents by 5 rand 90, and service charges for home-owners by 5 rand 50. Residents refused to pay. Two more councillors were burned that morning in Sebokeng and Evaton. In the course of the riots the police shot thirty people dead. The nationwide unrest sparked by the Vaal Uprising led to the imposition of a state of emergency, and ultimately to the capitulation of the apartheid regime.

Black municipal councils were the product of government half-measures designed to bring about a new South Africa on White terms. The aim was to make apartheid more efficient and delegate the increasingly burdensome responsibility of governing and financing the Black dormitory towns of South Africa. The economy was looking unhealthy and there had been unrest since the Soweto riots of 1976, when the police had shot dead several hundred rioters. Self-financing, all-Black local councils were established as a way of lightening the White man's burden while giving Black people a token degree of self-government.

The Black councils were seen as a sop to Black political aspirations, which indeed they were. Local elections were boycotted. People who took jobs as councillors were branded as sell-outs. Many were members of the conservative Black middle class, churchgoing men who owned businesses in the townships: funeral parlours, mini-markets, garages and liquor stores. Councillors were often wealthy, resented and envied by those around them.

The Black municipal councils walked straight from sham elections into a financial crisis. Because they were self-financing, and because commercial activity in the Black townships was all but proscribed by the government, all the extra revenue the council needed had to come from higher rent and service charges. The rent increases were the drop which overflowed the cup. Burning Black councillors became a national sport. Hundreds of councillors resigned in fear. The favourite method of execution was the 'necklace', a tyre filled with petrol which was placed over the victim's head and arms and set alight. The victim turned into a screaming, stumbling human torch, to jubilant cries of 'Tshis'inyama!' ('Barbecue the meat!').

Ernest Sotsu was a prominent figure in the leadership of the Vaal Civic Association at the time of the Vaal rebellion. The 'civic' led the rent boycott in the Vaal Triangle townships, demanding the resignation of the Black councils. 'People did not want councillors and "homelands",' says Sotsu. 'They wanted freedom. The tree of apartheid had been planted in the locations. People were trying to uproot it. This was done with violence. The main thing was to destroy the apartheid system within our communities. It would have been too dangerous to take the violence into the White areas. The system was too strong.'

Sotsu fled into exile when the army moved in to pacify the Vaal and the leaders of the Vaal rebellion were arrested and tried for treason and terrorism. Sotsu became an intelligence agent for the armed wing of the African National Congress, uMkhonto we Sizwe (MK for short). He organized recruits and guns, moving to Transkei to start MK cells and enlist homeland civil servants. 'My age enabled me to infiltrate,' says the old man gleefully. 'We did it right under their noses.'

In his present incarnation Ernest Sotsu, also known as the Reverend Sotsu, is the leader of a hard-line ANC faction in the Vaal. He is a courteous, quaint gentleman with playful eyes and a penchant for purple neckties and striped shirts. His enemies call him a warlord. Sotsu has earned the undying loyalty of thousands of heavily-armed Xhosa steel-workers in the Vaal hostels.

Sotsu trained as a preacher in the Brethren Mission Church. He speaks in ringing, rounded sentences with the meticulous, old-school elocution of the London Missionary Society. The son of a Xhosa goldminer who spent most of his life underground in the Transvaal, Sotsu grew up in rural Transkei, in the same district as Nelson Mandela. In his student days he joined the ANC and sympathized strongly with the Communist Party.

While he was still on the run from the South African security forces in the years after the Vaal rebellion, Sotsu made regular clandestine trips into South Africa to see his family. In 1986 he was shopped by an informer and arrested while visiting his wife one night in Boipatong. 'I was moving around, doing a lot of work. There were spies,' he shrugs. Sotsu was interrogated, sentenced to five years in jail for subversive activities and deported to Transkei, where he shared a prison cell with the future military dictator Brigadier Holomisa. 'We had some useful discussions,' he says with a wink. Transkei is now an important source of arms and military training for ANC-aligned 'self-defence units'.

In the same year that Sotsu was arrested, KwaMadala hostel, which had housed ISCOR's migrant workforce since 1945, was closed down. ISCOR's workers moved to a gigantic brand-new hostel, KwaMasiza ('the Place of Help'), next to the main Vaal township of Sebokeng. KwaMasiza consists of a couple of dozen three-storey buildings in spacious grounds, ringed by a wire security fence. ISCOR workers were also living in Sebokeng hostel, a government migrant-labour barracks nearby. The hostel-dwellers were migrants from the distant Black labour reserves or homelands. The majority came from Transkei, the larger of the two Xhosa tribal homelands. Others came from KwaZulu, the Zulu homeland. Until the end of the eighties there was relative harmony amongst the hostel-dwellers, while the youngsters battled the police in the townships outside.

Then, in 1989, Sotsu was amnestied by Brigadier Holomisa and returned to the Vaal. There he began to 'revive the political fire' which had been extinguished by a police clampdown and several years of martial law. In 1990 came the unexpected release of Nelson Mandela and the unbanning of Black political parties (outlawed for the previous thirty years). Once again the blue touchpaper ignited first in the Vaal Triangle, before spreading to the East Rand and the other townships around Johannesburg.

The soccer stadium in Zone Seven of Sebokeng township is a rectangular piece of grass scorched black by winter veldt-fires. A low wall surrounds battered goalposts and a couple of wooden stands. The stadium sits next to a wasteland on the edge of the township, surrounded by a large, bare expanse of red dust. Zone Seven stadium was the venue for the Inkatha Freedom Party's first rally in the Transvaal, South Africa's richest and most populous province.

Two months earlier, on Mayday 1990, Jay Naidoo, the leader of the hugely powerful Congress of South African Trade Unions (COSATU), had issued a declaration of war on Inkatha. He announced to a rally in Cape Town that he had learned about a meeting at which KwaZulu Chief Minister Buthelezi, the leader of Inkatha, told the *amaKosi*, the Zulu chiefs, to place themselves on a war footing. 'In the past,' Naidoo declared to a packed Athlone stadium, 'we had to be diplomatic when we explained the causes of violence because we hoped that the peace talks with Buthelezi would succeed. There is no more hope for peace with Buthelezi while he talks like this. Our enemy has two faces. One is that of Buthelezi and the other is that of de Klerk and the South African Police!'

Naidoo's speech sparked a furore amongst Inkatha-supporting Zulus. The word went round that Naidoo (a Natal Indian) had said the only solution to the violence was to kill the Zulus. A crisis meeting of Zulu men from the Transvaal was called on 1 July, the day before the planned COSATU stayaway. On a field next to the Mapetla hostel in Soweto, the Transvaal leadership of Inkatha, consisting of Pat Mchunu, Themba Khoza and Humphrey Ndhlovu, addressed thousands of Zulu men armed with spears and clubs. Enough was enough, they announced. The stayaway would not be observed, everyone must go to work and defend themselves against intimidation. 'We took a resolution to stand up and fight,' recalls IFP Transvaal leader Humphrey Ndhlovu, a former shoe repairman. 'We said "Blood is going to flow in South Africa!".'

'The Vaal was an ANC stronghold,' says Ernest Sotsu. 'Inkatha was so insignificant we never even bothered about it. Buthelezi was beginning to be known as a sell-out,' he sneers, 'serving Pretoria while claiming to lead a liberation movement.' Nevertheless, on the morning of the IFP rally in Sebokeng, curiosity got the better of Sotsu and he wandered over to the Zone Seven stadium.

Sebokeng was humming with tension that morning. There were rumours that Inkatha workers from the Sebokeng hostels were planning to wreak vengeance on the township. During the COSATU stayaway on 2 July the township 'comrades' (ANC-supporting youth) had burned several houses belonging to Inkatha supporters in the Vaal townships.

The stayaway had also inflamed the Vaal hostels. Inkatha-supporting Zulu workers from the KwaMasiza hostel begged the ISCOR steelworks management to allow them back into 'the Old Place', KwaMadala. They complained of friction with the majority Xhosa group at KwaMasiza hostel, saying their lives were in danger.

COSATU, which had an excellent system of intelligence in the Vaal factories, had warned township comrades that IFP officials had visited the hostels in order to mobilize retribution for the burned houses. Comrades patrolled the streets, looking out for signs of trouble. Supplies of petrol were kept handy.

'Eight houses had been burned in Small Farms, between Evaton and Sebokeng,' says Oupa Nhlapo, a local Inkatha official. 'The purpose of the rally was to show solidarity with people who lost their homes. Funds were collected at the stadium.' He adds implausibly: 'It was a prayer rally.'

A low wall separated 2000 Zulu hostel-dwellers from the jeering township youths outside. The comrades had demolished sections of the stadium's outer wall so they could keep an eye on proceedings. Feelings were running high. An Inkatha supporter had been shot dead as he got off his bus to remove a barricade on the road to Zone Seven stadium.

'I approached the police,' says Ernest Sotsu, 'asking why people were armed. The police said: "These people are harmless."' Inkatha supporters were still getting off buses outside the stadium. One group of Zulus overheard Sotsu's complaint to the police officer. 'I was grabbed,' says Sotsu indignantly. 'It had never happened to me before. I wondered "Are these people really going to kill me? And what for?"' Sotsu heard the policeman remark that if anyone interfered with the IFP the Zulus would kill them.

Several thousand highly charged Zulu hostel-dwellers heard speeches by Chief Biyela, the leader of the *amaKosi* (the Zulu chiefs), and C.J. Mthetwa, the KwaZulu Minister of Justice. In the midst of the proceedings Mrs Kubheka, a local Inkatha official who was the master of ceremonies at the rally, noticed smoke rising from her home nearby in Sebokeng, which had been set ablaze by the comrades. 'ANC youth stoned the rally,' recalls Nhlapo. 'They were waiting to fight at the entrance to the stadium.'

Fighting continued after the rally in the red-dust area outside. The

Justice Minister's bodyguard was hit in the head by a bullet. The IFP subsequently claimed that one of their supporters was killed in the fighting. The ANC claimed the dead man was one of theirs. The police fired teargas at the comrades. Some Inkatha supporters, who had travelled to Sebokeng from other hostels in the Transvaal, got into their buses and left. 'They were bussed in,' says Sotsu darkly, as if bussing were some fiendishly clever manoeuvre.

Inkatha supporters from the nearby Sebokeng hostel marched home under police escort. There was little doubt whose side the police were on. The police had been at war with the youth since 1976. Inkatha supporters were relatively docile and seen by the police as pro-Government.

While they were attending the rally, Zulus from the Sebokeng hostel had received a message from friends who had stayed behind. 'We got a message that they would attack the Zulus. We thought it was just a rumour,' says a former hostel resident. Other former inmates claim they were told by ANC-supporting Xhosa hostel-dwellers that if they went to the IFP rally they should not expect to be allowed back to their rooms in the hostel.

On the way back to the hostel the Inkatha column was harried by youths throwing stones and petrol bombs. The Zulus retaliated by smashing windows and burning houses on the edge of Sebokeng township. When they reached the entrance to the Sebokeng hostel they were confronted by a large crowd of Xhosa hostel-dwellers, wielding traditional weapons and reinforced by township youth.

'The police accompanied Inkatha to the hostel where they attacked the residents,' says Sotsu. 'People had come to the rally from all the hostels ... The idea was to drive people out and establish an IFP stronghold and bring people here from KwaZulu to take the jobs of those they drove out of the hostels, and give Inkatha a constituency.' While on the surface the confrontation was about political allegiances, the real stakes were jobs and beds for migrant workers in the city.

At dusk, after a two-hour stand-off, the rival mobs drew closer, shouting threats and abuse at one another. 'We told the police they must remove the Xhosas,' says a former resident of the hostel. 'But the groups were too close. There were thousands of them, from KwaMasiza and Sebokeng hostels and from the township. They were singing "Beat the dogs, beat the Zulus!" and screaming "Bulala!" ("Kill them!"). They started attacking the police.' The first casualty was Warrant Officer Petrus Jooste who fell, transfixed with a sharpened steel pole thrown by one of the Xhosa steelworkers. At this stage the police left. Whether they took fright or decided to 'let the two sides sort it out' is unclear. When they came back half an hour later there were fifteen corpses in the hostel yard.

'We tried to run away,' remembers a Zulu hostel-dweller. 'We went to the buses, but one of them was burning. So we went back to fight.' He smiles. 'If a snake runs away, and you follow it, it will fight.' The IFP side claimed all the dead were Xhosas or ANC. In spite of this, they did not succeed in regaining their hostel rooms that night. Most of the Zulus from Sebokeng hostel spent the night in the yard of a nearby police station.

The fighting continued until the end of the month. The remaining Zulus in Sebokeng hostel were thrown out. Reverend Sotsu claims there were Zulus in only 'one or two rooms'. Former hostel-dwellers say they numbered 200.

Some of the evicted hostel-dwellers, who had left with nothing but the clothes they stood up in, slept in Red Cross tents or in the open, on waste ground near the steelworks. Others took refuge in Zone Seventeen of Sebokeng township, in a safe house. There were revenge attacks on Sebokeng hostel, which was raked with machine-gun fire, reportedly by White men in balaclavas, killing nine residents. The 'safe' house in Zone Seventeen was attacked by a Xhosa war party from the hostels. The fugitives received advance information and ambushed the raiders, driving them back into the hostel. 'We saw it as an opportunity to recover the property which we had left behind,' says one of the former residents. 'But they regrouped.' Eventually 137 Zulus were surrounded and had to be rescued by the police and the army, who shot dead nine Xhosa hostel-dwellers in the process.

News of the conflict in the Vaal Triangle hostels set off a wave of faction fighting all over the Transvaal. As in 1984, the East Rand was the first area to be inflamed. The Red Cross took away the tents which the fugitives from the hostel had been using, saying they were needed elsewhere in the war zone.

In the second week of October several hundred homeless Zulu workers turned up at the old ISCOR KwaMadala hostel, which was being used as the steelworks' nursery. They forced open the front gates and occupied the hostel, with its 1500 concrete bunks. KwaMadala, 'the Old Place', became a haven for outcasts from the troubled townships of the Vaal. Later that month 400 Zulus fled to KwaMadala from the giant KwaMasiza hostel after the murder of a Zulu worker. 'Zulus were threatened by our kin,' says Sotsu smugly. 'They left KwaMasiza out of fear. KwaMadala,' he adds, 'became the most hated place in the Vaal.'

5 The Man from Umtata

Nobody can remember the name of the Xhosa man from Umtata, or much about him, except that his death triggered the civil war on the East Rand, a vast industrial zone in the shallow hills between the Vaal Triangle and Johannesburg. He was buried in a hill village in distant Transkei, far from the mayhem which followed. He was the first of thousands of migrant workers who returned home from the East Rand in cheap wooden coffins, or swathed in blankets, blood-stained bundles on the backs of pick-up trucks, bouncing along the winding dirt roads of Transkei and KwaZulu.

The man from Umtata was murdered on a winter night in August 1990, three Sundays after the fateful Inkatha Freedom Party rally at Zone Seven stadium in Sebokeng. The killing happened at Mpashlela's shebeen inside the massive Kalanyoni workers' hostel, in the East Rand.

Mpashlela's was a popular dive with three rooms, a TV, a sound system and fridges to keep the beer cool. It was a cosy, bright, pleasant place to be when the smog from tens of thousands of coal stoves descended on the East Rand at dusk. The grey pall obliterated the feeble glimmer of candles through net curtains, which was the only illumination in the shacks of neighbouring Phola Park. The edge of the shanty town was within spitting distance of the hostel walls. There were thousands of shacks out there, a whole city in the darkness. They were invisible behind the grey smoke. It was difficult to believe that 20 000 people were sleeping only metres away, five or six to a shack.

Everyone agrees the war started over a woman. She was the girlfriend of the man from Umtata and was living with him at the hostel. The man from Umtata ate stamp every day, the traditional Xhosa corn porridge. His Zulu room-mates regularly cooked meat. One day the woman couldn't resist the cooking smells any longer and asked one of the Zulu men for a piece of meat. They ended up in a relationship. The man from Umtata was still in love with her, and took it badly. His Xhosa friends told him he must demand the woman back. How could he allow his girlfriend to be stolen by *iChaka*, a Zulu? That Sunday night in August 1990 the man from Umtata went to find his rival at Mpashlela's shebeen.

It was by no means the first time there had been a disagreement over a woman. The men in the huge single-sex hostel, who were bachelors or had left their families far away in the rural homelands, used to flirt with the women of Phola Park who came to draw water at the taps in the hostel yard. Older men in Kalanyoni used to grumble about the liaisons. 'Where women are, there's a lot of shit,' mutters a former resident. 'It was the young guys who went for that kind of thing. Us older men didn't like it. But we couldn't stop the women coming in.' There were also grumbles from some of the Xhosa men in Phola Park, who were not pleased that 'their' women were dating dirty, uncircumcised Zulu men from the hostel.

These gripes had never previously marred the friendships between the men of Phola Park and the Kalanyoni hostel-dwellers. At weekends the men of Phola Park, who were predominantly Xhosa-speaking, but included Shangaans and Zulus, got drunk on *umKomboti* with the hostel-dwellers, who spoke a broad mixture of languages, with no particular group being dominant. A 2-litre plastic tub of the cloudy, frothy brew was passed round. Sometimes the men drank together at Mpashlela's or at shebeens in Phola Park until the early hours of the morning. At their closest point the hostel and the shacks were barely 3 metres apart.

That Sunday night the man from Umtata walked into Mpashlela's shebeen, the cosy place in Block Eight of the hostel, looking for his Zulu rival. A fight started and he was unlucky. The man from Umtata was hacked to death with *pangas*, the long, sharp machetes formerly used to harvest sugarcane. Friends of the dead Xhosa ran to their countrymen in Phola Park. An angry posse from the shanty town marched to Mpashlela's shebeen and jumped on the first Zulus they saw. The fighting spread throughout Block Eight. Rooms were set alight. A large crowd hovered outside the hostel gates. The Xhosa posse who had come to avenge their countryman were driven out by Zulu hostel-dwellers. In the fighting two Xhosas were killed, both from Block Eight. The other Xhosas living in the hostel panicked. Smoke could be seen pouring from the side of the building. Xhosa hostel-dwellers fled *en masse* into the pitch-dark alleyways of Phola Park.

They left everything behind: fridges, radios, guitars, blankets, all the things which made the years working away from home a little more bearable. No one was in any doubt that the Zulus were looting whatever they could get hold of. The more prudent hostel-dwellers packed their bags, suspecting that the events of that Sunday night might be the beginning of something serious.

As Monday dawned on the scorched walls of Block Eight and the twisted corpse of the man from Umtata, which was still lying where he had been tossed out of the hostel, people looked for explanations. People in both factions agree that the mood in the hostel had soured in the early evening, hours before the fight between the man from Umtata and his Zulu rival in Mpashlela's tavern.

There had been a meeting of Zulus in the hostel that Sunday evening before the murder. Routine residents' meetings took place in the hostel every weekend, but this one had been for Zulus only. Attending the meeting were men who had recently returned from a rally at George Gogh Stadium in Johannesburg. They had travelled the 25 kilometres to Johannesburg that morning to hear Chief Biyela, the head of the Zulu chiefs, address the Zulu men of the Transvaal. It was an emotional speech, containing a message from all the chiefs to the effect that Zulus must close ranks in these troubled times. The crowd, from hostels all over the Transvaal, was buzzing with rumours about July's attacks on Zulus in the Vaal Triangle.

The men who returned to Kalanyoni from the rally were seething with indignation. The meeting in the hostel that evening was tense. Non–Zulus were not welcome. The word was that Xhosas were planning to kill the Zulus in the hostel. Look what happened in Sebokeng, the men were saying. Zulus were expelled from the hostels by Xhosas. Now the Xhosas wanted revenge for their people who died in the fighting. The Zulus were worried, for they were in the minority in Kalanyoni hostel, as they had been in the Sebokeng hostels.

An old man at the back of the gathering listened to the rumour and hearsay and asked: 'Why should the Xhosas want to kill us when we weren't even in Sebokeng?' That made people think. The Zulus at the meeting decided to give the Xhosas the benefit of the doubt.

While this debate was in progress the Xhosas from Phola Park were holding a similar gathering, at the meeting place under the power pylons. An Inkatha official in the hostel was rumoured to have called all the Zulus together in order to plan an attack on the shacks of Phola Park. What other reason could there be for not allowing Xhosas into the meeting? People's worst fears were confirmed when someone informed the meeting that the Zulus were planning to attack Phola Park that night. 'It was the *tsotsis*, the gangsters, who spread the rumour,' said someone who was there. 'In fact the whole thing was organized by a bunch of criminals who went around spreading the rumour that the Zulus were going to attack the Xhosas.' Meanwhile the Xhosa hostel-dwellers were holding their own gathering, dominated by discussion of the recent killing of fifteen Xhosas at a West Rand hostel.

Elsewhere in Kalanyoni hostel the Zulus were dispersing to their rooms. Otto Masuku, the Inkatha official who had convened the meeting, was informed that people in Phola Park were saying he had summoned the Zulus to attack the shacks. Otto brushed aside the report, saying the Xhosas must be drunk. He walked out of the hostel at dusk to open Masuku's Tuck Shop, which he had set up in a shack in Phola Park. A crowd of Xhosa men stood watching him. Some of them wore blankets cloaked over their shoulders. Nothing was said.

When Otto shut his shop at eight o'clock and walked back to the hostel all was quiet. An hour later the confrontation broke out in Mpashlela's shebeen and the man from Umtata lay dying.

The whole of the Transvaal was ready to explode. Leaflets had been going round Soweto: 'We want to destroy the Zulus. We want to drive them out of the hostels as we did in Sebokeng. There will be no peace as long as the Zulus are still powerful. Let us destroy them all. Down with Zulus.' The leaflets bore an out-of-date African National Congress crest and were clearly forgeries. People didn't know why they were fighting. Everyone was scared. The only way to survive was to beat the other side to the punch.

6 The Blanket Men

On Monday, the day after the man from Umtata was killed, a war party from Phola Park entered the Kalanyoni hostel while most of the residents were at work. Six Zulus, jobless men and night-shift workers, were killed. Later that afternoon shots were fired at the shanty town from the hostel.

At nightfall the men of Phola Park patrolled the squatter camp as they had done the night before. They carried axes and spears, and wore blankets cloaked round their shoulders. After the killings on Sunday night people in Phola Park were watching Kalanyoni with hawk eyes. At two in the morning a war party came out of the hostel carrying axes and spears. They were intercepted by a police Casspir, a hulking, sarcophagus-like armoured vehicle. The war party from the hostel halted in the white glare of the vehicle's searchlight. The driver talked to them and the raiders turned round and walked back to the hostel.

Just before dawn they attacked again. A shot rang out inside Phola Park and people bolted from their shacks in a panic, racing through the dim alleyways, stumbling across the railway line on the edge of the camp and onto the tar road. The Phola Park patrol lay in wait inside the empty shacks. Four Zulus were ambushed and killed. Five men from Phola Park were shot dead.

That Tuesday morning, hours after the raid on Phola Park, several hundred Zulus in four platoons marched out of the gates of Mshayazafe ('beat him to death' in Zulu) hostel in Tokoza. Escorted by police in armoured vehicles, they headed south down Kumalo Street to relieve the besieged Zulus in Kalanyoni hostel.

Thirteen thousand migrant workers lived in the three Tokoza hostels at the north end of Kumalo Street: Mshayazafe, Kutuza and Madala, long, low barracks next to the railway line. At the outbreak of the war Tokoza, the township nearest Phola Park, was home to 140000 people, two-thirds of whom were under sixteen. At the south end of Kumalo Street, 4 kilometres from the hostels, lay the 3000 huddled shacks of Phola Park.

The *impi* (Zulu war party) from Mshayazafe tramped south to Kalanyoni, observed with bewilderment by the residents of Tokoza, who had never seen this kind of thing before. The *impi* turned into the hostel, leaving the police escort at the gates. The reinforcements sat down in a large circle with the Zulus from Kalanyoni and held a conference. The hostel's outer line of defence, a 2-metre-high wall of concrete blocks, had been breached in several places over the years to provide short cuts for people walking to work. Now Zulu pickets guarded the breaches. The walls of the hostel were charred where rooms had been petrol-bombed. The roof was buckled and twisted by fire.

While the Zulu faction was conferring inside the hostel shots rang out in Phola Park. Two men who had been sitting with a bottle of beer outside one of the shacks fell dying, and another man was slain by a bullet inside his shack. In Zola section a fourteen-year-old boy lay dying outside shack M45 from a bullet wound. A large toy pistol was tucked into his belt. When Phola Park residents asked policemen at the hostel gates why they had let the assassins run back into the hostel, they said it was too dangerous for them to go inside.

Meanwhile reinforcements had begun to arrive in Phola Park. AmaBhaca clansmen came by taxi from the Kutalo hostel in Germiston, an industrial centre nearby, and others trickled in from squatter camps in the area. The Xhosa pogrom, or the threat of a pogrom, had purged the nearby hostels of Xhosas. Some of the fugitives who had found shelter in Phola Park joined the assembling Xhosa war party. Razor-sharp, all-steel axes were hastily machined by men who worked in the engineering industry. *Pangas* were bought from Lucia's Shop on Kumalo Street. AK-47s were begged or borrowed. Handguns trickled in. But most of the weaponry consisted of spears, wooden clubs and sharpened steel reinforcing rods. A final solution to the threat posed by the Kalanyoni hostel was decided at a mass meeting held under the giant electricity pylons in Phola Park.

On Tuesday evening the Xhosa war party began to prepare for battle. Women were asked to leave and *intelezi* (battle-medicine) was brewed. The *inyanga*, the medicine man, supplied the *intelezi*, a bitter-tasting decoction of herbs and tree bark. All the men swigged from a large container of *intelezi*, then stuck their fingers down their throats to make themselves vomit. After they had thrown up the men became wild and fearless. The *inyanga* then cut two small, parallel nicks on each man's forehead with a quick flick of a razor blade. *Muti*, a bullet-proofing potion, was rubbed into the cuts. Some of the men tied plastic foam and cardboard round their forearms to fend off *panga* blows. Finally the men donned their traditional war blankets, the *abungubu*, rough woollen prison-issue blankets treated with *muti* and never washed.

The onslaught on Kalanyoni began at four in the morning on Wednesday. The man from Umtata had been dead for three days. Four a.m. was the traditional hour for surprise attacks, when the enemy was sleeping most heavily. The Phola Park *impi* invaded Kalanyoni through the breaches in the outer wall and took the hostel by storm. The blanket men made a weird buzzing noise as they slashed and stabbed their way through the hostel, killing more than twenty Zulus. Residents of Phola Park shudder at the memory. 'A sound like a swarm of bees came from inside the hostel,' remembers one resident. 'It was an eerie sound, like a horror movie.'

Panicked hostel-dwellers poured out of the windows and ran for their lives. The fighting continued in the twilight outside the hostel, under the bluegum trees and along the railway line. Bodies were strewn everywhere. A fat Zulu worker who was killed inside the hostel was slit open and his liver eaten by the blanket men while it was still warm, to boost the effects of the battle-medicine. 'The sound of the AK was too much for them,' says a Phola Park resident who took part in the raid. 'We had five AKs by then. They were armed with R1 rifles. But they couldn't shoot. They aimed between the eyes. The recoil threw their aim off and the bullets went over our heads. Most were hacked to death. Even some Zulu guys who supported us were killing their own brothers. We got fridges, beds, beer, anything we could lay our hands on.'

The police arrived on the scene once the worst of the fighting was over and shot teargas grenades at the Xhosas, who ran away. R1 rifles were seen changing hands between White policemen and hostel-dwellers. Phola Park complained that the police were handing out guns to the Zulus. The Zulus protested that the police were confiscating their guns as they came out to fight.

At dawn Phola Park massed for another attack. Once again they were dispersed with volleys of teargas. The Zulus decided to cut their losses and fled to Mshayazafe hostel, at the far end of Kumalo Street. The Xhosas wanted to go on fighting. They decided to pursue the Zulus and attack Mshayazafe hostel in Tokoza. Several hundred blanket men were intercepted in the township at lunchtime by the South African Defence Force. They were herded back through the streets of Tokoza by a dozen armoured vehicles, before being surrounded and disarmed on the football field outside Phola Park. The people of the East Rand didn't know what had hit them. Pitched battles had not been seen there since the Boer War in 1900. The police had captured truckloads of weaponry, from AKs to *assegais*. All together, 150 people had died that day in the East Rand.

That Wednesday morning the Nguni hostel in the nearby East Rand township of Vosloorus was brutally purged. Zulu hostel residents donned red headbands and moved through the hostel from room to room, smashing doors and slaughtering any Xhosas they found. Other non-Zulus who weren't nimble enough to join the mob were trapped inside their rooms and had to wait their turn to die too. 'It's weird, these guys don't scream when they get killed. They're like lambs to the slaughter,' said a press photographer who was on the scene. He remembers vividly 'the power of killing in their eyes'. The bodies of old and young alike lay sprawled on their beds where they were shot. A Xhosa man fled the hostel with his possessions in plastic shopping bags and was shot through the head with a hand gun. A petrol bomb spilled flames against one of the hostel walls as comrades from the nearby town tried to buy time for the Xhosas to escape. Twenty-five men died. The killing went on for two hours. The police station was across the road from the Nguni hostel. Survivors came to raise the alarm but found the police were not interested.

A few kilometres from Vosloorus, Kalanyoni hostel was overrun by looters. Anything of value was taken to Phola Park. Over the months the hostel was dismantled and removed piecemeal. Concrete blocks, roofing sheets and window frames were used for home improvements by the shack-dwellers.

The day after the wrecking of Kalanyoni an ANC peace meeting was held in Tokoza stadium. A large contingent from Phola Park listened sceptically as regional leaders made conciliatory noises, saying that a truce would have to be agreed with the IFP, and that problems would be addressed by negotiation. The last speaker to address the crowd screamed: 'Burn the hostel to the ground!' The crowd cheered wildly, taking up the chant: 'Burn the hostel, burn the hostel!' The peace meeting was abandoned and the crowd dispersed in high spirits, chanting and dancing the *toyi-toyi*, a jubilant, high-stepping dance imported from the guerilla training camps of Zimbabwe. The empty ruins of Kalanyoni were repeatedly set alight over the next few days.

Pitched battles between Phola Park and the hostels now became a daily routine. The blanket men of Phola Park would, in the vernacular, 'pay a visit' to Mshayazafe hostel. The hostel would repay the courtesy with a return 'visit' the next day. A stream of coffins from the East Rand poured into the poorest villages of KwaZulu and Transkei.

The opening battles of the East Rand civil war were waged by armies drawn from the ranks of the industrial workforce and unemployed rural migrants. For a number of years the apartheid system of migrant labour had been falling apart faster than it could safely be dismantled. As the government, desperate to preserve the edifice of White rule, tried to replace the structurally unsound pillars of apartheid, the roof caved in. The tangled ruins of apartheid's brave new White South Africa, the house that Hendrik Verwoerd built, became the battleground of the 1990s civil wars.

7 The Grudge

The grudge between hostel-dwellers and the people of the surrounding townships and shanty towns has a long history. By the time civil war broke out in 1990 the migrant workers' hostels in Johannesburg's industrial hinterland had already been suffering a profound internal crisis for several years. Access to the hostels had always been tightly controlled by the pass laws. Under the influx control system you could only get a bed in a hostel if you had a job. After 1986, when Pretoria abolished influx control and breached the dikes, the pass-law raids ceased and the hostels were flooded by the rural unemployed, women, children, criminals, refugees, and just about anyone who wasn't welcome in the townships.

The hostels played a vital role in South Africa's migrant labour system which moved Black males off the land and put them to work in the factories and goldmines. The precursors to the hostels were the diamond miners' 'compounds' in Kimberley in the 1880s. They looked exactly like prison labour camps except that workers could not be shot for trying to escape. The resemblance has endured down the years, and today's hostels look very much like shabby correctional institutions.

In the latter part of the nineteenth century the compound system spread to the goldmines of the Reef, south of Johannesburg. Some factories put up buildings lined with rows of concrete bunks. It was only after the Second World War, when the numbers of migrant factory workers doubled and tripled, that the government began to build its own gigantic barracks for migrant workers.

Hostels became part of the machinery of apartheid, a way to ensure that Blacks remained temporary citizens in South Africa. Blacks could live in barracks only so long as they were working. The worker had a numbered bed and a locker. When his contract with the factory expired he would take his things and leave, to be replaced by a fresh labour unit.

South Africa's hostels are vast, grim dormitories containing thousands of beds, connected by railway lines to the big cities and industrial areas. By 1990 the government had built 180 hostels, containing 600000 beds, with an average of two people sleeping in each bed.

In 1990 a large proportion, perhaps the majority, of hostel dwellers in the Johannesburg area were Zulu-speaking peasants from the KwaZulu homeland. They came from the poorest districts of KwaZulu: Msinga, Nkandla, Mahlabatini. Industry had a preference for Zulus because they were hard-working, compliant and respectful towards Whites. The Zulu peasantry also tended to be politically conservative and reluctant to join strikes or stayaways. Discipline was entrenched: obedience to the *induna* (headman) was unquestioning. If an employer could keep the headmen on side, they would deliver a docile workforce.

There were also large numbers of migrants from the other rural homelands: Xhosas, Suthus, Pedis, Shangaans, Tswanas. In the goldmines the established practice was to segregate the different ethnic groups in separate hostel blocks. Every few years there were bitter wars between the various ethnic dormitories, in which dozens of miners were killed. Some state hostels were ethnically segregated into Sotho and Nguni sections. Most, however, were mixed.

In the hundred years since the migrant labour system was born in the diamond mines of Kimberley in the Northern Cape, hostels have become a way of life for the South African peasantry. When influx control was abolished, not all hostel-dwellers rushed to bring their families to town. Zulu migrants, for instance, seemed quite comfortable with single-sex hostels. The traditional Zulu system of land tenure dictates that once a family vacates a plot of land, it forfeits its living rights and the land reverts back to the local chief, who allocates it to someone else. Zulu migrant labourers had to leave their wives and families on the land in order to retain living rights. Other Zulus decided to break their link with the land entirely.

People moved to the townships for various reasons. Some were misfits in the rigidly conservative system of Zulu custom. People who married into their own blood line, for instance, were shunned, as were men who didn't own any cattle. Becoming a 'township Zulu' indicated that you had broken your connection with the land and the ancestors. In the eyes of some traditionalists that made you a pariah. If you were a 'township Zulu' you no longer spoke 'proper' Natal Zulu, you used the township patois, a hybrid vernacular based on Zulu with plenty of Xhosa, Suthu, Tswana, English and Afrikaans words and phrases mixed in. You could tell straight away whether someone was from the township or the hostel by the way they turned their words. During the civil war speaking the wrong dialect was an automatic death sentence.

It's not clear exactly when the hatred began between the hostels and the townships. The first recorded clash was in Soweto in 1957. Residents of the Dube hostel, most of whom were Zulus, tangled with residents of Meadowlands township. There was another fracas in the winter of 1976, also in Soweto, when hostel-dwellers were harassed by township youth for going to work during a stayaway. The hostel was petrol-bombed and a war party from the hostel slaughtered several dozen township residents.

Further clashes occurred that winter in Cape Town, when Xhosa hostel-dwellers went on the rampage, burning 200 houses in Nyanga, after youths attacked the hostel.

As the townships began to mobilize against the government in the mid-eighties, friction increased once more. When the 1984 revolt against the Black local councillors spread from the Vaal Triangle to the East Rand, the Tsakane hostel was wrecked, the first of several Transvaal hostels to be pulverized by township residents.

Father Joseph Khanye, a young Anglican priest, was unemployed in Tsakane township at the time. 'People started to boycott rent,' he remembers. 'The fact that councillors had businesses – garages and shops – was resented. They were using the rent for their own purposes. There were no improvements in the township. Tsakane still had a bucket nightsoil system.'

Most of the municipal workers, including the men who collected the nightsoil buckets, lived in the Tsakane hostel. 'Some people saw the bucket men as lower-class people,' says Khanye. 'They were Zulus with ritual scars and looped ears. People used to make fun of them. Some of us suspected they didn't want a sewer system in the township because they didn't want to lose their jobs.'

In May 1985 a popular local trade union official, Andries Raditsela, died while in police custody. A stayaway was called to mark his funeral. 'Some hostel-dwellers ignored the call to stay away,' recalls Khanye. 'We heard they weren't happy. We organized meetings to air their grievances. Some hostel-dwellers said they were prepared to be part of the community. They left the hostel and built shacks in the township. But most said they had come to work for their families and would not take part in stayaways or rent-boycotts.'

As friction between the township residents and the Black councillors increased, there were attacks on young United Democratic Front activists at night. Several were murdered. The police did nothing. Youngsters in the township suspected that the vigilantes were being recruited from the hostel. 'The people in the hostels were vulnerable,' says Khanye. 'Their disagreements with the township people were exploited to eliminate activists.' The hostel-dwellers and the town councillors found common ground in opposition to the rent-boycotts and stayaways. As elsewhere in the Transvaal, the hostels became the Black councillors' natural constituency.

A Zulu hostel-dweller who went drinking in a shebeen in Tsakane one night was caught by youths, splashed with petrol and set alight. War parties from the hostel, wearing white scarves for identification, went on the rampage with spears and sharpened metal rods. People living near the hostel had their windows smashed. 'The mood was terrible,' says Khanye. 'You could feel it groaning with tension. The vigilantes were killing comrades and youngsters at night in their houses. The police did nothing about it. People would sleep with kettles boiling on their stoves as a means of defence.'

A decision was taken in September to demolish the hostel. 'We called a stayaway. No one would enter or leave the township. Barricades were erected and the entrances to the township were guarded. We explained to the police that we had decided to demolish the hostel, and our reasons,' says Khanye:

> It started at four in the morning, we went from house to house waking up the men. Even the local priest came along . . . Some of us were armed with pick-axe handles and shovels, others carried petrol. Just as it was getting light we smashed the windows of the hostel. People inside screamed and ran away. We entered the hostel and the rooms were looted and burned. Some hostel-dwellers resisted and they were killed. The police took the bodies away. The hostel people were helpless. They never came back. The Xhosas from the hostel moved into the township.

Father Khanye pauses, shaking his head culpably. 'I was also blackened by this anger, caught up in an emotional ecstasy.'

A pattern of attacks and counter-attacks between hostels and townships set in. During stayaways hostel-dwellers were prevented from travelling to work or to the shops by transport stoppages and harassment. People from the hostel were assaulted or abducted by members of the township 'street committee', a gang of youthful vigilantes.

A complaint was made to the hostel headman, who was answerable to a chief in KwaZulu for the safety of his subjects. He would decide whether to retaliate against the township. If a revenge attack was judged necessary, the hostel would be placed on a war footing, each room mobilizing its own armed unit in the traditional Zulu way.

The hostel-dwellers saw the entire area where an assault had taken place as anti-hostel, since the township residents had done nothing to restrain or punish the street committee. If shots were fired at the hostel from the township, for instance, it would be impossible to ascertain exactly where the shots came from. That entire section of the township would therefore be viewed as hostile.

From now on military logic takes over. The area in question must be cleaned out so that it becomes a no man's land in which nobody moves. A massive, highly visible retaliation is planned. The headman's defence unit, the *amaButhu*, forms a shield- and spear-carrying war party.

While the hostel is on a war footing a form of martial law applies. Security on the hostel gates is tightened. Every man in the hostel is mobilized. You either fight or you support the fighters, who are busy full-time and may even lose their jobs. Levies are raised to pay for firearms and battle-medicine. Guns are purchased or hired from professional gun-runners. Organized crime flourishes while the residents are busy trying to cope with the external threat. Rooms are robbed, women raped, raising the temperature still further. Warlords emerge and criminal gangs move into the hostel for protection. They help with the supply of weapons and bribe the headmen to let them stay.

The township lays siege to the hostel. Hostel-dwellers are singled out for attack in the streets, in taxis and on trains. There is massive retaliation. The hostels become fortresses, entirely cut off from the township. The railway, the hostel's only link with the outside world, comes under rifle fire and the track is sabotaged. Water and electricity are cut off. People trapped inside the hostel for three, four days, maybe a week, are losing their jobs. The ordinary sensible types are saying, we've had it, we're going back to Natal. Their beds are taken by unemployed hopefuls from Natal, gullible hillbillies who've been told there are jobs in Johannesburg, only to be press-ganged on arrival and sent on night raids against the township. The unlucky ones lie rotting in a city morgue for weeks. No one bothers to tell their relatives to come and collect them. Often no one even knows who they are. By now people are wondering whether township and hostel can ever live together in peace. People in the township want the hostel destroyed. The hard core in the hostel will fight to the last man. Both sides arm themselves for the final onslaught.

It all goes back to Hendrik's dikes. The crisis in the hostels was a direct result of the dismantling of the pass laws and influx control. The hostels filled up with jobless men and women, relatives from the homelands who came to stay. You couldn't really turn them away. Your brother might sleep on your bed while you were working night shifts. You might look after him and give him money for bus fares so he could look for a job. But there were no jobs to be had. The jobless people in the hostel stole food from your locker. They became a nuisance, a burden on those who had jobs. And when the youngsters in the township, most of whom were unemployed, called stayaway upon stayaway, you certainly weren't going to risk losing your job and becoming one of the loafers.

While the civil war was the bane of employed hostel-dwellers, whose daily journey to work became a nerve-racking chicken run, for the jobless drifters who bedded down on floors and in corridors it was an opportunity to establish themselves in the city. First of all, when Xhosas and ANC members, who were seen as the enemy's fifth column, fled from the hostels, beds became available. Secondly, the war created employment for idle hands. It provided jobless men with a mission, a way to become a respected somebody instead of a jobless nobody. Hundreds of previously idle men in the hostels became full-time combatants and troublemakers. With the ending of pass-law raids on the hostels the police were seldom seen. Many hostels became no-go areas for police, who did little to protect hostel-dwellers against harassment, and would interfere with plans to attack the township. White and Zulu policemen drew less hostility, but generally speaking the police weren't welcome. The hostels descended into anarchy.

The dismantling of the influx control system also widened the gaps between ethnic groups inside the hostels. Zulu men preferred to stay in barracks. They weren't fond of squatting and couldn't bring their families to join them, as this would mean forfeiting their claim to land back home. Besides, now that security on the hostel gates had become looser, girlfriends could move in with the men. Xhosas, on the other hand, seemed quite prepared to move out. Partly because some preferred not to be near Zulus. Partly because they would, if given the choice, bring their families over from Transkei. Partly because people were flooding to Johannesburg in their thousands from the Xhosa homelands and were settling in shanty towns where they could live in the company of clansmen from their home area.

Until 1990 no one really bothered much about politics in the hostels. There was Inkatha, a stuffy cultural organization for Zulus. There were the unions, which pretty much ignored the hostels and held their meetings in the townships. Politics was about township issues. And the hostels, and the villages where the hostel-dwellers had their homes, were of no interest to the mass urban movement fighting against apartheid. People in the townships were literate, better educated. Most hostel-dwellers had no education beyond herding cattle.

Politically, people in the townships had their eyes wide open, especially the youngsters. They identified with the Russian revolution, the Cuban revolution, the North Vietnamese, the Palestine Liberation Organization. All over South Africa they renamed the sections of their townships Beirut, Vietnam, Cuba, Moscow, Poland, Russia. The men in the hostels were middle-aged, working men who thought the youngsters were out of order. The way they saw it, you had headmen and chiefs and a king; you had the glorious history of the Zulus who had given the British a pasting. They were the ones who had started the fight against the White man, not these youngsters with their stayaways and their rude songs about Chief Buthelezi.

People in the townships had aspirations, they wanted things to change. They were fighting for a better life, more opportunities, more money, better schools and transport, better houses. They did the nicer jobs and left the heavy-duty industrial toil and the nasty shit-shovelling jobs to the hostel-dwellers. The townships were the home of South Africa's urban petty bourgeoisie, the hostels were the barracks of its semi-rural lumpenproletariat. The hostels were right inside the townships. Sooner or later there was bound to be trouble.

When Black politics was unbanned in 1990 and Hendrik's last dike came crashing down, the hostels became islands of resistance within the politically galvanized Transvaal townships. It was no great problem for the Inkatha Freedom Party (IFP) to mobilize tens of thousands of disgruntled Zulus to go out and hammer the ANC. The way the Zulus in the hostels saw it, the ANC youth wanted to bring their factories to a halt, destroy their jobs, destroy their hostels and drive them out of the townships altogether. Which was the way a lot of youngsters in the townships did see it, even if their political leaders made soothing noises in public.

Inkatha, which had been fighting ANC-supporting Zulus in Natal for years, became the rallying point for migrant Zulus. Even if you didn't feel particularly strongly about politics, you joined the IFP because everyone else joined. The worse the fighting became, the more people flocked to join. Soon membership of the Inkatha Freedom Party was all but compulsory, notwithstanding the IFP politicians' bland catchphrases about 'choice', 'freedom' and 'democracy'. Inside the hostels, and wherever else Inkatha was mobilizing at grass roots, there were no ifs or buts. If you didn't join you were a traitor to the Zulu nation. Your folks back home might suffer a nasty accident. There was actually no point in trying to remain neutral. Township youngsters assumed you were Inkatha anyway, because your Natal Zulu accent screamed 'country bumpkin', an invitation for the shampoo bottles full of petrol and the little boxes of matches to come out.

8 Kom, Zulu! Kom, Zulu!

A year after the abolition of the pass laws, in the winter of 1987, 150 families who were living in shacks in a coal yard near Tokoza township on the East Rand were evicted by the Tokoza Town Council. The land had been sold to developers. Influx control may have been abolished but the government still insisted on 'orderly urbanization'. These people who thought they could just trample the apartheid dikes and settle in tin huts wherever they liked were wrong. The government was busy toughening the penalties for illegal squatters. Meanwhile the squatters in the Tokoza coal yard were told to move to Site Two near the Tokoza water tower. They watched as their shacks were demolished. The lucky ones were able to salvage roofing sheets and window frames. The others spent two weeks sleeping rough before the Red Cross could provide tents.

Four months later the squatters who had obligingly moved to Site Two received a letter from the Tokoza Town Council. 'Your continued presence in the area is in the way of a future township development,' it said. The squatters were told to move to Site Three. They watched in disbelief as the bulldozers razed their shacks for the second time. After wandering round the debris in a daze they picked their things up and moved to Site Three, behind the Kalanyoni migrant labour hostel.

This time the Tokoza Town Council said they could stay, and promised to collect the rubbish and install water taps and sewers. The Red Cross donated more tents. The camp was nicknamed Dunuza, a Zulu word meaning 'stoop', because the women were always bending over to hammer in tent pegs. Soon shacks went up by the hundreds. They looked messy from the outside, built from an assortment of corrugated iron sheets nailed together over a wooden frame, the nails hammered through bottle tops so as not to tear the corries. Inside, though, the shacks were pristine, proud homes. The walls were papered with magazine or newspaper advertisements in neat, regular rows. 'Pictures' were made out of wire and bottle tops and hung on the walls. People brewed beer and flew kites. Dunuza became Phola Park, a place where people could *phola hier* (stay put and relax).

Different sorts of people came to live in the shacks. There were single men from Mozambique, refugees from the civil war which had raged since independence in 1975. The Mozambicans spoke Shangaan and excelled at sewing clothes, mending shoes, and doing perms. Some were trained fighters, who had fought with Frelimo in the Mozambican civil war. These men tended to make their living by illegal means.

Single men arrived from Transkei, the Xhosa 'homeland'. The Xhosas came to work in the factories and send money back home. Then there were the people who came from backyard shacks in Tokoza, the local Black town. The Tokoza Town Council, a self-financing Black local authority, had begun to tax people who rented out shacks in the back yards of their homes. Rents rose to accommodate the tax and most people decided they would rather live for free in a squatter camp. There was an exodus from the backyard shacks of Tokoza. Hundreds of families moved to Phola Park. The Town Council watched in dismay as thousands of potential ratepayers thumbed their noses and left.

In the autumn of 1989 the Tokoza Town Council, which had limited its services to painting numbers on the fronts of shacks, was in dire financial straits. Demands for rent were received by the shack-dwellers in Phola Park. The letter said: 'The Council at its recent meeting decided that every head of household in the area popularly known as Phola Park will pay a sum of R50.00 per month to the Council. This amount is payable on or before the seventh day of each month.' In return the Council promised to take the rubbish away and provide some taps and toilets. The residents of Phola

Park told the Council to get stuffed. The rent was too high and anyway the Council never kept its promises.

Six months later the Council changed its tune once more, desperate to raise some cash. 'The sale of industrial land upon which the squatter camp is situated has become a necessity,' it declared. 'The Council will not be able to market or sell the land before the squatters have been moved.'

The shack-dwellers of Phola Park were given six weeks to move. The Council had established an alternative site: Zonkizizwe, meaning 'people from all places', which was a bare piece of grassland on a farm 13 kilometres away from Phola Park. Each plot had a toilet in a corrugated iron cubicle, and a water tap. There was a rubbish removal service. Phola Park residents pointed out that Zonkizizwe was in the middle of nowhere, with no transport. But some squatters couldn't face the prospect of watching their shacks being demolished for the third time and accepted a plot at Zonkizizwe. Most of the Phola Park shack-dwellers refused to budge. This time, as the bulldozers and the police advanced on the shanty town, they fought back.

Hundreds of shacks were destroyed, then rebuilt overnight by their owners. A few days later the shacks were torn down again. And so it went on. Fights broke out between residents and police. Three squatters were shot dead and about fifty injured. Youngsters from Phola Park went on the rampage, stoning and burning trucks on the Old Vereeneging Road next to the camp. Young White lawyers from the Legal Resources Centre blocked the Council in the Supreme Court. There was a deadlock.

The bulldozers went away. The newspapers were full of pictures of Phola Park residents being pushed around by police while having their homes destroyed. The Minister of Law and Order turned puce and ordered the police to eradicate 'the evil of squatting'. But there were others in the government who believed the problem of squatting should be solved by building houses and turning squatters into home-owners.

In August 1990, as civil war was breaking out on the East Rand, the government established the Independent Development Trust, which was to play an ambiguous role in Phola Park's future. In the winter of 1990, however, the residents of Phola Park had other things besides community development on their mind.

After the destruction of Kalanyoni hostel in mid–August there had been a lull in the vendetta between Phola Park and the local Zulu migrants. Mshayazafe hostel, where the Zulus from Kalanyoni had taken refuge, was the new focus of hostility in the shanty town. It wasn't until the second week in September that the attacks resumed. They began with red tracer bullets streaking over the shacks from the direction of the brick factory, just after sunset. On three nights in succession Phola Park was invaded by dozens of bare-chested Zulu warriors wearing red or white headbands. Hundreds of shacks were exploded by means of mysterious and devastating incendiary devices. After the attack people remarked that the Zulus seemed more interested in burning shacks than in killing Xhosas. The strangest thing about September's night raids was the presence of White men in the ranks of the Zulu war parties.

During the second attack, one old lady heard a knock at her door and someone screaming in Zulu to open. Four men were standing in the doorway, three Black and one White. The White guy was wearing a balaclava and his face was blacked up. One of the Black guys asked in Zulu: 'What are you doing here?' The old lady told him she lived there. The man asked her why she lived there. She said because she lived there, she had nowhere else to go. Another Zulu guy said, nah, leave her, she's an old lady. The White guy told the Zulus in English no, they must hit her, so they slapped her across the face before taking her outside. The White guy took a step backwards and fired something at the shack, which burst into flames.

That night people all over Phola Park saw White men in balaclavas with faces smeared in black skin paint, blowing up shacks and egging on the Zulus in Afrikaans. 'Kom, Zulu, kom! Maak die Xhosa dood!' ('Come on Zulu, kill the Xhosa!') and 'Kom Rasta, Xhosas is hierdie kant!' ('Come on Rasta, the Xhosas are this side!') Armoured police vehicles (Casspirs) were seen driving around, playing their searchlights on the shacks. A helicopter hovered over the shanty town, also shining a searchlight. Once Phola Park was ablaze, the searchlights were switched off. The defenders tore down shacks to create fire-breaks, but a large section of Phola Park was burned to the ground.

By the morning of the third day one side of the camp was a mass of charred wreckage. Dozens of squatters were dead or maimed. Zulu corpses wearing red headbands were dragged out from between the shacks and laid out in a row on the edge of the shanty town. People came to vent their anger. Women screamed with rage and kicked the bodies. Men came forward and let fly with their wooden clubs, making a strange, dull sound on the dead flesh. 'Little children were playing with the corpses, calling them "uncircumcised",' remembers a shack-dweller. 'They poked sticks up the dead men's bottoms.'

Two of the balaclava-clad, blacked-up White assailants had been killed. One of the corpses was retrieved by a police Casspir in the middle of the night. The other was taken by the medicine men in the camp and used for *muti* (battle-medicine). Part of the White man's body was eaten on the spot, slivers of flesh shaved off and given to the defenders to chew. The vital organs were kept for later. One of the blanket men was proudly showing off the scalp. 'The big guys got the important parts,' says a resident. 'One guy from the Madiba clan (Nelson Mandela's kinsmen) was holding the brains. He went round drinking and boasting that he would overpower the White man with his own brains.' The *inyanga* placed the White man's

Vosloorus hostel, August 1990.
BELOW IFP-supporting Zulus attack non-Zulus trapped in their rooms.
RIGHT A victim of the purge lies dead.
(*Ken Oosterbroek/ The Star*)

OVERLEAF
Zulu *impi* return to the Vosloorus hostel after a raid on the township.
(*Ken Oosterbroek/ The Star*)

RIGHT Phola Park
in summer.
(*Daniel Reed*)

Phola Park, August 1990.
LEFT A boy lies dying,
shot only minutes before
by Zulu gunmen. The
pistol in his belt is a toy.
ABOVE Angry Xhosa
blanket-men gather to plan
the final assault on
Kalanyoni hostel. (*Ken
Oosterbroek/ The Star*)

RIGHT Soweto, 1992: Zulu hostel-dwellers attack commuters. (*Joao Silva/ The Star*)

BELOW Soweto, 1992:
a commuter leaps
between trains in a bid
to escape from the
hostel-dwellers.
(*Joao Silva/ The Star*)

BELOW East Rand, 1993:
blanket-men from the
Phola Park SDU (one
armed with an AK-47
rifle) run for cover.
(*Ruvan Boshoff/ The Star*)

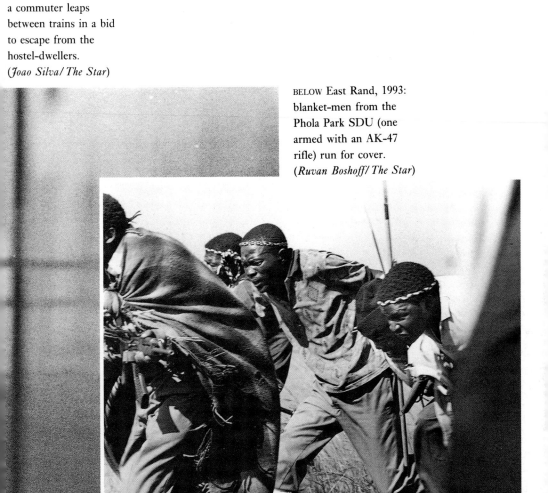

East Rand, 1993: South African
Defence Force armour patrols
Tokoza at dawn. (*Guy Adams/
The Weekly Mail*)

testicles and other vital organs on the roof of a shack to dry in the sun, so that they could be powdered later. 'The White man's young wife was losing her mind,' remembers a Phola Park resident. 'She came to Phola Park on foot saying she wanted even just a bone to give him a decent burial. She kept asking for "die been van die baas, die been van die baas" (the boss's bone). We laughed. We told her there's no *baas* here.'

Phola Park was tense after the September burn-out. There were constant rumours of attacks, particularly at weekends. People became paranoid. If the police patrolled the camp, searching for guns, Phola Park concluded that they were being softened up, disarmed in preparation for a Zulu attack. If the police stayed out of Phola Park, the silence grew deafening, and people drew the same conclusion but for the opposite reason: an attack was on the way because the police were leaving the coast clear for the Zulus. The men would gather with their weapons and fighting blankets. But the attack never came. And when an attack did come, it was never preceded by a rumour.

In the lull between major confrontations there were routine killings, usually involving the minibus taxis which plied the busy routes between the industrial parks and the townships of the East Rand. Most of the local taxi drivers were Zulus from the hostels. The day after the last Inkatha attack on Phola Park, a taxi driver who was stopped by shack-dwellers near the camp made the mistake of speaking Zulu. He was driven into Phola Park where a crowd gathered around the minibus. The driver protested that he was in fact Shangaan, not Zulu. Somebody asked: 'If you are Shangaan then why don't you speak your own language?' Before he could answer the driver was killed.

In November refugees began to arrive in Phola Park by the dozen, carrying their belongings in plastic bags and supermarket trolleys. They were running away from Zonkizizwe, the resettlement camp for 'people from all places', where they had been sent by the Tokoza Town Council earlier in the year. Fighting had broken out between Zulu fugitives from Kalanyoni hostel who had taken refuge at Zonkizizwe and the Xhosa group from Phola Park. Forty-five people had died. The IFP was in control of Zonkizizwe. The fugitives were bitter. They wanted revenge. A decisive onslaught on the Tokoza hostels was planned.

9 The Great War

Phola Park's Great War of December 1990 began at midnight, when an army set out from the shanty town under police escort to annihilate Mshayazafe ('beat him to death') hostel.

The new Xhosa *inyanga* (medicine man) from Umzimkulu had prepared special *muti* to make the warriors invulnerable. Instead of bullets, the Zulu guns would shoot harmless drops of water. The *inyanga* had a troubling premonition about the planned attack. He was heard to say that he might not come back. No one paid any attention at the time.

Xhosa policemen sympathetic to their clansmen in Phola Park were a key part of that night's operation. They entered Mshayazafe early in the evening and told the hostel-dwellers that the police were planning a raid that night. They advised them to stash their armaments. The Mshayazafe militiamen buried their firearms in a safe place round the back of the hostel, near the railway line, and went to sleep.

Meanwhile the war party from Phola Park, numbering 100 men, was joined by an additional fifty men from Tokoza township. They were accompanied by Xhosa-speaking policemen, who were in charge of the night shift while their Zulu-speaking colleagues were off-duty. Two armoured police vehicles escorted the Phola Park war party. More warriors were transported in trucks. The raiders surrounded the hostel shortly after midnight, covering all the exits.

The Mshayazafe hostel, like the two other hostels on Kumalo Street, consists of several long, low barrack blocks, known familiarly as 'trains'. The trains were dark at night, with no lights in the smashed window panes, as the electricity supply to the hostels had been switched off.

First to penetrate the hostel was the medicine man from Umzimkulu. He was disguised as a Zulu *inyanga*, with red and white beads draped across his chest and in bands round his wrists and ankles. His task was to sprinkle *muti* around the hostel, a mixture of herbs designed to spike the Zulu guns. Once he had done this he left by way of a window at the back of one of the trains. This proved to be a mistake.

At the war conference in Phola Park, it had been agreed that all the exits from the hostel would be sealed off, leaving a single exit through which a detachment of gunmen could penetrate the hostel and leave once they had completed the attack. Perhaps no one had allowed for the medicine man's undercover mission. The pickets in the ring of steel round the hostel spotted what looked like a Zulu escaping out of a window. The disguise of red and white Zulu beads clinched it. The medicine man from Umzimkulu had foreseen his own death. He was shot dead next to the hostel, as the attack began.

Hostel-dwellers were woken by automatic gunfire aimed into their rooms from the outside windows. As they fled into the hostel yard they were cut down by gunmen who had entered the hostel. Hand grenades were tossed into the dormitory rooms. Some Zulus managed to run behind the hostel to fetch their firearms but the Xhosas stationed there were waiting for them. The classic two-pronged attack was going like clockwork. The Xhosa-speaking policemen were fighting shoulder to shoulder with the Xhosa blanket men, gunning down the hostel residents in the yard, which soon filled with gunsmoke. Zulus who managed to grab their guns found that the medicine man's herbal treatment had rendered them inoperable. 'There was a massacre,' recalls a Phola Park man.

Meanwhile the Zulu policemen beginning their shift at the police station were growing suspicious. Their Xhosa colleagues had disappeared without saying where they were going. The Zulu constables decided to check the hostels. They arrived just as the blanket men were retreating out of Mshayazafe. They had expended all their ammunition on the hostel-dwellers, only to discover that the man carrying the AK magazines had wandered off somewhere with all the spare bullets. 'The Zulu police took us out of our rooms to go and fight,' recalls a hostel-dweller. 'They couldn't let us be butchered by Xhosa policemen and their brothers.' The arrival of the Zulu policemen perked up the hostel-dwellers, but by then the attack was over and a dozen Zulus lay dead. A couple of White cops sat chatting in a car near the Kutuza hostel gates, without a care in the world. Kumalo Street usually gets busy well before dawn with taxis and people walking to work. That morning the street was still.

Day broke on Kumalo Street to reveal small groups of men with white headbands guarding the hostel gates. Inside Mshayazafe a huge meeting of local Zulu hostel-dwellers was in progress. A contingent had come from Kwesine hostel in neighbouring Katlehong. Themba Khoza, the Inkatha Freedom Party's Transvaal strongman, was there. When he heard how the hostel-dwellers had been caught napping he threw a tantrum. 'He was very furious,' remembers one of the hostel-dwellers. 'He threw down his pen and hurled down his jacket. He didn't know what to do.'

In a nearby street a solitary factory worker in blue overalls was walking to work. He was challenged by one of the guards wearing white headbands, but pretended he hadn't heard. A woman lobbed a stone at him and he skipped into one of the front yards for safety. Before he could hide, a silver grey Toyota Cressida tooled past and two shots were fired. The man in overalls lay dying, watched by a group of bystanders. 'Is he a Xhosa?' asked an old man. People just shrugged.

Meanwhile the gathering at Mshayazafe hostel had decided to retaliate against Phola Park. All the men stood up and yelled the battle shout. Battle-medicine was quaffed and sprinkled. They jogged out of the hostel towards Phola Park chanting a battle song: 'Is'ghubu Asasazani! Sikhulela Entabeni!' ('The wild animals don't know each other, but they all grew up together on the mountain.') The Is'ghubu song is sung to raise morale when a war party is made up of people who don't usually fight side by side. The men from the Katlehong and Tokoza hostels joined in the singing together as they marched on Phola Park.

'The road was black with a cloud of men fully armed to wipe away the uncultured creatures,' recollects a hostel dweller:

We went straight to Phola Park. There were all kinds of policemen. But when we got there the police disappeared to the location. I think they were giving us a chance of revenging. There was no one in Phola Park. They had all run away. We burned their shacks. As we were about to finish we saw a crowd of Xhosas under a bridge, sitting with their women and children. All the municipal police who were helping them were no longer there, they were some distance away in their police vans. All the guns they were using to shoot us were no longer there. What happened then will never leave my mind. It was difficult even to walk because their bodies were strewn all over the place.

That morning the blanket men were defenceless. They had used up all their ammunition in the previous night's attack. The police stood watching as they fled this way and that, while the AKs went rat-tat-tat, hammering on inside the shanty town for what seemed like an eternity. The police watched as Xhosa men were chased into a patch of marshy ground and slaughtered in the reeds.

The only policemen who did anything were Coloured policemen from Eden Park, the Coloured township next to Phola Park. They tried to hold off the second Zulu attack. A Coloured policeman perched in a tree in Eden Park used his automatic rifle on the Zulus, yelling at the fleeing Phola Park men to stand their ground. But the carnage was only halted by the arrival of a large force of police armoured vehicles, who pacified the attackers with teargas and herded them back to Mshayazafe. The smoke cleared to reveal the smouldering wreckage of the shanty town, bodies lying everywhere. At least thirty men had died. The local morgues filled up once more with truckloads of corpses.

That day the women and children of Phola Park packed their possessions and took shelter in churches nearby. Several hundred women found refuge in the brick factory next to the shanty town, sleeping on the drying racks and in the showers. The men of Phola Park stayed in the camp, out of sight.

A dead silence hung over the burnt-out shacks. At dusk it began to rain. When it rains in South Africa the fighting stops.

Next morning the South African Defence Force threw a ring of steel round the camp. A soldier stood guard every 30 metres and an armoured vehicle every 100 metres. The troops were tense. For many of the young conscripts it was their first day in the East Rand battle zone.

10 Prince's New Dawn

Shortly before noon, two days after the second, devastating raid of the Great War, a convoy of new BMWs entered Phola Park, trailed by the largest contingent of international press the squatters had ever seen. Nelson Mandela, the President of the African National Congress, had arrived to deliver a pep-talk to the people of Phola Park. A crowd of several thousand gathered to listen to his message. People climbed on the roofs of shacks to get a better view of their leader, causing several of the frail structures to collapse.

Meanwhile at the other end of Kumalo Street Dr Buthelezi, Chief Minister of KwaZulu and champion of the Inkatha Freedom Party, was addressing an even larger crowd of angry hostel-dwellers. He outdid Nelson's convoy of BMWs and Mercedes, arriving by helicopter with the South African Minister of Law and Order, Adriaan Vlok.

Mandela stayed in Phola Park for twenty minutes. He spoke in English, for the benefit of the assembled media. It seemed incongruous since he was a Xhosa, as were most of the people in Phola Park. In the end, though, it hardly mattered, because his voice didn't carry and no one could hear what he said.

As Mandela's motorcade made its way out past the twisted remains of incinerated shacks on the edge of the camp, a rumble went round the crowd that there was a Zulu in the camp. Phola Park turned on the suspect, eager to burn him. An American aid worker who was on the scene shielded the man with his body, while Prince Mhlambi, a community leader, reasoned with the mob. 'Who says he's a Zulu?' he barked. 'Who says?' Nobody could answer. The press photographers fingered their shutter releases in readiness for blood and the front page. But Prince faced the people down and the mob dispersed sheepishly, allowing the suspected Zulu to leave.

By no means all the residents of Phola Park, however, were interested

57

in war. There was a desire amongst many shack-dwellers, particularly those who lived in Phola Park with their families, to put down roots, build homes and get on with making a better life. This was particularly true of the families who had moved from backyard shacks in Tokoza when the Council started to tax their landlords. They were modern township people, who wanted to live in houses. They formed organizations and committees, elected along democratic lines. Their champion was Prince.

Prince, who was in his late twenties, had lived in Phola Park from the very beginning, when he was a student leader on the run during the second state of emergency. By the time of his assassination, five years later, he had become the public face of Phola Park. He was the darling of the media, adored by the press and the foreign embassies.

Prince had fled his parents' house in nearby Tokoza in the late eighties to find safety in Phola Park. Before long, however, Prince began to see Phola Park as more than a bolt-hole. It became his personal mission, a vehicle for the energy, talent and ambition which everyone admired in him. The crusade to uplift the squatters, often in spite of themselves, became Prince's life's work. And there was no doubt that he genuinely did care.

Prince buttonholed all the embassies and consulates in Johannesburg and Pretoria on behalf of Phola Park. Convincing, passionate, well-dressed, well-spoken, Prince made a good impression on foreign diplomats, particularly at the British and American consulates. They enjoyed his company, and the insights he provided into a way of life so far removed from their own. He took them round Phola Park and made them feel they had a role to play in the welfare of the community. Donations were requested for the poor of Phola Park. Little by little money began to flow in.

To handle the money, Prince founded KWASA ('Dawn' in Zulu), an organization which provided soup kitchens, pre-school centres, adult literacy classes and free legal advice to the shack-dwellers. Another of KWASA's aims was to 'encourage self-empowerment' through a candle-making project, a silk-screening project, a carpentry project and a knitting project.

Prince became the main man in the camp. He chaired the residents' committee. He got things done. He was Phola Park's bridge to the outside world, to the media, to the welfare organizations and the ANC. The ANC was popular in Phola Park because it was in favour of squatters' land rights, and opposed the Black councils, who were trying to move squatters off the land. The 'civics' (the local civic associations), which were pro-ANC, also supported the squatters' demands. An additional factor was the presence in Phola Park of a majority of traditionally ANC-supporting Xhosas. Winnie Mandela was a frequent visitor, who gained credibility after reportedly dishing out guns from her house in Soweto during one of the early crises. Phola Park was known as the most militant ANC stronghold in the Transvaal.

Prince, who kept close to Winnie, organized bread and shelter for those made homeless by the fighting. He helped bereaved families with funeral arrangements and paid for the bodies to go back to Transkei. When shacks were being torn down by the Council, or the police were shooting at the residents, Prince would rush to the advice office and dial an emergency list of numbers he always kept with him on a piece of paper: journalists, priests, aid workers, any outsider whose arm could be twisted into dropping whatever he or she was doing and driving straight to Phola Park to be a witness to the latest outrage. The presence of members of the press, or other White outsiders became the residents' secret weapon against forced removal by the Council.

Prince was sometimes resented for his bossy manner and his need always to be at the centre of things. His critics observed that he surrounded himself with yes-men, who didn't speak English and would let him do the talking. There were rumours that Prince was 'fond of money'. He flatly refused to account for donations to KWASA, claiming that KWASA's funds were his private concern. When it was pointed out that KWASA raised funds on behalf of Phola Park, not Prince, he just shrugged, saying he was working full-time for the community and needed to support himself.

By Christmas 1990, as the first year of civil war drew to a close, Phola Park and its arch-rival Mshayazafe hostel were ringed with razor wire and placed under twenty-four-hour armed guard by the South African Defence Force. No one entered or left the squatter camp without being searched. With the army separating the two warring factions, the era of pitched battles between massed regiments faded into history. The rolls of razor wire encircling the camp were festooned with rubbish. People were getting into the habit of walking up to the perimeter wire with their trash and lobbing it outside the army's 'ring of steel'.

11 The Vaal Monster

On Boxing Day evening 1990, Victor 'Khetisi' Kheswa and Daniel Mabote, leaders of the Khetisi gang in Zone Seven of Sebokeng township, were summoned to a meeting by the local ANC-supporting 'comrades'. They went to pick up 'Lucky' Mboyane on the way.

At the meeting they were accused of fighting with members of the Cameroon Squad at Ramsay's Inn on Christmas Day. The Cameroon

Squad was another Sebokeng gang which included a number of ANC activists. The local ANC 'people's court', a vigilante group set up to combat crime, wanted an explanation.

Kheswa denied the charges and went to fetch the two boys who had been involved. The boys admitted that they had indeed fought the Cameroon Squad at Ramsay's Inn on Christmas Day. However, as the boys were explaining the reasons for the fight, the meeting was interrupted by a second group of comrades, who had heard that Kheswa was armed. The new arrivals insisted on searching the members of the Khetisi gang and the two boys. When Kheswa's turn came, he refused to be searched. A group of comrades jumped on him and found a loaded gun. One of them went outside and fired the gun to check that it was working. He then returned and shot Kheswa in the stomach.

While Kheswa lay on the floor bleeding, the comrades took Daniel Mabote's car keys and reversed his car into the yard of the house. The other members of the gang were handcuffed. The comrades forced two of them into the boot of the car, and told Lucky to put Kheswa in the boot with them. Lucky himself was then ordered into the boot. The boot was full, and he was told to sit in the back of the car. At this point Lucky ran for his life and was chased for 200 metres by the comrades before escaping. In the confusion Kheswa and the others also escaped. When the police arrived Mabote's car was burning.

It wasn't the first time Victor Kheswa (also known as 'the Vaal Monster') had been in trouble with the comrades. The comrades had accused him of shooting a boy dead in Zone Seven in March. In August they said he had killed a woman by forcing her to drink acid. Christopher Nangalembe, a member of the ANC's anti-crime campaign, had seen him do it.

Two days after Victor was shot, the Khetisi gang had a meeting at a house in Zone Three. Victor was recovering in Boxburg hospital. The men wondered what to do about the comrades. 'Silwane' Kubheka was there. Silwane was Daniel Mabote's cousin, and a member of the Inkatha Freedom party. Silwane's mother was Mrs Kubheka, the IFP official whose house had been petrol-bombed by the comrades while she was hosting the fateful IFP rally in July at Zone Seven stadium. Silwane said his mother had suggested that the gang should seek help from Inkatha members in their fight against the comrades. Silwane then allegedly suggested that the gang should point out the leaders of the comrades to members of Inkatha, who could assassinate them. The younger comrades would then calm down. Daniel, Lucky and the others said nothing. Silwane shrugged and left. The men discussed his suggestion and decided that it was better to keep Inkatha out of it.

On New Year's Day, however, Mrs Hannah Ndhlovu, who lived next door to Victor Kheswa's mother, noticed that eight men in grey overcoats had moved into the Kheswa home. Every time she or her husband turned on the outside light on their house after dark, the men came out and told them to switch it off. One day Johnny Kheswa, Victor's nine-year-old brother, told Mrs Ndhlovu that the strange men were members of the IFP, who were guarding the Kheswa house in case the comrades attacked. They had a whole pile of AK-47s in the bedroom, under a blanket, he chirped.

The day after New Year's, comrades came under AK-47 fire in Zone Seven from three cars hurtling through the township. No one was hit. Victor (who had been discharged from hospital) and some other gang members, accompanied by Victor's mother Emma, had decided to shoot the comrades whom they thought were planning to kill Victor. After the drive-by shooting the comrades went to Kheswa's house as they had recognized his car, but came under fire once more when the cars returned with a police van. That night one of the comrades was woken by policemen accompanied by members of the Khetisi gang. He was held at the police station, where, he claims, he was beaten up by gang members in front of the police.

The next day, Victor and his mother Emma were arrested by the police, who had discovered AK-47s and ammunition in Kheswa's car. They were released four days later.

Meanwhile Christopher Nangalembe, the ANC activist who was said to have witnessed Kheswa force the woman to drink acid, had been abducted. His body was discovered the next day on a rubbish heap near Boipatong township. He had been strangled with wire.

Mandla Nangalembe, who had been warned of a possible attack at the forthcoming night vigil for his brother, contacted the Vanderbijlpark CID. There were strange men patrolling in cars outside the house, he told the police. He was being followed, and feared for his life. The police promised to send a unit to the vigil.

A friend of the Nangalembe family, Mr Ncube, had made his front yard available for the night vigil marquee, where mourners could sit through the night with Christopher's body. Marshals were stationed along the tar road in front of the house and rocks were laid across the road as barricades.

During the night one of the marshals saw men fire shots in the air from a yellow Ford with no numberplates. He recognized the car as one of the vehicles which usually stood in the front yard of the Kheswa house. The car drove off and was not seen again.

That night Daniel Mabote allegedly went to fetch sixteen men from the KwaMadala hostel in the ISCOR steelworks. At least two of the men were former inmates of Sebokeng hostel. The group drove to Kheswa's house, where they were joined by three other members of the Khetisi gang. After a discussion the men drove to Evaton stadium, where they parked their cars and walked towards the night vigil.

A couple of hours before dawn the marshals were guarding the area, chatting in a group by the road several hundred metres from the marquee where the vigil was being held. The night had been uneventful, apart from the brief appearance of the yellow car. One of the marshals, 'Hellboy', decided to walk back to the marquee where the vigil was being held. He was 70 metres from the marquee when he saw a group of twenty men walking towards the tent, singing an ANC hymn 'Senzeni na?' ('What have we done?'). As they got closer to the tent, two men wearing long overcoats came to the front of the group. Hellboy started to walk backwards, away from the marquee. The two men had long shapes under their coats. They fired shots in the air. The other men in the group opened fire on the marquee. Hellboy recognized one of the two men at the front as a member of the Khetisi gang. Three hand grenades were lobbed into the marquee. Thirty-nine mourners were killed and twenty-six injured.

Mrs Ndhlovu's daughter woke up at seven a.m. the day after the night vigil massacre. It was a clear, hot January morning. Oddly, none of the three cars which were usually parked in front of the Kheswa house, including the yellow Ford, was there. The cars never came back. The Kheswa house was burned down that afternoon.

Kheswa and ten associates were arrested and charged with involvement in the night vigil massacre. At least one of the suspects was tortured by police. They were later acquitted for lack of evidence. Victor 'Khetisi' Kheswa and most of the Khetisi gang fled to KwaMadala hostel (the Old Place), where they joined several hundred fugitives from the Vaal townships who had been forced to flee from their homes by the comrades.

'They were outcasts,' comments Ernest Sotsu sourly. 'That was the common denominator.' As the local ANC strongman in Boipatong, the township closest to KwaMadala hostel, Sotsu watched in alarm as the hostel turned into a militant IFP stronghold. It was around the time of the Sebokeng night vigil massacre that people in the townships and hostels of the Vaal Triangle started to form heavily armed self-defence units (SDUs). The formation of armed militias was internally sanctioned by the ANC in November 1990, in response to the growing threat from the IFP. 'People acquired guns on their own,' says Ernest Sotsu:

> They collected money and bought guns on the black market. To begin with, most of the guns were kept at the Sebokeng hostel. People live there without wives or families. They think as men defending themselves think. They could afford to buy guns. If you were driven out you lost your job. The people who ran away from the hostel had lost their jobs. Their jobs were taken by Inkatha workers, whom the ISCOR management preferred, as they wouldn't make demands for higher wages.

The Xhosa-speaking hostel-dwellers from the Sebokeng and KwaMasiza hostels, reveals Sotsu, obtained guns from the Xhosa-dominated Phola

Park squatter camp in the East Rand, which had formed the best-equipped self-defence unit in the country. 'People from the hostels developed a relationship with Phola Park,' he says. 'They were all from Transkei and had brothers and sisters there. The guns came from Phola Park. The blood relationship is very strong. If you have brothers like that you'll go to them and get what you want,' grins Sotsu.

12 The Eyes of the White Man are Lighter

In the summer of 1991 the Reverend Ernest Sotsu was attending an ANC conference in Durban, the first since the organization had been unbanned, when he received a phone call advising him to return to the Vaal Triangle immediately. He found that his home, a tiny three-roomed house on a dusty street in Boipatong, had been gutted by fire. His wife, daughter and grandson had been killed, and two of his sons, aged ten and twelve, were in hospital.

'I lost my mind,' he says. 'I couldn't believe it.' Sotsu went to visit his sons to try to find out what happened. They were too shocked to make any sense of what they had seen. On Sotsu's third visit to the hospital, however, the boys said, 'It's Khetisi.' Sotsu asked why they thought it was Khetisi. 'We know him,' they replied. The police showed the children a series of mugshots, but Sotsu insisted on an identity parade. Both the boys identified Victor 'Khetisi' Kheswa (a.k.a. the Vaal Monster) as the leader of the gunmen.

From his sons' accounts Sotsu pieced together the story of that night. Between eight and nine o'clock there was a knock on the door of the house in Boipatong, the township adjacent to the ISCOR steelworks. An innocent-sounding voice called some familiar name. Sotsu's wife Constance opened the door to find two men armed with AK-47 rifles. Taken by surprise, Constance and the three children were hustled to a bedroom. The house was ransacked. Constance and her children were then locked in the lavatory. 'They realized they were going to be killed,' says Sotsu.

One of the intruders went to fetch a tin of petrol, which was sprayed throughout the house. The man identified as Kheswa then said, 'Shoot!'

'They shot them in the lavatory,' says Sotsu. 'As the children, who were sitting on the bath, fell over, one of them kicked the door shut. It saved the children's lives.'

The women died instantly. The gunmen fired shots through the door. The house was set alight. The children escaped, the ten-year-old pulling the wounded twelve-year-old through the window, his thigh riddled with bullets. As they left, the gunmen fired into the shack at the back of the house, where Sotsu's son, his wife and grandchild had been asleep. A bullet hit the three-year-old child as he lay in bed and ripped open his stomach.

Sotsu looks tired, devoid of his usual cockiness. 'The police were involved in the killing of my family,' he asserts grimly. 'The police had a score to settle with me because I was released from jail.'

The Xhosa steelworkers at the nearby KwaMasiza and Sebokeng hostels rallied round. 'It was my turn to be consoled, to be looked after,' says Sotsu. 'It made me more popular. I was taken to KwaMasiza for a month. Then the comrades gave me a place to live at Sebokeng hostel. Nowadays they guard me and move me around.'

Meanwhile tensions between the fugitives living in the KwaMadala hostel (The Old Place) and the local township residents were coming to a head. Sotsu and the comrades in Boipatong believed that IFP Zulus in KwaMadala wanted to overrun the township. In the time-honoured South African way, a pre-emptive backlash was organized. 'Anyone associated with Inkatha became an enemy,' admits Sotsu. 'There was a cycle of revenge killings.'

Township residents disappeared into the hostel, never to be seen again. The familiar barbecue smell of burning Inkatha sympathizers wafted through Boipatong and Sebokeng. The week before Soweto day in 1992, Sotsu heard reports from the steelworks that people had been bussed in from KwaZulu to the KwaMadala hostel and promised work at ISCOR, but told they must attack the township first. Sotsu's informers at ISCOR had observed an increase in the numbers within the hostel, but had no details of the date or time of the attack. Rumours of the planned raid by KwaMadala spread to Boipatong. That weekend three suspected Inkatha supporters were burned in the township.

Miriam Molefe, a Boipatong resident, was warned by ANC-supporting comrades to leave the shebeen where she lived, for her own safety. If they found any Inkatha supporters drinking there, they said, the house would be attacked. She and her husband, who worked at Baldwin's Steel, moved to her sister's place in the Slovo Park shanty town adjoining Boipatong.

Miriam's husband was in bed one night wearing his stripy boxer shorts, and she was washing, when they heard a crashing noise behind the shack. They looked through a crack between the corrugated-iron wall panels and saw people wearing white headbands moving through the alley. While they had their eyes glued to the peephole, a group of men smashed their way through the front door and attacked Miriam's husband. Miriam grabbed her three-year-old daughter and ran outside. On the way out she bumped into a man who cut her with a panga and hacked the child's head in two.

Miriam fell, moaning that she was dying with her child. Some men asked her in Zulu where the guns were. She answered that she had none.

The strange thing about the man who stabbed her and hacked her daughter, remembers Miriam, was not that he wore a rollneck jersey, a black balaclava and gloves. Or even that he didn't make a sound as he swung the machete. The strangest thing about him was his eyes. In the bright orange glare of the sodium projectors high above the shacks, she saw that her attacker's eyes were light in colour. 'The eyes of the White man are lighter,' she says with conviction. She also noticed pale skin in the eye-holes of the balaclava. Miriam's husband had disappeared. She heard the Zulu war chant 'Usuthu! Usuthu!' in the distance. She decided to put a dressing on the child's head so its brains wouldn't fall out. Her sister led her to safety on the rubbish dump behind Slovo Park. Later that night the comrades told her a man in stripy boxer shorts had been found dead in the street. Forty-four other Boipatong residents and six attackers had been killed.

Miriam was not the only resident of Boipatong to have seen a White man taking part in the attack. The petrol pump attendant at the Trek filling station pressed the panic button as 400 heavily armed Zulus tramped past the smiling concrete zebra on the crossroads that night. He told a constable on the local police force what he had seen. In a later testimony to the Goldstone Commission he amended his story, testifying that he had seen police Casspirs escorting the Zulus. A member of the Boipatong Self-Defence Unit who watched helplessly as the war party approached, saw Casspirs patrolling before the attack, then returning after the attack, but no Casspirs during the attack. He did, however, see White men wearing red headbands shouting 'Time up! Time up!' shortly before the attackers trooped back to KwaMadala. 'I had heard about such a thing as a massacre,' said the youth, 'but I had never imagined anything like this.'

The presence of balaclava-clad White men and police Casspirs amongst the assailants remained an enigma, adding to the catalogue of similar reports from other townships in the Transvaal. Thirty-two inmates of the KwaMadala hostel were arrested for the Boipatong killings. One former inmate who turned state witness testified that Prince Zulu, the IFP headman at the hostel, had prepared a 25-litre container of *intelezi* (battle-medicine) on the evening of the massacre and handed out white headbands for identification. He also testified that 400 Zulus had marched from KwaMadala to Boipatong in several groups, carrying an assortment of weapons including a large number of AK-47s, shotguns, spears, pistols and wooden clubs. After the massacre they returned to the hostel laden with TVs, hi-fi and home appliances looted from the township. The next day they gathered to sing 'uMkhonto uMbomvu Ngegazi' ('the spear is red with blood').

It began to emerge that state witnesses were being intimidated by the local Vanderbijlpark police, who beat the men and forced guns into their mouths, threatening to kill them if they did not implicate fellow hostel-dwellers in the massacre. They were also threatened with being 'fed' to ANC supporters, who would necklace them if they didn't spill the beans.

One of the key state witnesses was killed by mysterious gunmen. Victor 'Khetisi' Kheswa, a.k.a. the Vaal Monster, died in police custody of mysterious causes. Daniel Mabote, his close associate and one of the Boipatong accused, became very frightened. He complained to his lawyer that he was being threatened by police. Shortly afterwards he too died in police custody. Daniel Mabote and three others had been removed from prison after a White police sergeant persuaded the prison officers to hand the men over. The judge who remanded them in custody had given strict instructions that the men should not be removed from prison. According to Mabote's lawyer, the sergeant had told the men, 'We're taking four of you out, but not all four of you are coming back.' On the highway, Mabote apparently jumped out of the car and under the wheels of the police car behind. He died in hospital.

'I've a strong suspicion he was assassinated,' says the IFP's defence lawyer on the Boipatong case:

> The police are being totally ruthless. They are intimidating the witnesses. My clients are all very scared. They don't know when next the police are going to rock up, arrest them, threaten to kill them and the next moment another one will be dead. Perhaps they know more than is good for the police. That is the only possibility I can think of. The police are in a panic. There is something more going on than meets the eye.

13 Shovels and Operators

In the summer of 1991, while Phola Park was still locked inside a security force 'ring of steel', a supply of shovels was organized by the Shangaans. Every shack contributed a small sum of money, some as little as 2 rand. Young men, Shangaans and Xhosas from the villages of Transkei, were deployed in each section of the camp, A to H, and trained in the basic skills of handling and maintaining a shovel. These young men were known as the operators.

A 'shovel' is a Russian-made AK-47 automatic assault rifle. It was also referred to as *umShangaan*, because it was the Shangaans who brought the weapons into Phola Park and knew how to handle and maintain them. Many Shangaans were illegal immigrants from the neighbouring state of Mozambique, ex-fighters in the Frelimo movement. The Mozambican civil war was burning itself out. The country was destitute and former guerilla fighters were selling their weapons for the price of a few loaves of bread. Getting hold of shovels was not a problem.

Each of the eight sections of the camp formed its own militia, with several operators and two commanders, whose job was to organize and coordinate activities with the other sections. A whistle or a gunshot would summon the operators from all the sections within minutes. The South African Police Riot Unit soon learned to recognize the 'AK whistles' before they came under fire in Phola Park, which happened frequently.

The Phola Park Self-Defence Unit (SDU) was joined by soldiers of uMkhonto we Sizwe (MK), the armed wing of the ANC, who were pouring back into the country from exile in Mozambique, Angola, Uganda. Many settled in Phola Park simply because they had nowhere else to go in the city, or had been rejected by their families in nearby townships.

The Phola Park SDU became the strongest private militia in the country. It had more guns and better training than any other SDU. The Phola Park 'heavy mob' took part in township battles all over the Johannesburg area, from Soweto to Alexandra. If the assistance of the Phola Park SDU was needed in one of the embattled Johannesburg townships, approaches would be made by the local civic association, or 'civic'. Most civics by this time had a 'defence minister' in charge of coordinating the defence of the township in conjunction with the local militias and the SDUs. If there was a particularly heavy battle in one area, against a well-armed hostel, for instance, reinforcements were summoned from other townships. The arrangements were reciprocal. If Soweto helped out in Tokoza, Phola Park would help out in Killarney.

Training AK-47 operators for other SDUs became a cottage industry in Phola Park. Men came from the Vaal Triangle, Soweto and all over the East Rand. If Ernest Sotsu's Xhosas were in trouble in KwaMasiza hostel in Sebokeng, for instance, they went straight to Phola Park for training and guns. Phola Park acquired the largest concentration of illegal firearms in the country. The demolition of Kalanyoni hostel and the pitched battles against Inkatha had covered Phola Park in glory. The men of the Phola Park SDU were celebrated as the shock troops of the liberation struggle.

In reality, however, the Phola Park SDU was a law unto itself. While several of the section commanders were members or sympathizers of the ANC and the Pan Africanist Congress of Azania, and while they were certainly not pro-Inkatha, there was no direct political control over their activities. Several SDU section commanders were more renowned for their criminal activities than their political zeal. As dozens upon dozens of automatic weapons arrived in Phola Park, it became difficult for those residents who were unemployed and trained in warfare to resist the temptation to use their skills to make some money. Some operators touted their services as paid assassins or hired guns. Others became gangsters. In the same way as the hostels, the squatter camps of the East Rand – Holomisa Park, Mandela Park and especially Phola Park – had become heavily militarized. The foot-soldiers were the Xhosa blanket men, traditional rural migrants, much like the Zulu hostel-dwellers.

In March and April the violence seemed to have ebbed away from the East Rand to other townships on the Reef, although the riot police had a presence in Phola Park every hour of the day and night. The hand-to-hand pitched battles of 1990 belonged to the past. The East Rand had been saturated with troops and riot police, and the two sides could no longer launch their regiments into battle.

New military strategies were devised, involving small, mobile hit squads using heavier weaponry. From 1991 onwards, both hostel-dwellers and squatters bought quantities of automatic rifles, hand grenades, bazookas and limpet mines. A war of attrition began, in which the factions tried to wear each other down by terrorizing 'civilians' and assassinating leaders.

Phola Park found allies in the township youth, who acquired guns from the shanty town. The hostels in Tokoza and Katlehong forged links with the other hostels in the area. Taxi drivers became heavily involved on both sides, transporting weapons and supplies, chauffeuring hit squads and taking part in the fighting in heavily armed 'taxi squads'.

This was the climate in which a group of young, enlightened White town planners arrived in Phola Park to launch the most expensive and ambitious community development project South Africa had ever seen.

14 Workshopping the Community to Death

Conflict-ridden Phola Park had been visible in the South African media and overseas. Prince was an outstanding publicist for the camp, coralling the media to witness the aftermath of attacks, flatly denying reports of any acts of aggression perpetrated by Phola Park. The people of Phola Park were always the victims, never the culprits. In the eyes of well-meaning progressive South Africans, Phola Park became an icon of the liberation struggle, a beacon of solidarity and resistance against the forces of apartheid. Sociologists and town planners in South Africa's non-governmental welfare and development consultancies began to see Phola Park as an opportunity to put into practice a new, progressive approach, backed by massive funding from the Independent Development Trust (IDT). Created by the South African government in 1990, the IDT was inspired by the 'new thinking' within the establishment. Instead of tearing down shanty towns, which was a Sisyphean task and created a huge stink in the media, let's give the squatters what they want: houses, streets, a proper town.

Progressive town planners and consultants began to ponder ways of transforming Phola Park from a higgledy-piggledy maze of shacks into a model new South African town. The Black towns designed by apartheid planners had been a disaster in every way. In the new South Africa a new approach would have to be found. Here was a chance to show how it should be done. Phola Park was going to be *the* new South African development.

Here, for the first time in South Africa, argued the sociologists, was a really coherent community. It had demonstrated its ability to resist determined onslaughts by the state and its proxies. They concluded that Phola Park must have an organizational structure imbued with discipline. Moreover the shanty town was of a manageable size – 3500 shack units – and occupied a clearly demarcated area. In the jargon: all the parameters of a successful community-driven project were there. The challenge, pointed out the sociologists, was to transform the energy of resistance into the energy of development.

The Phola Park project was enthusiastically taken up by Planact, an organization whose mission was to provide 'consultancy to community organizations on the transition process from pre- to post-apartheid structures'. Planact had started out as a group of volunteers, young White professionals who donated their expertise to the task of improving the lives of the Black poor in the heaving cities of the Pretoria–Witwatersrand–Vaal (PWV) area, where most people in South Africa lived. Planact was growing, becoming more professional, with a 'staff collective' of forty, mostly young, well-educated Whites. Phola Park became Planact's baby.

Planact submitted a funding proposal to the Independent Development Trust. The IDT was excited. They saw it as a way to deal with 'a major conflict area'. There were other attractive aspects: the Planact proposal was not merely about building toilets and taps ('site and service') but had also come up with ways to 'consolidate site and service' into 'housing units'. The Independent Development Trust was sold on the idea. Phola Park would be the IDT's baby too. It funded the project's budget to the hilt: 21 million rand (£4.2 million), or 7500 rand per shack.

Having spent the last two years trying to remove Phola Park from the map, the government was now paying for it to become a permanent town.

More than that, the success or failure of the Phola Park development would have decisive implications for other large-scale development projects. Phola Park was the test case for the new South Africa. It had all the ingredients: money, progressive planning, careful research, a community approach. It had to work.

A key figure on the planning side was an ambitious, progressive young town planner, Julian Baskin. 'My role at Planact is to develop planning methodologies which take cognisance of empowerment,' explains Julian, a shy, good-looking man dressed casually in shorts and trainers. 'This was *the* project,' he remembers:

> This project quite frankly was being seen around the country as the pilot for that real, community-driven process. This time it was community-driven but also had enough resources behind it. And we were looking at the development of a new planning methodology. We were looking at the development of a methodology that basically says outside actors are there to *enable* a community-driven process. So it was the real first example of a breakaway from a top-down to a bottom-up approach.

If the Phola Park scheme worked, in other words, the problem of eradicating Black poverty in South Africa would become merely a matter of time, money and political will. A blueprint for uplifting the Black poor, South Africa's ten million shack-dwellers, would have been found. Phola Park became the showcase project for the new South Africa. Before they dug a single trench or laid a single pipe Planact set out to discover exactly what sort of town the people of Phola Park wanted.

> 'We engaged in a detailed planning exercise,' says Julian: Some people were accusing us of workshopping the community to death. We had workshops on every issue. We had a residents' committee and a development committee. The development committee was itself subdivided into four working groups, each with a core grouping of four people, under which were a whole load of programmes. We had a working group looking at the physical development of Phola Park, things like housing, sewage, basic services. We had a working group on community finance and local economic development. We had a working group on community education and liaison. Throughout the planning process we had workshops, with targeted groups of people. We had mass meetings with mandates and feedbacks. We had walkabouts which meant we used to walk around and whoever was in the area could come and discuss particular issues. A plan was drawn up and approved. It was a plan which had a whole new look at how these places could be. It put forward new standards, new plot sizes, whole different concepts of the use of streets and recreational space.

We brought in an incredibly talented team of professionals to back the whole programme up. The optimism was so high. Phola Park was a winner.

Naturally everyone wanted to back a winner. Trees for Africa created an environmental grouping in Phola Park around the issue of planting trees. The Women's Development Bank arranged credit for the women of Phola Park so that they could launch businesses. The Legal Resources Centre helped with documenting land tenure. The future of Phola Park looked bright.

'It was a winner,' Julian adds generously, 'because they had the most dynamic person working at the head of the development committee, a very young guy who was eventually killed, Prince Mhlambi. He had enormous energy and just got things happening. So we were working with a group of people who had really dedicated their lives to this development.'

The winter months of 1991 were the quietest Phola Park had known for a long time. Prince and his Phola Park Residents' Committee went from strength to strength, meeting the planners, orchestrating support, preparing for the day the bulldozers would move in to transform Phola Park into a radiant new South African town.

15 House 2044

Early in the morning on the second Sunday of September 1991 the section commanders of the Phola Park Self-Defence Unit (SDU) held a meeting by the water tank. On the agenda were some disturbing developments. Firstly, there were rumours that Phola Park residents were being abducted by Zulu taxi drivers, who drove their victims into the hostels to be butchered. Their bodies were then left for the dogs at the back of Mshayazafe hostel. These rumours had provoked a feeling of helplessness and anger in the shanty town. But there was a more serious danger, which threatened to swing the balance of power in the area.

Rumours indicated that these same taxi drivers in Tokoza were distributing leaflets to their passengers. The leaflets announced an Inkatha Freedom Party peace rally in the Tokoza stadium. Their message was that the hostels had no quarrel with the residents of Tokoza, that the war was strictly between the hostels and the squatters of Phola Park. All township residents above the age of seventeen were invited to the peace meeting. The Phola Park section commanders saw right through the hostel's strategy. It was a cunning political manoeuvre. The aim was to weaken Phola Park by driving a wedge between the township and the shanty town. Something had to be done, the section commanders agreed. They made a plan. Operators would be deployed at the four corners of the stadium, and inside the stadium. Once the stadium had filled with hostel-dwellers, the assembled masses would be scythed with AK-47s.

The stadium was recced early in the morning. Residents of the adjacent Tokoza Gardens housing estate were told to sit tight and watch TV. Phola Park was placed on a war footing, in case of retaliation. The war blankets came out. The operators took their AK-47s to the stadium.

Later that morning men from Mshayazafe and the other two hostels in Tokoza marched peaceably down Kumalo Street towards the stadium, each group led by its *induna* or headman. A smaller group of men from the Scaw Metals hostel gathered near the southern entrance of the stadium.

As the march approached the stadium Michael 'Mbotho' Phama, a section commander and one of three operators who were standing in the front garden of house 2044, Kumalo Street, opened fire unexpectedly on the procession with his AK at point-blank range. The other two gunmen let fly almost simultaneously. Sixteen Zulus died on the spot and thirteen were wounded, some of whom died later in hospital. As the firing started, the men from Scaw Metals were also attacked by blanket men, and two were hacked to death. The attack was blamed by many in the press and the liberation movements on the 'third force'.

Ironically Michael Phama's action had saved a great many lives. The plan had been to wait till the stadium was full to begin the massacre. 'Michael acted out of emotion,' says a Phola Park man. 'He had seen so much blood. We have people who feel uneasy if there's a single quiet night. He disappointed everyone by shooting first. So people were angry with him.' A witness identified Phama by his drooping eyelid and he was arrested.

At his trial Phama was found guilty of shooting dead twenty-one people, including the sixteen Inkatha supporters on the march in Tokoza. He became the biggest convicted mass-murderer in South African history. In his defence Phama said, 'People must defend themselves to keep the killers at bay.' The psychologist at the trial concluded in mitigation that Phama was suffering from war psychosis. In spite of his crimes many in the ANC still privately regard Phama as a hero.

A new cycle of violence began, in which it became difficult to distinguish between criminal acts of violence and the political and ethnic vendetta against the hostels. A large number of the AK-47 operators and several Self-Defence Unit section commanders were notorious gangsters, members of a criminal fraternity known as the *amaSela*. In fact the backbone of the

Phola Park SDU consisted of Xhosa hoods from the hills of Transkei. Herds of livestock were stolen from nearby farms and driven into the camp, where they were slaughtered. Prostitutes appeared on the Old Vereeneging Road. Cars were hijacked in nearby White towns, their owners murdered and their firearms stolen.

Once they reached the safety of the shacks any fugitive from the police, including mobsters from outside Phola Park, knew they were safe. Guns or stolen goods were dumped in a shack. When the police arrived everyone would step outside their shacks and stand uncooperatively in the alleyways. Even if the stolen goods were found, they could never be tied to a particular person, as no one would admit to owning the shack. In the words of one resident, 'Phola Park became a Sodom and Gomorrah.'

Law enforcement in Phola Park was ineffectual. Indeed the police were perceived to be one of the main causes of violence. A week after the Tokoza stadium massacre an armoured Casspir vehicle of the notorious SAP Riot Unit 19 entered Phola Park in the middle of the night. All was quiet. In the course of the patrol they stopped the Casspir and got out to take a piss. One of the men was shot in the leg by a sniper. The patrol returned fire and killed someone.

The next day Unit 19 came back for the body. Residents tried to stop them removing what they considered to be incriminating evidence against the Riot Unit. A man from Phola Park was shot in the back. Determined to avoid more casualties on a second return visit, Prince and two friends grabbed the cadaver and ran into the alleyways, where the body was hidden in a shack. After talks between the police and Prince, a coroner's van came to fetch the body. A detective drove to Phola Park to take a statement. It was noticed that his car didn't have matching numberplates. The deaths were never investigated.

Complaints mounted about the Riot Unit kidnapping people and looting shacks. It was impossible to identify the men, as police vehicles bore no numberplates or identification. The young, blond Afrikaners in the Riot Unit were famed in the townships for their childish pranks. They threw stones on the roofs of shacks at night to wake people. They shouted abuse through loud-hailers, or sat in their Casspirs with the sirens switched on for ten, twenty minutes in the dead of night. They stole money during searches and played chicken with cars in their 20-ton Casspirs, slamming on the brakes at the last moment. At least one visitor to Phola Park was crushed to death in this way. The fresh-faced youths of the Riot Unit (renamed the Internal Stability Unit in 1992) swerved their Casspirs drunkenly round the dirt roads between the shacks and had a habit of shooting residents dead for no apparent reason.

In 1991 the Phola Park Residents' Committee began a series of peace meetings with the Riot Unit and the South African Defence Force. Prince set out the community's grievances. The Riot Unit representatives agreed that policemen should wear name tags and paint identification numbers on all the vehicles. A system was devised whereby police vehicles would check at the Residents' Committee office on their way in or out of Phola Park. Brigadier Venter, who shook hands on the deal, was enthusiastic. 'We're inventing community policing for the rest of South Africa,' he gushed. Phola Park had produced yet another South African first. 'Solving problems together,' beamed Venter.

Four weeks later he crawled back to the Peace Committee, apologizing profusely, saying he was obliged to end the agreement. Brigadiers in Pretoria had heard – quite how they had heard was unclear – that Phola Park residents were boasting that the camp was a no-go area for the Riot Unit. Venter had almost lost his job over it. To the people of Phola Park, Prince and the Residents' Committee's ineffectual negotiations with the police were beginning to look like appeasement.

At the next meeting a Major Drosky assured Prince and the Committee that all vehicles had now been clearly marked with identification numbers painted on the sides, and that he should tell the residents. Prince chose to trust Major Drosky, but warned: 'Make it work, or we're out.' Drosky assured him the vehicles were already standing at base with fresh, clear markings painted on the sides. Prince put the word round Phola Park. At eleven o'clock two unmarked Riot Unit Casspirs drove into Phola Park and shot someone dead.

Next morning the same two Riot Unit Casspirs, with no numberplates and mud plastered over their identification numbers, returned to the shanty town. 'We came looking for stolen cars last night,' said a young riot policeman. 'We're still looking.' When questioned about the agreement to make the vehicles clearly identifiable, the men claimed they were not part of the agreement.

By Christmas Brigadier Venter and Major Drosky had been transferred from the East Rand. Venter was promoted to the post of Commissioner of Police in the minute homeland of QwaQwa. The shambolic peace efforts had left Prince exposed to criticism from the shack-dwellers. He was seen to be getting too close to the police. His credibility in Phola Park had worn paper-thin.

The war of attrition between the Zulu and Xhosa peasantry ground on. Early one February morning in 1992 a rumour flashed down the long line of people walking beside the railway tracks from Phola Park to Angus Station. Gunmen in a white minibus taxi had opened fire on the station platform. Three AK-47 operators ran to the roadside and sprayed the taxi with bullets. As it came to a standstill a posse of onlookers advanced across the railway line from Phola Park. One of the passengers was shot as he alighted from the taxi. Blood splashed on the white bodywork and the man fell into the ditch by the railway line. Three other passengers who had not managed to escape from the minibus were butchered by the crowd from Phola Park, some of whom thought that the shanty town was under attack when they heard stray bullets hitting the branches of the bluegum trees.

The Goldstone Commission, entrusted by the government with the task of investigating the causes of violence in South Africa, concluded that the incident was a premeditated attack on the taxi driver, who was the son of a local Inkatha official. The crowd from Phola Park who had slaughtered the surviving passengers became involved, the Commission found, 'out of a combination of inquisitiveness, militancy and fear generated by rumour, persecution mania and coincidence'.

The sixteen section commanders of the SDU had become despots in Phola Park. Those who questioned their decisions were denounced as police spies, *impimpi*. The punishment for an *impimpi* was to be locked inside an abandoned freight container overnight, awaiting trial. The next morning someone went round the camp with a whistle, summoning people to the meeting place by the water tanks. A show trial was staged. If, at the end of the trial, the women were shooed away and the children told to go and play football, everyone knew the sentence was death.

The presumed informer's hands were tied behind his back with wire. He would be told 'Run, we don't want to see you here!' and pushed in the direction of the ruins of Kalanyoni hostel. As the prisoner stumbled through the broken foundations, he would be intercepted by a group of men and murdered.

One of the first residents to be lynched by the Self-Defence Unit in the new year was Majola, a member of the Residents' Committee and an ally of Prince's. He had criticized the Self-Defence Unit for unnecessarily gunning down passengers on a bus. Prince's position as a leader in Phola Park was looking more precarious by the day.

16 'Down with the Committee, Up with AK!'

In March 1992 the Phola Park development team was putting the finishing touches to plans for the pioneering new town of Phola Park. The project was about to become a reality. Forty-eight sites had been marked out on the wasteland where the Kalanyoni hostel had once stood. The people in the shacks next to the wasteland were to move to the new sites of their own accord. Weeks passed and nobody moved. People procrastinated and delayed, then refused point blank to move onto the hostel land, a few metres from where they lived. It was Zulu land, they said. If they occupied it, the hostel-dwellers would attack.

Criticism of Prince and the Committee was growing. There were rumours that he was embezzling the development money, which couldn't be true as no money had been spent. But the allegations stuck. Prince thought he could paper over the cracks and pretend nothing was wrong.

The problem was that not everyone in Phola Park supported the idea of turning the shanty town into a model of urban development. Not everyone wanted a house with a tap and a toilet on a private plot in a straight, well-lit street, even if they received the title deed at no cost. What the planners had not realized, and Prince felt he could not reveal for fear of delaying the scheme, was that a large number of the shack-dwellers actually preferred to live in a shanty town.

The planners and sociologists had perceived a strong unity amongst the people of Phola Park. This cohesion had enabled them to survive successive onslaughts by the police and Inkatha. However, when it came to tearing down the shanty town and building something new in its place, deep divisions emerged. Alliances were dissolved as groups discovered they had different vested interests. Disagreements over the development project began to shake the previously stable foundations of Phola Park.

The Shangaans were threatened by the scheme. Being illegal immigrants from Mozambique, they would not qualify for the housing subsidy. The squatter camp was their refuge from the police.

The Xhosa blanket men had no desire to own a house in the city, if that meant they had to pay service charges. They were single men who had come to the city, like the Zulu hostel-dwellers, for no other reason than to scrape together some money to send home to the villages. Their allegiance was to a rural way of life, governed by medicine men and traditional chiefs. Suddenly they were also asking questions. They wanted cash instead of houses, so they could build homes in Transkei.

The *amaSela* mobsters ('people with different urban intentions', read the politically correct Planact post mortem document) were the most dangerous opponents of the scheme. In the new Phola Park, with its orderly pattern of streets, high-mast lighting and numbered houses, there would be nowhere to hide from the police.

None of these recalcitrant factions had been to any of the workshops. Most could not speak English. Their leaders sneered at Prince's clique. The planners had relied on Prince to deliver 'the community'. Prince had said nothing about Shangaan AK-47 operators or Xhosa criminal fraternities. As far as the planners were concerned, these dissenters were invisible. Out of nowhere a crisis had materialized.

The first Julian Baskin heard of the coup was a phone call one Sunday in March 1992 from a lawyer who represented residents of Phola Park, warning him not to go near the place. Later on Prince and the Residents' Committee came to Julian's office to explain what had happened.

That Sunday, literally one day before the bulldozers were due to start work, a posse of men wearing balaclavas and carrying AKs walked into the Residents' Committee office and told everyone to get out. Having got rid of the leadership, the men drove around Phola Park in a pick-up truck shouting their new slogans through a megaphone: 'No more Whites in Phola Park!', 'Down with the Committee, up with AKs!' Prince was devastated. He went into hiding.

Julian's dream crumbled before his eyes. 'This is the part I don't like talking about,' he winces. 'This is where it got really vicious, vicious, vicious.' You can still sense the fear in his voice:

> It was incredibly dangerous. You had a situation where the Residents' Committee had been kicked out at a fundamental development stage. You're talking 21 million rand for an informal settlement. That's unheard of in this country. And that was just the money from the IDT, let alone all the other funding we were securing all over the place. We were talking about a major development programme here, with resources behind it and a lot of enthusiasm all over the show.

Julian shakes his head in disbelief. 'We were out. We couldn't move. We'd lost our client.'

'What seems to have happened,' he explains soberly, 'is that we started from the assumption that because we had mandates and workshops etc. that we had reached the broad mass of the community. We met the 75 per cent of people who wanted to urbanize, people who had a vested interest in the development, who wanted to bring their families, who wanted schools, who wanted just a normal life.' He pauses:

> This is where it gets incredibly complex. What happened was, it became apparent that the development committee only represented the people who wanted to be represented by them. What we didn't reach was the other 25 per cent who had no vested interest in the development, who never came to our workshops. A drift process happened, a process which we never accessed. As soon as their vested interests were challenged they came to the fore and showed who really had power in that particular settlement.
>
> We tried to develop a new development committee in Phola Park. If the new grouping could demonstrate they had popular support and there was a mass movement towards it, we would work with them. We tried meeting after meeting after meeting. We brought in every mediator we could. Different people turned up every time. Eventually we gave up.

Julian shakes his head sadly. 'It was pretty hard. It had never happened before. No one had really worked out the vested interests. It's quite a brutal thing to say about ourselves, but even though we work with community organizations, we're still outsiders. I don't think we realized just how vicious it could get,' he adds with a shudder.

It was to become more vicious still. Prince had been sentenced to death by a faction in the Phola Park Self-Defence Unit (SDU). He tried to work his way back into Phola Park, pulling every available political string. Chris Hani, a former Commander in Chief of Umkhonto we Sizwe, the ANC's military wing, came to reason with the shack-dwellers on Prince's behalf. Tokyo Sexwale, the charismatic regional chairman of the ANC, drove to Phola Park to talk some sense into the people. He took Prince into the shanty town with him. Johnson Mbathane, one of the section commanders of the Phola Park SDU walked up to Tokyo, jabbing his finger venomously at Prince: 'Nobody will talk to you as long as this dog is here!' he said. Tokyo drew his gun and shielded Prince with his body. Shots were fired at his car as they fled for their lives.

Attempts by the police to discredit Prince continued. The police would line up suspects in an identity parade on the football field near Phola Park. Using a megaphone, so that everyone in Phola Park could hear, a policeman would ask: 'Prince, is that him? Prince, is this the man?'

In the course of a subsequent inquiry the police admitted that one of the coup leaders in Phola Park, a notorious car thief and a section commander of the SDU by the name of 'Nyati' Ceba, was a paid informer. Johnson Mbathane, another ringleader of the coup against Prince, later admitted that he too had been working for the police. It became obvious that the leadership of the most powerful self-defence unit in South Africa had been deeply infiltrated by the police.

Prince was gunned down in the Beirut section of Tokoza in November 1992. Three other passengers in his car were also killed. The crowd which accompanied his coffin was one of the biggest the shanty town had ever seen. The coup leaders in Phola Park themselves became victims of a coup. Most were killed. Some fled and were assassinated in Mandela Park, another squatter camp nearby. The war with the hostels continued. Fear continued to reign, as it had always done in Phola Park. Some fought the fear by buying more AKs. Others barricaded themselves in the tiny shacks, too frightened to move. 'Phola Park people are afraid to leave their shacks,' says one resident. 'They are afraid and don't want to come out. There are many who have not set foot outside Phola Park since 1989.'

17 Everybody Proves Each Other's Complicity

In May 1993 the civil war on the East Rand entered its most vicious phase. A full-scale territorial war was in progress, and the fighting swept through the twin townships of Tokoza and Katlehong, section by section. The hostel-dwellers, who had overrun a large area in the first weeks of the battle, failed to hold onto their territorial gains and were driven back inside the hostels by the ANC-supporting comrades. Katlehong township began a ruthless blockade of the Katlehong hostels, choking off their links with the outside world. The aim of the stranglehold was to starve the hostels into submission, then destroy them once and for all.

To get to the Katlehong hostels from Johannesburg you take the skyway past the flat-topped mountains of goldmine waste and veer south-east onto the Heidelberg Road, which takes you between the abattoir and the market, through Electron and Steeldale, to the giant industrial park of Alrode.

Well before you see the tops of the large bluegum trees and the huddled shacks of Phola Park, you take a right turn in the direction of Alrode and the White suburb of Brackendown, before doubling back over the road bridge into Katlehong township. If you drive fast and there's no traffic, the journey from Johannesburg takes twenty minutes.

Once over the bridge, you see an army watchtower on your left. Through the thick blue-tinted windows, two soldiers watch Mandela Park squatter camp.

A convoy of Buffels, khaki armoured bathtubs on wheels, patrols in the vicinity of Natalspruit Hospital. Buffels are tall, chunky troop carriers used by the army. The driver sits in a tiny cab with tinted windows, while the troops perch uncomfortably on the edges of the bathtub, which has sloping sides to deflect the blast of landmines. Being so tall, Buffels have a tendency to roll over when taking a corner at speed, and some township residents have been inconvenienced by these 20-ton armoured vehicles cartwheeling through their front gardens. The more experienced soldiers get into the habit of buckling up whenever the Buffel sets off on a car chase.

Nudge through the crowd at the taxi rank outside the hospital, and take a right at the traffic lights. As you enter Schoeman Street, which stretches south to the hostels, you may feel the need to remove your seat belt, to speed your exit if the car comes under fire.

Schoeman Street runs north to south for 7 kilometres, between the townships of Katlehong and Tokoza. The front line runs down the centre of Schoeman Street for about 4 kilometres, before heading off down a side street. There are other, shorter battle lines lurking in the quiet cross-streets. They shift nightly as sections of the township are overrun, held for a few days, then change hands again. Schoeman Street has been a stable frontier between ANC and IFP zones for some weeks, since the houses on either side were cleaned out.

The north end of Schoeman Street, close to Natalspruit Hospital, is relatively safe during the daytime. The streets of Katlehong are reassuringly busy, with shoppers, children, taxis and a few cars. Drive another 50 metres towards the hostels and you cross an invisible line. Suddenly Katlehong is dead. The houses on either side of the road appear deserted. The silence is unsettling. Nothing and nobody moves.

Further on, every second or third house displays smashed windows fringed with scorch marks. Here and there the flames have buckled the roof, or spread to the garage. For 2½ kilometres each and every smart four- or five-roomed home lies desolate and empty. These are privately owned properties, not the average matchbox-type township dwelling. No two houses are the same, each one is lovingly designed. Brick facing is popular. Some of the bungalows have arches, some have round windows edged with bricks. The gardens are still neat, the rose bushes trim. Neighbouring houses rival one another for the most imaginative variation on steel garden railings. Each home is a picture of domestic pride. You find yourself wondering what happened to the owners. On the right-hand side of Schoeman street, the Tokoza side, is a 30-metre-wide strip of waste ground, planted with a long row of power lines. Beyond that is the next row of houses. These, too, appear to be completely deserted.

Nearer the hostel the road is potholed, and looks as though it has been dug up in order to slow approaching vehicles. From behind another row of deserted, white-walled houses appear the stark, geometric blocks of Buyafuthi hostel. The road turns to dirt next to a battered chicken-wire fence. Two dried-out cow's skulls hang side by side like trophies on the chicken-wire fence. Across the wasteland from the hostel, on the Tokoza side of Schoeman Street, some of the houses show a faint trail of smoke from the chimneys. There are other signs of life: a woman in a headscarf carrying a tub of washing, a few distant figures. The silence around the hostel is broken only by a cock crow.

Buyafuthi, the nearest of the three Katlehong hostels to Schoeman Street, is laid out in squares of two-storey buildings built of bare cement blocks, orderly and spartan, with sloping roofs of corrugated iron. The walls are bare and unmarked, the only graffiti is 'IFP': three tall, spindly letters on the ends of blocks. Not angry protest graffiti, more like factory markings. This hostel is Inkatha's place, the letters say.

The hostel yard is a huge expanse of dry red dust, with small patches of discoloured, matted grass. A fruit tree here and there breaks up the relentless geometrical progression of the blocks. The place is deserted, with a few men buying offal. Intestines and stomachs are slopped in revolting piles on a steel shelf, exposed to the crisp, cutting winter sunlight. A supermarket trolley contains more guts and a couple of cows' heads. Black roosters wander in the yards beneath the long row of windows, out-numbering the men. It's a Sunday morning and most of the hostel-dwellers are still asleep.

Township 'bubblegum' music blares in the yards, which are littered with old engine parts. A cowhide, stained with dirt and blood, dries against a wall. Old, battered cars and minibuses wait for the end of the war. If a group of young men starts up one of the cars you know they're not going far, perhaps for a joyride through the hostel grounds, to break the monotony of the siege. Others lounge on the staircases chatting, or sway to the music while standing at the windows of their rooms. There's a man with a guitar in almost every yard, standing around with friends, but no one has the heart to sing. The rituals of Sunday morning are carried on even though the hostel is under siege. The guitarist plucks a few diffident notes from a traditional tune.

Nearby, hostel-dwellers play dice in the bright, staring sunshine, clustering around the table in their overcoats. 'We are not dwellers, we are residents,' stresses an official of the Hostel Residents Association, which was until recently the Hostel-Dwellers Association. But somehow the word residence seems ludicrous when applied to these crude barracks, straddling the railway line to the factories of the East Rand. People don't reside here, they dwell.

Men perform their regular Sunday chores in the safety of the hostel yards. They emerge in twos and threes with their washing, chatting as they drape their overalls and shirts on long wire lines. In the shade of a small tree sits the clothes repair man, working quietly at his foot-operated Singer. There are women here too, and children splashing each other while dogs drink from the large puddles of water left over from the last rain.

Breakfast is cooked on an electric hob in a bare concrete room furnished with steel tables. A string of little paper flags festooned across the room advertises Smirnoff Vodka. A man wearing strings of red and white beads sits eating porridge at one of the tables. The beads identify him as an *inyanga*, a medicine man. Two men interrupt his breakfast to consult him about a kidnapping, and the word *amaXhosa* comes up several times. The man scowls and digs into his porridge.

Out in the middle of the wide open space on the north side of Buyafuthi hostel, a group of *indunas*, or headmen, are holding a meeting, sitting in a semicircle with a bottle of lemonade. About 100 metres away, between the perimeter fence and the first row of abandoned houses, an army convoy trundles past. Some of the houses have tell-tale fringes of soot round the windows. Those abandoned white-walled bungalows, row upon row of them standing empty and silent under a wide blue sky, are one of the most haunting images of South Africa's civil war.

'Those houses have been taken over. There were ANC people there, but they ran away,' says Jeff, looking slightly embarrassed. Jeff is the Inkatha Freedom Party youth organizer in the area. He claims to be looking after 30 000 members inside the hostels and in the surrounding township. 'It weighs on my shoulders,' he says with a long-suffering smile. 'In June we were trapped for almost a week. During Chris Hani's funeral we were also attacked and the hostel residents were stopped from going to work. The same during Tambo's funeral and the attempted AWB [Afrikaner Resistance Movement] putsch at the World Trade Centre.'

The word 'putsch' has an incongruous ring inside the hostel. Putsch is a word you might expect to hear in the township, amongst the politically aware comrades. Jeff is a more sophisticated brand of hostel-dweller.

Jeff grew up in Umlazi, Durban's biggest township, but had to leave in 1989 when the civil war broke out again. He went to Johannesburg to read law at the University of South Africa, and was in his second year when the latest round of unrest on the East Rand forced him to suspend his studies. 'It's too dangerous to move outside the hostel,' complains Jeff. 'I can't go to the library or attend tutorials.' The comrades in Katlehong don't believe Jeff is a student. They say students don't stay in hostels, and that he's been assigned to the hostel by Inkatha.

As an IFP youth organizer, Jeff has a tiny room to himself at the hostel. A room with a door is considered a luxury, as most dwellers bed down in tiny cubicles screened off from the corridor by a curtain. In Jeff's 2.5 metre square cell, behind a battered steel door, are two beds: bed number 2365 and bed number 2366. Between the beds is a two-bar heater and a small table artfully decorated with burgundy Drink-o-Pop labels. On the wall, next to the postcards of smiling Zulu warriors and bare-breasted Zulu maidens, and the photograph of Mandela and Buthelezi embracing stiffly at a meeting in Durban, is a home-made poster. The headline, in neat felt-tip, reads: 'Everybody proves each other's complicity.' Underneath are three photographs, clipped from newspapers, each with a line of explanation.

Next to a photo of an armed posse preparing to finish off a writhing man outside what looks like a hostel dormitory, the comment reads: 'A/ ANC ask who is responsible for killing our people? Answer is IFP.'

A youth hurls a large chunk of concrete onto the head of a prostrate old woman, who tries weakly to shield herself with one hand. The shutter captures the rock in mid-flight. 'B/ IFP ask 'Who is that "our people" and not ours?' Their answer is ANC "People's Courts".'

A White policeman stands coolly firing a hand gun into a fleeing crowd. The legend reads: 'C/ Does a Third Force which is alleged to perpetrate the killings exist? South African Police in Pretoria – NO.'

At the bottom of the poster Jeff has penned in bold letters: 'I don't believe that our thousands of pictures can be wrong.'

A Peace Accord poster above Jeff's bed demands 'Human Rights For All', and a large fluorescent orange label bears the words 'Monitor – Wits/Vaal Peace Secretariat'. Jeff is the Peace Secetariat contact in the Katlehong hostels, and carries a Peace Secretariat walkie-talkie wherever he goes. He makes daily visits to the Peace Secretariat's operations centre in the Natalspruit Hospital but doesn't trust the other monitors, who are all ANC. He politely turns down lifts in their cars, preferring to make the return trip down Schoeman Street in the safety of a police escort.

In this most recent spasm of the East Rand civil war, which began in May 1993, the Katlehong hostels have been under total siege. The hostel-dwellers – some 15–20 000 – are vastly outnumbered by the half million township residents of Katlehong who are blockading them.

'All the Alrode factory workers have quit their jobs,' says Jeff. 'They can't get to work, they're not safe. The taxis from Alrode make a U-turn in the middle of the township. They won't come near the hostels.' Jeff looks haggard, his face chapped by the dry Transvaal climate. He fingers the walkie-talkie nervously. 'Then you have to walk back to the hostel. Countless people have been attacked. The only men who still have jobs are the ones working in Germiston, who use the railway line.'

Like the majority of IFP members in the area, Jeff is adamant that the slaughter in Katlehong is motivated by ethnic hatred of Zulus. 'I don't find a logic. We are also victims of apartheid. If they were killing IFP members I would say it was a power struggle. But they just kill anyone who is a Zulu, irrespective of affiliation. Even ANC members are attacked, whereas IFP Suthus in the no-go areas of Katlehong are not attacked.' Jeff's composure is slipping. He sits up on bed 2365 and the tiny cell fills with angry gestures: 'Zulus are attacked just because they are Zulus. Most people killed in the townships today are Zulus. Leaders talk politics. But on the ground people fight because of ethnic issues.'

The whole thing, explains Jeff, started in 1990:

Before that we lived together with Xhosas. Maybe half the hostel-dwellers were Xhosas from Transkei and Ciskei. They stayed in A block and other blocks. All the rooms were packed. We had 8000 people staying in each of the three hostels, with only 5000 beds. Some Xhosas moved to the township when they found jobs, but many stayed in the hostel.

The whole thing started with the taxi war. One local taxi association was dominated by people from the township. The other association was dominated by Zulus from the hostel. It was a question of business and the way it was divided up. Residents attacked Zulu-owned taxis. Zulu drivers were killed. We retaliated against them. We went as a mob to confront them. Group confronted group.

Then Kalanyoni hostel near Phola Park was destroyed by the ANC in 1990 with hand grenades. The concrete blocks were used by the squatters to build houses. Kalanyoni was a large hostel. But it was too mixed. We were outnumbered.

News of the faction fight at Kalanyoni hostel, a couple of kilometres away, spread panic amongst the Xhosa residents in the Katlehong hostels. 'It was so terrible,' Jeff remembers. 'The Xhosas all left in one week. They fled under attack. There was nobody left. Some ran away in the clothes they stood up in. In Zulu, *Buyafuthi* means "come again",' he says with a mischievous grin. 'We are still calling the Xhosas to come again.'

'Then it became an ethnic war,' Jeff continues. 'In their meetings they said publicly that Zulus should go back to Natal. Why does nobody say that the Xhosas should go back to Transkei? Thirty per cent of the workers in Natal are from Transkei. They are not being driven from Natal. But in Transvaal they don't want Zulus. The civics in the township have called for all the hostels to be demolished. Why? Where did we go wrong?' he asks, looking puzzled.

Jeff turns up the 'bubblegum' music on the small Taiwanese cassette player by his bed, as if to shut out the hostile outside world. Like many Inkatha cadres in the Transvaal workers' hostels, he adopts a posture of militant Zulu nationalism, a schizoid blend of triumphalism and paranoia: 'Part of the Transvaal is Zulu territory,' he declares. 'Our kings demarcated it years ago. No one will tell us where our borders are! We know our natural borders and we want them back!' The gentle, conciliatory Jeff, the champion of peace and human rights, begins to sound shrill and petulant: 'Before the election we will go to Pretoria and demand our land back. We cannot vote against our own existence.'

In the minds of embattled hostel-dwellers, the increasingly pointless tooth-and-nail struggle to hang onto a few squalid barracks in the city, their last foothold in the Transvaal, is part of a glorious history of resistance which stretches back to the Zulu wars against Britain.

'The British Queen knows our borders. The British took our land. That was wrong. We will ask them to explain where our borders are. If we are not satisfied . . . ' says Jeff darkly, 'it is possible that we will engage in war. We have traditional weapons,' he pulls a stick from under his bed. 'It's our culture. We are trained to fight. When we look after cattle as young boys we divide into groups and fight.'

Then he remembers that Chief Minister Buthelezi has influential admirers in Britain and adopts a more conciliatory tone: 'We like Margaret Thatcher. We like Britain. Britain made us known to the world. We know no one except Britain,' he enthuses, adding cryptically: 'They took our land. They will be giving us back our land.'

Jeff gets up to go, he has things to do. His wife, who is staying in a township nearby, has received death threats from the locals, and he must arrange for her to move to the Eastern Transvaal. Then there is the fiasco at the Germiston government mortuary, where 180 unclaimed bodies lie heaped on top of one another, many of them burned and disfigured beyond recognition. 'We don't know what to do with the bodies,' Jeff admits. 'The morgue wants to bury them. We are making a video of them,' he explains, adjusting his Inkatha headband, 'so that relatives can identify them after the burial.'

18 This World is Not Our Home

Kwesine, the oldest hostel of the three in Katlehong, is Inkatha's strongest toehold in the township. 'If Kwesine falls,' says the inmates, 'we have to go.' As a place to live, Kwesine makes Buyafuthi next door look desirable.

The hostel consists of eleven narrow dormitories, each one 125 metres in length, laid out in a semicircular fan shape. The huge empty spaces in between the blocks are strewn with rubble. In the middle of the central compound is a large container overflowing with rubbish. The place looks like the bombed-out remains of a prisoner-of-war camp or a battery chicken farm.

The hostel-dwellers sit around in twos and threes, tiny knots of men lost in the wide open spaces. Others stand behind the dormitory blocks drinking sorghum beer from plastic buckets. A giant tattered billboard shows a young Black couple sipping glasses of iced Coke, with the caption: 'You can't beat the feeling!' This dilapidated barracks with its huge littered yards and its few thousand listless, dejected inmates is the place which has aroused so much fear in the 500000 residents of Katlehong township.

'The hostel-dwellers used to have dances,' remembers Max Sibeko, a member of the Katlehong Civic Association. 'We made friends. Some of us had relatives in the hostels. It will never be like that again. Every time the violence erupts it spreads from the hostels.'

Sibeko, an unemployed clerk, is a lean, thoughtful middle-aged man. 'The township residents of Tokoza and Katlehong took a resolution at an official meeting called by the Katlehong Civic Association in mid-1990 that the hostels must be demolished,' he says crisply. 'We wanted the government to remove them. Now we're saying we're going to do it ourselves. The only thing stopping us is the security forces.'

The conquest or reconquest of a particular section of the township in the war of May 1993 was routinely followed by purges. House by house, street by street, the faction which had gained control of the area systematically killed, burned and expelled families loyal to the opposing faction. Thousands of township residents were displaced. Several hundred Zulu families took refuge in Kwesine hostel.

The refugees live in a large community hall in the main compound of the hostel. Around the edges of the hall, on the polished concrete floor, lie dozens of mattresses, bundles of clothing and paraffin stoves. One family has salvaged the entire contents of their home. A large wooden dresser stands next to a king-size bed, with a pink plush bedstead and two ornate, matching bedside tables. One item which every single family seems to have rescued is a pair of matching porcelain dogs.

At the far end of the hall a woman is cooking porridge for her three sons, in a cloud of flies. She fled Katlehong township after some houses near where she lived were burned by township youth. She is going back to Natal, as there are no jobs in the Transvaal any more. Why was her family attacked? 'Because we are Zulus.' What's to be done? She smiles helplessly. Two dispirited-looking women sitting next to her on the double bed say they will go back to Natal as soon as they can get some money together. A fourth woman says that in her opinion the fighting is political, not ethnic. No one disagrees.

On the opposite side of the vast compound from dormitories A to H is the beer hall, where sorghum beer is dispensed into buckets from two taps the thickness of a man's wrist. Men bask in the pale winter sunshine on improvised stools consisting of two bricks balanced on top of each other in the shape of a T. Conversation is minimal.

Between the beer hall and the dormitories is Kwesine Station. The shops next to the station, and all the stalls on the diagonal dirt path across the compound, are deserted. Kwesine and the two adjacent hostels are being slowly throttled by the township comrades. There is a complete blockade in force, in which neither goods nor people can enter the hostel. Taxi drivers who worked the hostel routes have gone bankrupt and have had their vehicles repossessed, increasing the market share of township taxi owners. Any hostel-dwellers caught outside the hostel are automatically put to death by the comrades, usually by burning them alive.

The proportion of employed men in the hostels began to dwindle when transport routes through the surrounding township were severed. Absences of several days or weeks ensured that a great many workers lost their jobs. Supplies of food were cut off, apart from the small amounts brought in by police or army convoys. Hunger in the hostels is now widespread. The Katlehong hostels' sole remaining lifeline is the railway.

Kwesine Station is deserted, except for half a dozen security men armed with shotguns. The trains are running today. The line to Germiston is perilous, particularly early in the morning. Gangs rampage through the carriages shooting people and pushing them out of the doors. Train carriages have become segregated, with hostel-dwellers travelling in certain coaches and township residents in others. If you get in the wrong carriage you are likely to be killed and your body thrown from the train.

'People from the hostels stab township residents when they get on the train. Then vice versa. Also people shoot from the trains onto the platforms once the train starts to move,' says the Springbok Patrols security guard. Dozens of commuters were murdered on the East Rand railway lines in the siege of mid-1993.

When hostel-dwellers take the train north to the factories of Germiston, they enter hostile territory almost immediately. The first two stops are Pilot and Lindela, where a hostel was destroyed shortly after Kalanyoni in 1990. Between Kwesine and Lindela is where most of the sabotage takes place. Piles of boulders appear on the line, forcing the trains to stop. When train drivers and security guards attempt to clear the line they come under sniper fire. Lindela and Pilot Stations have both been petrol-bombed.

In their attempt to cut the hostels off completely, the township youth have resorted to severing the railway line with a blow torch and unscrewing the bolts securing the rails to the sleepers. One Sunday in September 1993 they finally succeeded in derailing a train. Four coaches were set ablaze and the line was shut down. The stranglehold on the hostels became complete. Three days later an attack on a taxi rank in the nearby Wadeville industrial area killed twenty-three commuters and injured twenty-two. Men from Kwesine hostel were spotted at the scene of the massacre, shortly before the gunmen opened fire. An ANC spokesperson blamed the attack on the 'third force'.

The line was repaired and ten days later rail services resumed, despite protests by ANC leaders in Katlehong that the railway would be used to bring supplies and reinforcements to the hostels.

Weary night-shift workers returning from Germiston to Kwesine bunch nervously together in one coach. They keep watch on the station platform every time the train stops. The line takes them from Germiston past the chemical plants and squatter camps of Kutalo, past the birch wood on the edge of the town and the bridge which says 'Mods suck', and into the townships. As the train travels south the first gutted bungalows appear amongst the regular rows of white Lego houses.

At midday the station platforms are empty, except for heavy army patrols, moving awkwardly in their body armour. Amongst the other slogans on one of the shelters ('Kill the Boer', 'Viva ANC', 'Viva Liverpool'), someone has scratched the words 'This world is not our home'.

From Kwesine a walkway crosses the tracks, allowing access to Mazibuko, the third hostel, on the other side. The sides of the bridge are made of thick steel, and this is where people take cover to wait for the trains, when the sniping gets bad in the mornings. From the walkway you can see the naked, reddish hills of the East Rand in the far distance, under a glaring blue sky. In the middle distance are the houses of Vosloorus township, also at war.

'We are losing our hold on Katlehong,' says David Radebe, an Inkatha official at Mazibuko hostel. 'We can't defend our members any more.'

'We lost Sali section this week,' chips in one of the headmen, cutting thick slices of white bread for a peanut butter sandwich. The walls of the Hostel Residents Association are decorated with the obligatory picture of Emperor Shaka, leaning on his spear. Ritual feathers and animal tails dangle from the walls, next to a hard hat and a pair of overalls.

Six or seven *indunas* (headmen) cluster around the table in the centre of the room, listening intently to Radebe. 'We want the police to patrol the borders of our areas,' he says. 'Instead, the Internal Stability Unit blocks the exits from the hostels during ANC attacks, so we can't go to the rescue of our members.'

'This is a war,' asserts Radebe. An old man brings him tea, touching his forearm with his free hand in the traditional sign of respect. 'You can see that by the orchestration, the arms that are used. Cuba and the PLO are supplying the ANC with arms. You can see their fighters are well trained. They aim straight between the eyes. Then you must die . . . whether it's raining or not!' he laughs.

'The self-defence units attack at night, just about the time we go to sleep,' says an *induna*.

'They crawl long distances,' adds Radebe. 'The shots come suddenly in a volley. But we can respond very quickly.' He pauses to bite into a huge slab of white bread. 'We are not going to wait for heavy stones,' he continues, the Zulu idioms coming thick and fast. 'We need an army. We may have to bring in trained men to defend our people.'

'I am prepared to sacrifice lives to defend this area and the jobs,' says one *induna* quietly. 'We must give a good account of ourselves.'

'We are not going back to the area of their choice,' bursts out someone else. 'We know our own borders. The Transvaal is part of Zululand.'

'Many people feel they belong in Transvaal,' explains Radebe. 'Not Zulus alone. Xhosas don't want to return to Transkei either.'

'In Zululand no one will destroy the economy by marching for no reason. Our people don't like to strike,' says the first man bitterly.

Radebe, who is jobless after leaving his job as a production manager at Donald Cook Chilled Foods, moved into the hostel from the township when the Internal Stability Unit burned his house. 'I received a warning from the lookouts, but they broke down the door before I could escape,' he recalls:

I locked myself in my bedroom. When I looked there were two White riot policemen in the kitchen. They stole eggs from my fridge. Then they went into my kids' bedroom, and I ran out and hid. Smoke started pouring out of the house. I saw them get into a Casspir, carrying my stove which they had stolen, and I managed to take the registration number. On my way to the police station to report them I saw policemen from the same Casspir kicking down the doors of other houses which they thought were empty. One of them took out a pram. They played with the pram, pushing it backwards and forwards and laughing. Then a day later I found someone had sprayed 'ANC' on the walls of my house.

'The way to resolve this question is to make a committee of hostel residents and township residents,' says an *induna*. 'We had such a committee in 1990 but the civics dismantled it.'

'The ANC is behind the whole crisis,' says the wizened old man who brought the tea. He wears blue company overalls and his earlobes are pierced and enlarged, hanging in loops which flap when he moves his head. 'But the war is between Xhosas and Zulus.'

'The ANC only supports the Xhosas. They don't care which party you belong to. If you are a Zulu they burn you,' says the quiet *induna*.

'The ANC paints its slogans and colours on the area they occupy,' rejoins the old man, shaking his earlobes.

'We were labelled government surrogates,' interrupts Radebe. 'Then we were labelled Conservative Party and AWB [Afrikaner Resistance Movement] supporters. Meanwhile the ANC was in bed with the government. The ANC is coming out of the bushes with the government!'

'It's better to start mobilizing beforehand, to make the elections unworkable,' says a man at the back. 'We're not strong but we'll form an alliance. Can't say with whom,' he adds conspiratorially.

The old man shakes his head again. 'People talk about war all the time,' he says. 'It's become everyday talk.'

19 MK Lives in Slovo Section

From the ghostly streets of Katlehong, over Schoeman Street, and across a strip of waste ground 40 metres wide, are the equally deserted streets of Tokoza, the smaller township west of Katlehong. It's a bitterly cold, foggy morning and a peace meeting has been arranged for nine o'clock, in the middle of the waste ground. The Katlehong side of Schoeman Street is ANC, the Tokoza side is Inkatha. The two sides have agreed to discuss a ceasefire.

In Henry Zondi's house, on the Tokoza side, the men have gathered in the sitting room to discuss the meeting. The walls are bare, except for the obligatory print of King Shaka leaning on his spear. In the garage next door the young tenant is still asleep. With an hour to go before the meeting, a hand grenade explodes outside the front door, echoing right down the length of Schoeman street. This is followed by AK-47 fire, bashing chunks of plaster out of the back wall of the room. The tenant in the garage next door jumps with fright when a bottle of Shield deodorant next to his bed explodes into small pieces. The bullet shreds a 10 rand note and smacks into the wall behind his head.

'These people in Katlehong are always attacking us,' grumbles Zondi, standing outside his house with the other men in the freezing fog. An army lieutenant picks up the cartridge cases and drops them methodically into a small plastic sachet, as if he were picking strawberries. 'The same thing happened three houses down,' says Zondi. Two White national servicemen stand ruddy-faced next to the lieutenant, their weapons at the ready. Nobody says a word. A chunk of concrete has been gouged out of the front path by the grenade dust. One of the men whistles a sad tune.

Two streets away, in Sabi Street, the Mabasos' house lies empty. Mr Mabaso was shot dead last week in front of his wife and children. Men from the Mshayazafe hostel had been making threats and demanding money from him for two weeks. Mabaso was a Zulu, but his loyalties lay with the ANC.

'We parted at six o'clock that morning,' says Ivan, a Xhosa-speaking neighbour of Mabaso's, who fled after his murder. 'Men from the hostels were standing armed on the street corners. They stopped us from going to work,' he explains. 'Mabaso was furious, and said in a loud voice that we were going to lose our jobs, and that people from other sections of the township would take them over. He was very angry. Someone must have heard and reported him to the hostel. That night he was killed. Four families in my street have left, all Xhosas.' Sabi Street is in Penduka section, known unofficially as Mandela section. Recently Penduka was renamed Ulundi, after the Zulu capital city.

One street away, on Tshabalala Street, a knot of nervous-looking IFP youths in ragged clothes cluster on the street corner, armed with wooden clubs, spears and huge broad-bladed machetes. The north end of Tshabalala Street is in Ulundi section, which is Inkatha territory, while the south part is in Slovo section, which is held by the ANC. The front line on Tshabalala Street moves one block forward, one block back, almost every night. Today ANC territory ends at the junction with Ndebele Street, where some houses were burned last night.

Every so often one of the boys will peer gingerly round the corner, checking the cross-street. Women walk by, carrying the bare essentials in plastic bags, casually fleeing this morning's war zone. The boys don't even notice them. They are looking out for the comrades, who are rumoured to be planning an attack. A woman bolts out of one of the streets in fright and everyone stands back from the corner, seeking cover behind the fences. It's one of dozens of false alarms.

'I don't know why I joined the IFP,' says one teenager. After thinking about it, he says, 'Because I live in an IFP section.' After thinking some more, he adds; 'If you are a Zulu and you join the ANC, they kill you.'

'We are killed because we are Zulus. The other side are Xhosa and Shangaan. All these animals are against us,' mutters another boy. The IFP youths complain that whenever the police Hippos (Casspirs) come to disperse them they are attacked immediately afterwards by the ANC comrades. 'The ANC uses R1s and R5s, security force guns. We don't know where they get them. On this side we only have knobkerries,' complains one boy, holding up a small wooden club.

'The soldiers go around with two ANC members inside the Hippos,' protests another. 'The soldiers are selling us out. We tell them they should clear the area and let us fight. We can defend ourselves. The army should let us get on with it. We've got traditional weapons and *intelezi*.' The boys' laughter echoes in the shabby street.

Soldiers appear silently from one of the streets, moving fast, checking over their shoulders nervously. They ignore the boys, striding past them as if they were not there. The squaddies look disgruntled, their faces red with cold. The corporal, who wears a balaclava, urges his men to move faster. An armoured vehicle arrives, with two Black teenagers huddled amongst the soldiers in the back. They wear baseball caps and appear fairly relaxed, chatting to the soldiers. 'ANC!' murmurs one of the Inkatha boys, with a helpless shrug. As the Casspir trundles down the street, the boys in the back appear to be pointing out houses, which are then searched by the army. The patrol moves down Tshabalala Street, and one of the IFP youngsters points out a slow-moving white minibus which seems to be waiting at the south end of Tshabalala Street, in the ANC zone. 'The SADF are going. Now the ANC are moving their guns back,' says the boy knowingly.

The comrades at the southern end of Tshabalala Street are infinitely better organized than the sorry IFP rabble with their sticks and meat cleavers on the north side. In Nhlapo Street, which intersects with Tshabalala, rows of boulders cross the street every 10 or 20 metres, like a series of speed bumps. The bright logos on the electricity junction box leave you in little doubt as to who controls the street. In fresh, glossy paint, with equal space allocated to the three main 'Patriotic Front' parties, the box displays the black, green and gold of the ANC, the Communist Party hammer and sickle and the radiant Africa symbol of the Pan Africanist Congress, together with the slogan 'One Settler, One Bullet' in black letters. The front of the junction box is painted with a huge AK-47, beneath the words 'MK lives in Slovo Section'.

When shots ring out a few streets away Skumbuzo jumps on top of the outside toilet in his father's back yard to get a better view. His father is still complaining about the way the police kicked down his door in the middle of the night. 'They said they would come back and fix it, but they haven't been yet,' he says. 'A couple of hours after the army left, two Zulu-speaking guys carrying pangas came looking for Skumbuzo. They were dressed in old clothes and sneakers, and looked like *tsotsis* (gangsters). Never seen them before. They asked me for my reference ID book. They looked at it for a long time, then left.'

Sipho, a youngster with a radiant, angelic face speculates that it might have been the Kumalo gang. 'They only kill young boys. They all stay in Mdakane Street,' he says, pointing in the direction of the Tokoza hostels, a few streets away. 'They are Inkatha. They started shooting people last year,' he says with a sweet smile. 'Two youths were kidnapped from this street and taken to the hostel. They were killed.' He counts under his breath. 'Five people have been killed in this street since December. Aaron Shongwe and Pani Sibiso were killed on New Year's Day. Pani's brother was also wounded.'

The house next door to Skumbuzo's has been reduced to a few charred bricks and twisted roofing sheets. 'One of Mbatha's relatives,' explains Skumbuzo. 'Mbatha used to visit there. He killed two of our neighbours. On the way back from the funeral the youth burned his house.'

A whistle sends the boys vaulting over the fences to take up their positions. Some are armed, and clutch their back pockets as they disperse. The army Buffels arrive, negotiating the barricades at a snail's pace. Two women carrying a hi-fi set and other belongings walk past on their way to find safety.

Once the false alarm is over, people come back out to gossip. There is a street party atmosphere, with excited chatter and laughter. Today's gossip is that the army searched the hearses and dug up the graves at the funeral of two boys from the street, to make sure that corpses were being buried, and not guns.

Women standing at their front gates curse Inkatha. 'Phola Park must deal with them,' says one impatiently. In Nhlapo Street, politics seems to be more of an issue than ethnicity.

Skumbuzo points out that he is a Zulu. 'Township Zulus are not a problem,' concludes Sipho cheerily.

'But if we see a Zulu from Ulundi and we catch him . . .' laughs another youth, a visitor from Beirut section, 'no questions asked . . .'

20 More than Peaceful

'There's going to be more chaos in Tokoza,' laments Louis Sibeko. 'People are armed to the teeth. Known criminals are walking the streets.' He waves a thin hand in desperation. 'Criminals are comfortable with this chaos. They can do whatever they like. They can rob without being identified.'

Louis lives in a large, empty, modern house, just off the southern, ANC-held part of Kumalo Street. He is a skinny man in his mid-thirties, although he looks ten years older. His gaunt face shows the strain. Louis is the only civic leader in Tokoza to have survived the three years of civil war.

'People are idle in the townships,' he says candidly. 'Those who don't work need to eat, have nice cars, clothes . . . There is a large number of criminals in the hostels and in Phola Park. Some police are involved in criminal activities. They tell criminals about complaints, so people don't want to report crimes any more . . . People have had to take the law into their own hands.'

'Sometimes the youth don't think straight,' observes the commander of Tokoza's Self-Defence Unit, a burly local businessman in his late thirties. 'They kill people if they feel threatened. If they see you talking to the police, you are *impimpi*, an informer. If they think you're *impimpi*, they kill you,' he says bluntly. 'Life is complicated. It's dangerous to know who controls the youth. Since the violence intensified, they don't go along with ANC policy. They wonder why the ANC isn't helping them to fight,' sighs the commander. 'The Self-Defence Unit controls the youth to some extent,' he admits. 'I give them advice. But I don't want to bring them too close. They might rob me with that AK-47 tomorrow,' he says, glancing at his grocery store.

'There is a serious problem with the Azanian People's Liberation Army (APLA) youth here,' confirms Louis. 'Policemen who stay in the township are becoming victims. Most criminals claim to be APLA members. APLA kill policemen.'

Louis' spacious new lounge contains little more than a large dining room table, chairs, a dresser. ANC election posters are the only decoration on otherwise bare walls. A net curtain hangs in the open doorway from the back yard. Louis tenses every time people walk past or look into the room.

'There were no formal defence structures until now,' he says. 'Now we're organized. It's not easy to come and harass us now.'

There is no sense of triumph in his voice, only apprehension:

> We resisted the pressure for as long as we could. We knew that if we organized it would come back to us. If you let people have guns they will harass the community. But now we have no choice. As a resident I paid 50 rand, even though it's against my principles. The contributions are voluntary. But there is no normal person who didn't contribute. Moderates have become hard-liners. We couldn't sleep here in Tokoza.
>
> Now, just because we are organized, the police are doing their work. More than twenty comrades have been arrested in the last two weeks. They are still being held without charge under the 'unrest area' regulations. The police don't find any guns. They merely harass people. The Internal Stability Unit are the worst. They have an attitude.

Defiance turns to anxiety once more on Louis' drawn face. 'There are no trained people guiding these youngsters,' he frets. 'We are going to have a serious problem with those guns. Almost everyone has a gun.'

The Tokoza Civic Association did not come into being, however, with the purpose of arming youngsters in the war against the hostels. Civics were originally launched to campaign against the Black town councils which were introduced in the mid-1980s. The councils were seen as corrupt, ineffective and illegitimate, mere proxies for the White government. Civics were initially conceived as non-political organizations which would campaign on behalf of everyone who lived in the townships, including the hostel-dwellers. People marched to protest against the lack of improvements in the townships, against rent increases and other domestic grievances.

'In 1990 we had a very successful march against councillors in the Black Local Authority,' says Louis proudly:

> Some houses were petrol-bombed. It wasn't an ANC march, it was a march by township residents. The hostel-dwellers marched with us. In our central committee meetings we sat with delegates from the hostels and Inkatha to discuss services.
>
> The councillors were selling land illegally . . . If you followed the proper channels you'd never get a business site. All the money went to a clique in the council. My brother-in-law had a dispute with a councillor who took his money but didn't sell him the land. There was no improvement in the township facilities. Councillors were becoming successful businessmen. Some were taken to court for corruption.

The SDU commander puts it concisely: 'What caused the trouble between the community and the councillors was that the councillors were not providing good services. They were asked to resign. They refused and opted to join Inkatha for protection. The youth burned the councillors' houses.'

'The councillors were furious about the support for the civics,' says Louis. 'It was like saying to them "shut up shop". They wanted to create an opposing bloc. They started influencing people in the hostels to be hostile to us. The councillors and the town clerk found their power base in the hostels. The hostel-dwellers started coming to us saying the civic was ANC.'

'Before 1990,' sighs Louis, 'we used to play football with the hostel people. Township residents used to take showers in the hostel, where there was hot water. Relations were . . . is there a word for "more than peaceful"?'

'The heavy violence started in 1990, shortly after Nelson Mandela's release. It started with the taxis, then it got into politics,' remembers the SDU commander. 'Before that Tokoza was a nice place to live.'

'Here in Tokoza we had two taxi associations,' explains Solly Ramukhotwane, who owned four taxis at the time. 'The taxi war broke out because people didn't understand each other. In fact,' he adds, 'the taxi war came from Katlehong to Tokoza. The hostel and the township supported different taxi associations.'

'The problem was amongst the drivers,' says Solly, a Suthu-speaker:

> They said if you weren't a Zulu you were a woman. I saw the attitude of the Zulu nation. They were unfriendly. But taxi drivers had been killing each other before then, out of jealousy. It was normal. Then one day they took one of my taxis. I was hijacked at gunpoint. Another

of my taxis was burned. That's the day I realized it was a taxi war. It was September 1990.

It became Zulu-speaking drivers from the hostel and Inkatha drivers from the township versus mostly non-Zulu-speaking township residents. The people from the township would prefer taxis that were clean, driven by people who were clean. The Zulu drivers didn't care. They smelled bad. They were rude to the women. These dirty men proposed to women, it was embarrassing.

Even if people had been queuing for the taxi they would wait till a better one came. People flocked to the clean taxis. Up to then there had been no choice. Then the clean taxis came in, driven by people from the township. The Zulu drivers became jealous. They started the violence. Mine was the first taxi to be stolen. Other people got involved. It became Inkatha versus ANC.

We still thought it was a taxi war. Then we heard rumours that there was a Zulu–Xhosa war. The hostel-dwellers were on their way to launch an attack on Phola Park, when they told us they were fighting the Xhosas. Then the taxis started transporting hostel-dwellers to attack Phola Park.

The feud between the Tokoza hostels and Phola Park ignited an already tense Tokoza into all-out war.

'On their way to Phola Park,' says Louis, 'the hostel-dwellers would attack Xhosas or ANC members in the streets of Tokoza. The whole community got involved.'

Tokoza became one of the most hotly contested areas in the membership race between the ANC and the IFP. 'We heard that Inkatha intended to make Tokoza their stronghold,' explains Louis. 'Their way of recruiting was unacceptable. They forced people to join the IFP . . . Mandela section next to the hostel was renamed Ulundi. The areas next to the hostels have become no-go areas for us,' he says angrily. He admits, however, that the ANC had its own recruitment campaign, and that 'some unruly elements used force'.

Louis doesn't stop to talk to people in the street any more. His neighbours keep a careful eye on his house. He can't remember all the names of his close colleagues who have been assassinated since thirty-one-year-old Sam Ntuli, the leader of the Tokoza Civic Association, was slain by a hit squad on Kumalo Street in September 1991.

'Philip Mbatha, Mike Masupa, Vusi Tshabalala, Jack Malinga, Dennis Makanya . . . ' Louis struggles to remember. 'Themba Mabaso. Killed in his home,' he adds. 'All ANC members. They were mostly shot in the street, during the day. No arrests have been made. The police are not interested. I am the last surviving elected member of the Civic executive.'

Civic leader Ntuli was the first to die, after two failed assassination attempts that year. In the first, a hand grenade was thrown into his father's house. Two months later, when men from the hostel came looking for Ntuli at a friend's house, two women were dragged from the house into Mshayazafe hostel where they were shot and stabbed. One survived by playing dead.

Finally, three weeks after the massacre of hostel-dwellers by Phola Park gunmen outside house 2044, Ntuli was driving down Kumalo Street when a large blue Chevrolet pulled out behind him and flicked its headlights. Ntuli ignored the signal and his car was forced off the road. An AK-47 was fired at close range into Ntuli's car from the front passenger seat of the Chevrolet.

Ntuli's funeral was one of the biggest ever on the East Rand, attended by thousands of township residents and blanket men from the shack towns. After the traditional washing of the hands at Ntuli's parental home, the crowd dispersed, the blanket men from Mandela Park and Holomisa Park making their way north past the taxi ranks outside the Natalspruit Hospital.

As the blanket men passed through the taxi rank some of them attacked the Zulu taxi drivers, who were not observing a voluntary stayaway called as a mark of respect for Ntuli. A passenger who tried to flee was shot dead and taxi drivers were stabbed. Almost immediately after the fighting broke out in the taxi rank, a carefully coordinated AK-47 attack from passing cars cut down several dozen blanket men in an open space near the taxi rank. The attackers were members of a heavily armed taxi drivers' defence unit called the KAPTA Squad. No arrests were made. Revenge for the attack outside house 2044 was suggested as a possible motive, but no one knows for sure.

'There must be control of the people who live in the hostels,' says Louis, shrill with exasperation. 'I'm overloaded. I've disconnected my phone. I can't sleep. People call me in tears, complaining of harassment. People are still missing. There are rumours that their bodies were taken to the hostel. I don't have peace of mind. Things are beyond control. I didn't think it would turn out this way . . . ' There is a hint of despair in the thin man's voice, a feeling that he is holding on to his sanity by a thread. He recovers his composure rapidly.

'The residents feel they want the hostel-dwellers to leave,' he says. 'In 1990 we said there must be upgrading. Now we are talking about demolition. To destroy the hostels would be the best solution. Employers should build hostels near the workplace. Most of the people in the hostels are not working. Mshayazafe is out of control. Anybody can live there. There are people in the hostels who are not interested in peace. They have different agendas: crime and fomenting violence.'

Louis describes himself as a 'township Zulu'. He says he understands the pressures on hostel-dwellers:

The problem for Zulus in the hostels is that if you don't toe the line here they will get your family at home. The other problem is that they don't question their leaders. Zulus respect their leaders, come what may. Leaders have taken advantage of their illiteracy.

In the township the attitude is "I don't trust those people". There is no direct contact any more with the people from the hostels. People bring their personal grudges into it. There are people in the township who are killing Zulus.

Despair returns to Louis' face.

'The people of Tokoza don't have any hope,' he says. 'They're not sure if they will see the new South Africa. There is no more tolerance. People have lost interest in peace.'

21 Happiness for Husbands and Wives

About 1000 metres down Kumalo Street from Louis' house, several of the front windows of the Mzizi home are riddled with bullet-holes. The Mzizis are Tokoza's most controversial couple.

Abram, a former town councillor, is the chairman of the Inkatha Freedom Party in Tokoza. He speaks with a clipped, posh accent and used to play golf regularly. His wife Gertrude, the leader of the local IFP Women's Brigade, is a dynamic, handsome woman, who is constantly busy attending to some emergency in the Tokoza hostels. Gertrude has become the queen of the hostel-dwellers.

While Abram lathers his car in front of the house, whistling quietly to himself, Gertrude perches on a bashed paint tin in the hostel yard, in a semicircle of worried-looking middle-aged *indunas* (hostel headmen). The yard is black with coal dust and strewn with car parts. Chickens strut in circles amid the junk. The Tokoza hostels outdo even Kwesine in neighbouring Katlehong for sheer squalor. Every window pane in the long, low 'trains' is shattered. Thick white smoke pours from the tin chimneys. Gertrude talks and the headmen listen.

'They say a man can have twenty women,' she jokes later. 'Well, I have twenty men.' It has been a relatively quiet day. Gertrude summarizes the situation:

IFP people are being kidnapped from their homes. We buried two today. They were shot and burned. An eighty-seven-year-old woman who was shot in her house on Mdakane Street by ANC youth. And Mr Ndazi. He was taken out of his house and shot in the street in Unit F. Since April hundreds have died, with many missing. It's been total war in Tokoza since August 1990. People are so scared. Life is no longer sweet for them.

The war in Tokoza, as in Katlehong, is about territory. 'Unit F and Nthabanzimbo – Steel Mountain – are mixed areas. The ANC are trying to make those areas their stronghold.' Gertrude's defiant tone softens fractionally as she sinks back into the leatherette couch with the bullet-hole. The room is stark, with bare concrete floors. A leaflet explaining the new South African Defence Force uniform lies next to the telephone. The few books on the shelf include *Happiness for Husbands and Wives* and *Adventures in English Literature*. The only concession to comfort is the three-piece black leatherette suite.

From her front room Gertrude can observe the gates of Kutuza hostel, across the road. 'We discourage people from retaliation. You lose one man, you retaliate, you lose two more. And many IFP guys have been arrested. The only unfortunate person who doesn't rest is me,' she laughs, in mock self-pity. 'The men can't sit and take decisions on their own. They have to call on me.'

The event which triggered the war of early 1993 in Tokoza was an ANC march down Kumalo Street, past the Tokoza hostels. The leaders of the march were determined to take the Kumalo Street route to deliver a memorandum to Alberton Police Station.

'The streets are for everybody' insisted the commander of the Phola Park Self-Defence Unit, one of the leaders of the march. Peace monitors and the police had urged him to choose a different route, saying that the hostel-dwellers were mobilizing in preparation for the march. 'We heard the rubbish from the Goldstone Commission say we weren't supposed to go there, saying it was an IFP route,' he said. 'The IFP use the same route to the cemetery. We don't do anything to them.'

The marchers included a heavily armed contingent of blanket men from Phola Park, shielded from the police by men with traditional weapons. As they passed the Mshayazafe hostel a mysterious detachment of ten men opened fire on the hostel-dwellers from the rear of the hostel. They were photographed from a civilian helicopter which was carrying out surveillance on behalf of the police. No one knows who they were. One of the Phola Park shack-dwellers admits that 'the shooting was activated from Phola Park. Our people shot first. It was psychological. It happened on impulse.' The hostel-dwellers, who didn't know where the attack was coming from, returned fire on the marchers at the front of the hostel. Eleven marchers and two hostel-dwellers were killed.

Gertrude Mzizi had been warned by a friend in the ANC that there was going to be trouble that Saturday. Her children had been sent away for safety. Abram, her husband, was trapped by marchers in his car on the way back from Alberton, but rescued by police. Gertrude sat on her black leatherette sofa and waited. As the marchers went past in a big crowd of youths and blanket men, the Mzizi house was stoned. Somewhere in the house a window-pane shattered. Hand grenades detonated in the street. The first bullet ripped through the net curtain, the black leatherette sofa and the matching armchair before smacking into the wall. ('Shots came from Mzizi's house through the big window,' fibbed the Phola Park SDU commander. 'My people just tried to fire back.')

Gertrude ducked into her kitchen and out into the back yard, hoping to find cover in the outbuildings. The doors were locked, and there was gunfire which sounded like another attack coming from behind the house. Gertrude decided to crawl back inside. 'I thought, I prefer to die in my house,' she says. 'What they do to leaders is they kill you and take your corpse. If I die here they'll find it very hard to take my corpse.' On her hands and knees she made her way up a narrow alleyway to her front door. A bullet smashed the light over the door and the bulb fell on her head. Another bullet was stopped by the electricity meter. Even the narrow steel spokes of the front gate were ripped. Gertrude decided against going back into her house, and nipped out of the gate into the street.

Meanwhile the Stability Unit were blasting the hostel-dwellers with buckshot from a Casspir which was blocking the hostel entrance, 20 metres from Gertrude's front door. 'If the ANC come to burn my house, the police will seal off the hostel first. They are scared of the ANC,' says Gertrude bitterly.

As Gertrude turned her back on the Casspir she heard one of the policemen standing on top of the vehicle shout, 'Skiet! Maak die vrou dood!' ('Shoot that woman dead!') She stumbled and her back started to burn. 'It feels like a bucket of hot water,' says Gertrude. 'I was shot by the police with thirty-seven pellets. I still have some in my bum,' she adds coyly.

'I don't enjoy being followed like a queen,' complains Gertrude, who is a Suthu princess by birth. She has been in the local Inkatha leadership since 1984, and the troubles in Tokoza have stamped her face with a permanently defiant look. 'It started in 1990 when everyone was forced to join the ANC, to attend ANC meetings and marches. A group of youths would come to your house and say, "We are marching, you must join our march."' ANC youth stole Abram's Ford Sierra and burned Gertrude's Renault Five. 'They were told by their leaders that they were the young lions,' she says scornfully.

In August, around the time of the first clashes in Phola Park, Gertrude was walking home from the butcher's in Tokoza, carrying her nine-month-old baby, when she was confronted on the street corner by a crowd of more than 100 youths. 'We've been looking for you. We're going to roast you, Gatsha's dog!'

'I didn't try to plead with them,' remembers Gertrude. 'They told me to put the baby down. "The child must watch you burn," they said to me.'

There was a delay as a tyre and petrol were fetched. 'I couldn't do anything,' says Gertrude. 'I just stood there. I was told to fold my arms and pray to Buthelezi to rescue me.'

The petrol arrived in a 20-litre container. It was poured over Gertrude's head. 'The smell was terrible,' she recalls. The boys were laughing as they placed a car tyre round her neck. 'I had nothing on my mind except accepting to die.'

At this point the youngsters realized they did not have any matches. 'The last thing I heard,' says Gertrude, 'was someone saying "Go to the house and look for matches."'

The delay saved her life. A police Casspir arrived and the youths fled. Gertrude was treated for shock. She can still taste the petrol to this day.

A few months later the Mzizis' house was burned down, and they moved to a safer address opposite the hostels.

22 Tokoza is Cooking

It's dusk in Tokoza and an army Buffel has capsized in a side street. The driver, who was chasing a suspect car, took the corner too fast and rolled the Buffel into a front yard, flattening the garden fence. The huge armoured vehicle lies on its side as the East Rand smog descends, while reinforcements pour in to protect the salvage crew. Dusk is the most dangerous time in South Africa. A dozen armoured vehicles defend the street where the Buffel is being eased upright in the glare of the salvage crane's searchlight. Plain clothes policemen stand around chatting, with torches taped to their assault rifles. 'It's handy for house searches,' explains a blond man in jeans and trainers.

'Tokoza is cooking,' says a cheerful South African Defence Force sergeant. 'Both sides are heavily armed. They're well trained, they know what they're doing. They'll put up a fight if there are enough of them. If they are outnumbered they don't just run away. They won't shoot over their shoulder. They return negative fire.'

The sergeant has just spent three months in the East Rand, three times longer than the usual tour of duty. He volunteered because of the excitement and the danger money, 15 rand a day. It's not as much as the guys in the Internal Stability Unit, who get 60 rand, but enough to make a difference. A Black lieutenant walks up, seething with frustration. 'The guns are in there,' he mutters, glancing at the hostel, 'but we can't get at them.'

The sergeant shakes his head. 'If you could get them all together in one place,' he says thoughtfully, 'like the Chinese army did in Tiananmen Square, you could get rid of the whole problem at one stroke.'

The peace monitors from the Peace Secretariat's Joint Operations Control Centre in Katlehong knock off at dusk. In a small, shabby office in the grounds of Natalspruit Hospital, the Peace Secretariat controller on night duty tries to contact Jeff Sibiya at Kwesine hostel. 'Jeff, Jeff, this is Gold One, do you copy?' A two-bar heater glows on the tattered floral carpet. Maps of Tokoza and Katlehong hang on the walls. There is a flip chart bearing the dates and locations of forthcoming funerals. No names are given, only the political affiliation of each funeral march: 'IFP' or 'ANC'. 'That's the sadness of it,' says Mandla, the controller on duty for the night. 'You never know who they're burying.'

'Jeff responding to Gold One!' bleats the radio. People at Kwesine are extremely worried, crackles Jeff, about one of their members, Bongani Mbatha, who was kidnapped from a taxi rank and taken to Phola Park. Mandla reassures Jeff that Mbatha has been released into the custody of the Goldstone Commission, who have taken him to a safe house.

'We don't even know if the guy they released is the right guy,' he admits with a sigh after Jeff has signed off. The Tokoza ANC branch, on the same radio frequency, begins a long dialogue with Jeff, reassuring him that Mbatha is unharmed. That afternoon senior officers in the South African Defence Force had telephoned the Control Centre in a panic, wanting to know where the man was being kept.

At a special press conference in Phola Park that morning Mbatha had been paraded in front of the media, who heard his 'confession'. Reporters were told that Mbatha was found inside Phola Park, and that he was an Inkatha spy. Mbatha, who was trembling so violently that he almost fell off his chair, spoke through chattering teeth. He revealed that the police had distributed guns and uniforms to hostel-dwellers in Tokoza before a recent massacre. He was then taken to hospital, where it was found that his legs had been gouged with sharpened steel rods, and the wounds smeared with a substance which made them go septic. 'He stank to high heaven,' said one of the peace monitors who accompanied him to hospital.

Mandla shakes his head. 'Those guys are capable of doing anything with a human body,' he says. The Peace Secretariat Control Centre, staffed by volunteers, has been monitoring the conflict in the East Rand for months, typing every reported incident into a daily log on the computer next to the controller's two-way radio.

'Group conflicts are less now,' says Mandla. 'We can prevent those. Now it's individuals kidnapped and killed. The face of violence changes. Families avenge their dead, their burned houses. Criminals exploit the chaos. Society has fallen apart.' Mandla is silent while the IFP and the ANC natter on the radio. 'We pick up the bodies in the morning,' he says. 'The burned bodies are usually hostel-dwellers or IFP. The IFP doesn't have a tradition of burning people. Violence like this has been happening all over the Reef, in the Vaal, Soweto . . . But it all started in Natal.'

PART THREE

Natal

23 The Trouble with Harry

In the middle of Pietermaritzburg, the hub of the Zulu civil war in Natal, stands a bronze statue of Mahatma Gandhi, the Indian peacemaker. He wears a loincloth of bronze, with a fob watch, and carries a staff. His right hand is raised in a solemn gesture. His eyes are deep-set, horror-struck, although the sculptor meant to fill them with the milk of human pity. The dowdy shoppers of this resolutely English capital of the Natal Midlands waddle past on their errands.

The plinth reads: 'This statue marks the centenary of an event on the night of 7 June 1893 when Mahatma Gandhi was forcibly removed from a train compartment at the Pietermaritzburg station because of discrimination based on race.' This is followed by a quote from Gandhi: 'My active non-violence began from that date . . . The path of true non-violence requires much more courage than violence.'

Gandhi, a British-trained barrister, had arrived in South Africa to represent an Indian trading firm in a Supreme Court action. He ended up staying for twenty-one years, before returning to India to lead the mass campaigns of passive resistance for which he became famous. Gandhi founded the Natal Indian Congress and led the first pass law protests in South Africa, five years before the ANC was formed. The early leaders of the ANC were inspired by Gandhi's concept of passive resistance. Harry Gwala, chairman of the African National Congress in the Natal Midlands, has a more robust approach.

Harry denies that he is a warlord. His home is a large, comfortable suburban villa on a dirt road in the dilapidated Pietermaritzburg township of Dumbuza. Young men cluster in the driveway. Rumour has it that there are bodyguards perched in the trees. Harry is bespectacled and quietly spoken. He is a connoisseur of English literature. 'You can't compare Shakespeare to the others. He was in his own class,' he observes. He admires Thomas Gray and Robert Burns. A particular favourite is Burns's poem 'A man's a man for all that'.

England has a special place in Harry's heart. 'The English countryside is fascinating. So charming, so well-organized,' he enthuses. 'Hitler couldn't conquer this spirit.' On a recent visit Harry fell in love with Canterbury, but was puzzled and upset to hear that Jaguar had been taken over by Ford. 'British people are strange,' he says, bemused.

Harry Gwala has no time for the IFP's brand of Zulu jingoism. He sneers from behind his thick spectacles. 'Some people think freedom means going back to the traditional way of life and the great kings. Traditionalists who dream of the past belong to Inkatha. Those who go into the ANC are urban youth and industrial workers.'

Gwala describes himself as a Marxist who believes in democracy and respects Lincoln, Roosevelt and Churchill. He is believed by some comrades in the ANC to have a sneaking admiration for Joseph Stalin.

'We are the most advanced country on this continent,' he intones. 'I believe in the working class. I believe that those who produce should benefit from the products of their own labour.'

Dwelling nostalgically in the nineteenth-century heyday of the Zulu empire, in the manner of Inkatha leaders, is certainly not one of Harry's failings. But his grip on the reality of present-day, largely rural Natal is not particularly firm either. He inhabits a different bygone age, the crisis-torn industrial landscapes of 1930s Europe and the grand certainties of the struggle against fascism. His speeches, delivered in Zulu to an African audience, bristle with stirring references to Munich and Stalingrad. When the Red Army turned the tide of the Second World War at Stalingrad, Harry had already been a member of the Communist Party for more than a year.

'When Hitler made a putsch they called him a disgruntled Austrian corporal. When Mussolini marched on Rome they called him a ridiculous clown,' he warns, drawing parallels with Buthelezi. 'Inkatha started as an innocuous body, a cultural organization. As time went on Buthelezi found he was filling the gap created by the ANC. He saw himself as the heir to Chief Luthuli [a highly respected Zulu statesman and former President of the ANC]' he says. 'When the ANC was unbanned it was too much for him to take. He reacted by attacking the ANC. Buthelezi has been absorbed into the system,' Harry pauses. 'I don't want to speculate on who controls him.'

For Harry the civil war in Natal is not a power struggle between the ANC and Inkatha. It is a struggle between the people and apartheid. 'The people organized themselves into defensive groups. They considered themselves ANC,' he says. 'It's not the ANC that is attacking Inkatha. The fighting is there. The suspension of the armed struggle has become theoretical. They say I'm a warlord. I earned the name when I started organizing self-defence.'

Harry, a schoolteacher by training, had been a successful trade unionist when he was arrested in 1964 on charges of sabotage and recruiting young men into uMkhonto we Sizwe ('MK'), the ANC's military wing, for training. He spent most of the next twenty-two years as a political prisoner on Robben Island, emerging fifteen months before the ANC was unbanned.

The Natal Midlands he returned to was a war zone. 'It was real war . . . involving thousands of people.'

Despite the nervous wasting disease which deprived him of the use of his hands, Harry threw himself into the thick of the fight. 'We asked our comrades with military training for lessons in defence theory. They supplied their own weapons.' Harry earned himself a nationwide reputation as a hard-liner, committed to the use of force. He is bitter about the ANC's decision to suspend the armed struggle in August 1990, as a preliminary to beginning peace talks with the government. 'I was overruled,' he grumbles.

In 1993 Gwala could be seen touring South Africa's trouble spots, to the discomfiture of ANC pragmatists, preaching war to crowds of bitter youngsters. He cut an unmistakable figure at the microphone, dressed in a Soviet-style grey overcoat and scarf, a stirring orator whose arms hung limply at his sides.

'Harry Gwala doesn't like me,' murmurs his arch-rival David Ntombela with mock chagrin. 'He's an old man. If he can change his ways he can be my older brother. But he says there is no God. So there is nothing I can discuss with him.'

David Ntombela also denies that he is a warlord. 'The ANC say I'm the one who leads the attacks,' he complains. 'They call me the number one warlord, to ruin my credibility. I've never told people to arm themselves. If I wasn't poor I would sue those who call me a warlord,' he says, with a look that says he would like to do more than sue them.

Ntombela, the Natal Midlands IFP chairman, chain-smokes Rothmans in the old-fashioned flat cardboard packets and wears a kipper tie in IFP colours with a broad grey pinstripe. He is a Methodist, staunch without being pious. 'The wind and the sun are controlled by God,' he says in a rough, tobacco voice. 'Before I go to bed I think of God and ask myself, when will this violence stop?'

A compact man with an energetic frame and grey-flecked hair, Ntombela has the air of a rough-hewn village patriarch. 'They believe that once they kill me that will be the end of the IFP in the region. I've been attacked many times. My car still has bullet-holes,' he says hoarsely. Ntombela has become adept at tumbling out of his car under fire, pretending to be hit, while surreptitiously grabbing his rifle. Like all IFP chiefs, he carries a KwaZulu Police issue G3 next to the car seat.

Ntombela describes a recent attempt to kill him:

After Reggie Hadebe [a local ANC leader] was assassinated I was driving to work when I saw two guys standing next to the road. I thought they were pissing. One was looking away, the other was watching the road, as if they were talking. The one facing away suddenly turned and fired. I stopped the car and fell as if I was hit. My rifle is always next to me. I pulled my rifle out. They ran off and I fired at them but missed. Let me tell you . . . I'm not scared. If someone fires at me I'll stop my car, I don't care how many they are, I'll take my rifle . . . I've never troubled anyone. I've never killed anyone, but when someone fights me I'll fight back.

Feeling that perhaps he hasn't made the point convincingly enough, he looks for support to the Old Testament: 'If I do something bad to you because I have power, and one day God decides you will fight me, then you will take a small stone and hit me in the eye and I will die.'

Ntombela flares suddenly. 'The ANC want power. We try to defend the people. That's why they want to assassinate us.'

He describes how his twenty-three-year-old son Drake, a policeman, was shot dead in his front yard, one of a catalogue of killings he lays at the door of the ANC:

Goba, the IFP branch chairman at Inxwati was killed last night. His house was surrounded by men in camouflage uniforms, like those worn by the Internal Stability Unit. They asked him to open the door, and while he was talking to them someone broke in through the back window. As he turned round to look who it was, they shot him. Before that we had an IFP meeting at Mafuza. The buses were ambushed on their way back to Sweet Water. Eighteen people were killed. Harry Gwala said, yes, when the IFP attack us we will kill them to the last man.

Gwala doesn't care about his life. He tells his followers to arm themselves. He doesn't worry about going to jail. They believe in the armed struggle. They believe that to get freedom is to kill and grab power.

When Harry Gwala emerged from prison Ntombela had already been caught up in the civil war for some time. His involvement began during a strike in 1985 at a British-owned rubber factory at Howick, near Pietermaritzburg, when striking union members were sacked by a Thatcherite management team from the UK. At the time Ntombela was a local *induna* (headman), whose relatives were amongst the 'scabs' recruited to replace the sacked factory workers.

Inkatha backed the scab labourers. 'If you're hungry and you see a vacancy you'll take the job,' shrugs Ntombela. There were battles outside the rubber factory and in township streets as strikers fought against the scabs. 'That was the beginning of violence in this region,' says Ntombela. 'That violence spread all over. The strikers were from Mpopomeni. Scabs from there were killed and their houses burned.' He stops to think. 'In my heart I thought taking the strikers' jobs was wrong. But it was wrong to assault or kill those who took the jobs.'

In the course of the Howick strike Ntombela's father, who had four grandchildren amongst the scabs, was murdered by strikers. 'My father died trying to bring peace to the factions in the factory. He lived in the area and went to separate them. The youngsters threw stones and ran away. But he was an old man and couldn't run. He just shouted "Stop, stop!" Then someone came with an *assegai* and stabbed him many times.'

The men who killed Ntombela's father were arrested. 'I didn't go to the magistrate's court for the hearings,' says Ntombela. 'I didn't want to see the faces of the people who murdered my father. I didn't want to know their names.' The suspects were acquitted for lack of evidence. Ntombela claims he did not try to seek vengeance. 'Defend yourself immediately you're attacked. If you don't then forget it. If you go home and arm yourself, then innocent people will die. Both sides have made that mistake.'

Gwala and Ntombela's first major confrontation was the 'Seven Day War' in 1990. The clash ignited a full-scale civil war in the Natal Midlands involving organized armies of thousands of combatants.

Two weeks after his release from jail in February 1990 Nelson Mandela held a hugely successful rally at King's Park stadium in Durban. The ANC estimated the crowd at 200 000, the largest ever in Natal. A month later, Inkatha 's counter-rally, at the very same stadium, drew barely 10 000. Even allowing for the heavy rain which had discouraged many Inkatha supporters, the rally was a humiliating setback.

'I ordered 105 buses from KwaZulu Transport for my area,' remembers Ntombela. 'It began to rain. People got wet and the buses turned back. The first eight buses were stoned and shot at as they passed through Edendale, an ANC stronghold.' The police had asked Ntombela to take a different route but he had insisted on using the Edendale Road, saying his people could defend themselves. 'Tyres were burning near the hospital, the roads were blocked.'

'Inkatha's rally was not successful,' says Harry Gwala. 'They took it out on people in Edendale. The *amaButhu* [warriors] got out of their buses near the hospital. People retaliated with stones. David Ntombela was in charge of the Seven Day War which followed.'

There are differing stories about how the battle began. Another version is that the Inkatha supporters in one of the buses stopped for a drink in Edendale township and got into a fight with the locals, who torched their bus.

That evening Ntombela drove to Ulundi to report on the day's events to the KwaZulu Legislative Assembly. The next morning he received a telephone call saying that workers were being attacked on their way past Edendale. KwaZulu Transport stopped the buses in Ntombela's area. 'When I got back there were thousands gathered around my house, waiting for me,' says Ntombela. 'While I was discussing the transport situation with them, Chief Zondi came to see me. He had survived an attack on his *bakkie* [pick-up truck] in KwaShange, an ANC stronghold. They were using an alternative route to avoid the Edendale Road. One man, Poswa, was burned alive inside the *bakkie*.'

Ntombela advised the people in his area to take any means of transport available, but to use the KwaShange route. Later that week, according to Ntombela, the Inkatha stronghold of Mboxwana was burned, triggering off a revenge attack on ANC areas. 'KwaShange was burning with a big flame. I wouldn't know who burned those houses. The people from Mboxwana might have retaliated, because you can't burn your own house,' admits Ntombela reluctantly. 'Most of the houses at KwaShange were burned. The people of KwaShange fled to Edendale. They called it the Seven Day War. I don't know how many died.'

KwaShange township, near Pietermaritzburg, was traditionally a dissident area. It was close to town, a freehold area where people were better educated. A force of 3000 tribesmen descended on KwaShange from Chief Zondi's area and devastated the township. When they attacked neighbouring Edendale, however, they were repulsed.

The chairman of the ANC in Edendale was Sifiso Ntombela, David Ntombela's cousin. 'We used to be very close,' says Sifiso. 'Most of our family is ANC. David was ANC too. He joined Inkatha because he happened to be an *induna*, and the chiefs fall under the KwaZulu government. We were friendly until the ANC was unbanned. Then David started to call me a traitor. He said I had deserted the Zulu party and joined the Xhosa party.'

Edendale had become a non-tribal, Black freehold area when land was granted to local families in return for fighting on the British side during the Boer War. Church land had also been granted to locals, and the population of Edendale, which lay on the outskirts of Pietermaritzburg, became wealthier and better educated. In 1990 Edendale became the ANC's stronghold in the Pietermaritzburg area, a bastion of resistance against the tribal war parties from the surrounding hills.

'Youngsters were in the ANC front line,' says Sifiso, who works at a bread factory near Pietermaritzburg. 'We had a liberated zone here in Edendale. Thousands took refuge there from the chiefdoms. We were using stones and home-made guns. They had automatic weapons and were assisted by the riot police. There is no ANC–IFP conflict,' he recites. 'It's between democratic movements and the system. The system is using the IFP to create conflict and stall our liberation.'

24 Combat Intelligence

A short distance from Gandhi's statue in the pedestrian section of Pietermaritzburg's Church Street, which could be York or Guildford in England, stands an imposing corporate tower, the Southern Life Building. The ANC offices in Pietermaritzburg occupy a fifth-floor corporate suite. The walls are festooned with struggle posters in primary colours, and some new-look campaign flyers in softer pastel shades. Charts explaining 'Democracy' and 'What is voting?' overlap black-bordered obituaries of slain ANC regional leaders. One of the victims wears a guerilla's battledress and stands rigidly to attention. The exhortation reads: 'Take up his spear!' In the offices smartly dressed secretaries answer the telephone in a brisk, corporate manner while a dozen young men in floral shirts lounge on chairs in the waiting room outside.

By contrast the Inkatha Freedom party's offices are hidden in a small alleyway, also a short distance from Gandhi's statue but in the opposite direction. The corporate air-conditioned feel is lacking here. The walls are bare except for two portraits of Chief Minister Buthelezi. One, a black and white photograph, is captioned 'The man you can trust'. The other is a faded colour print of the Chief Minister, grinning uncertainly in a safari suit, wearing a necklace of traditional beads.

Philip Powell rummages busily through papers on his desk, preparing the Chief Minister's speech for that evening. The laser printer churns out copies of a memorandum explaining how to form a Self-Protection Unit. The headings include 'Military Theory', 'Combat Intelligence' and 'Topography'. Powell has a slight limp, from an assassination attempt in 1992. 'On the way back from an IFP rally in Imbali . . . It took any glamour there might have been out of my job,' he says. 'After the shooting my wife told me I had to choose between our marriage and the job. Eventually she said "cheers". My friends said I must be crazy. I've paid a high personal price. It's made me realize it's not a game.'

He adds: 'I've got involved at the rockface, which is something not many Whites have done. I've lost so many friends. You get involved with people, you work with them and get close to them and they are killed in front of you, or twenty minutes after you say goodbye, on the way home.' A bullet, the tip of it squashed, lies in the ashtray on his desk. 'A guy was shot at in his home yesterday while shaving. He brought the bullet to show he wasn't bullshitting.'

Powell is the Natal Midlands Regional Secretary of the IFP, an IFP Central Committee member and a KwaZulu representative. 'A political appointment,' he explains. 'I keep the Chief Minister in touch with what's happening in the Midlands outside the KwaZulu areas.' ('Philip Powell is a policeman. He spent time at university organizing right-wing students. He's one of the most backward elements we have ever come across,' sneers Harry Gwala.)

Powell, in his early thirties, went to work for the IFP when the party opened its ranks to Whites in 1990. In his days at the Pietermaritzburg campus of Natal University Powell was President of the National Students Federation. 'It was the equivalent of the Federation of Conservative Students in the UK or the Young Republicans in the States. Our politics were free-market, right-of-centre. I was very controversial at university,' he explains with an almost imperceptible stammer. 'Now I'm older and, I hope, wiser.' After university Powell did his national service in the South African Police. 'I never killed or detained people,' he hastens to add. 'I was employed as an analyst at SAP headquarters.' Unsubstantiated rumours allege that Powell was employed at some stage by the security police.

In his spare time Powell is writing a PhD thesis on the roots of the violence. 'For the first two years I couldn't understand why people were killing each other with such enthusiasm. I asked myself, what is the detonator? Why do communities turn on one another?'

Powell came to the conclusion that it was a mistake to see all the violence in political terms:

Ninety-eight per cent of the fighting in Natal has nothing to do with ideology. It's about buses, transport, schools, faction fights. It's a clash between modern and anti-modern forces. For every youth who aspires to a Malcolm-X T-shirt and a box haircut there is another who wants to marry three women and carry a spear. It's also a class conflict: the petty bourgeoisie and the youth are ANC, the lumpenproletariat – the rural peasants, the squatters, the migrant labourers – are IFP.

Workers don't kill each other because of ideology . . . Unskilled workers from the villages are willing to work for less than the unionized labour aristocracy in the factories. When you have stayaways the ANC blocks the roads from the rural areas into the cities. If people miss three days' work they are often fired. School-teachers can't get to the schools, and in KwaZulu the schools are paid for half by the parents and half by the government. So parents in rural areas get agitated when teachers can't get to school.

The ANC articulates the aspirations of the haves. They laugh at our people because they wear old clothes, because they're illiterate. During consumer boycotts a person from the rural areas, who feels he has his dignity and self-respect, comes into town to collect his shopping and is confronted by ANC youth and called 'sell-out' or 'teleweni' [after the punitive regiment whose job was to throw traitors off cliffs in Shaka's day]. It creates resentment, a feeling amongst rural IFP supporters of isolation of being ridiculous.

Powell spends much of his time in the trouble spots of the Natal Midlands, sleeping on floors in the homes of families who are under threat, rallying the IFP's supporters in the villages. He has been seen with assault rifles in the back of his car and remains contemptuous of the apathy of White farmers ('they're spineless') and dismayed by the number of branch-level IFP officials who have been assassinated. 'At least 150 in the Natal Midlands alone. In a given area all the branch officials will be systematically assassinated: secretary, deputy secretary, treasurer and so on. We've failed to protect our people, and it's something I for one feel deeply ashamed of. We've lost so many potential candidates for local government posts.'

Powell claims that the ANC is sending large numbers of youths for military training in the neighbouring Xhosa homeland of Transkei. 'Harry Gwala has been personally involved in recruitment in the last seven or eight months.'

Speaking in precise, energetic sentences, he paints a picture of the ANC as a highly organized and well-armed adversary:

> The pattern of violence changed from March 1992. Self-defence units were organized and reinforced by MK guerillas returning from exile, and the violence became much more selective and sophisticated. The ANC in Natal adopted a strategy of killing IFP leaders and massacres. There have been eighteen massacres since then, usually of women and children in IFP strongholds. Massacres are a way of putting pressure on community leaders to let refugees back into areas from which ANC supporters were driven out. The attacks are led by people who used to live in the area, so they are very well targeted.
>
> The three main supply routes for weapons from Transkei are the Port Shepstone road, the Bulwer road and the Richmond road. That's why there are so many massacres on these routes. We don't have a trained, paid army, that's the problem.

Powell is suddenly diffident. 'We've reached the end of the road. We've got nothing left to fight with.'

Police in heavy bullet-proof vests pace the empty night streets outside Pietermaritzburg City Hall. Chief Minister Buthelezi is inside, wooing the White English-speaking middle class of Pietermaritzburg from a lectern in the high-ceilinged Victorian hall. Half the audience consists of Black supporters from the rural areas who speak no English. The other half are

White Maritzburgers and farmers from the drought-stricken surrounding valleys, many of whom see Buthelezi as their last hope for security in the new South Africa.

The Chief Minister sets out his reasons for deciding to quit the multi-party talks in Johannesburg, and why he wants KwaZulu–Natal to be an autonomous state in a federal South Africa. He gives an assurance that his regional government will stamp out corruption and reduce taxes to boost market forces. Buthelezi is no orator and the speech is rambling and insipid.

Applause is led enthusiastically from the back of the hall by a small group of Whites. One red-faced, long-haired farmer bawls out like a supporter at a rugby game: 'Lots of White people support you! Please help us!' As the applause dies down in the ornate Victorian hall with its Boer War plaques and busts of British generals, a Zulu praise-singer gets to his feet, an old man in a tatty suit, croaking the Chief Minister's praises while the White audience looks baffled but sympathetic.

At question time a burly, flushed White man walks to the front of the hall trailing a powerful odour of cheap aftershave. 'I'm an Afrikaner,' he exclaims breathlessly. 'We Afrikaners are a proud nation. Zulus are proud people too. Why don't the Zulus just go ahead and declare independence?' There is a roar of laughter and plaudits in the hall. Buthelezi smiles, leaning cocksurely on the lectern, and waits for the applause to die down. 'I'll go away and think about it,' he quips. The audience loves it. Another rapturous surge of applause washes over the bronze British generals in the empty lobby outside.

25 This War is Forever

The rush hour in Table Mountain, near Pietermaritzburg in the Natal Midlands, is a gaggle of thirty uniformed schoolchildren walking down the long, straight dirt road which plunges into one of the most beautiful valleys in KwaZulu. On their way home they skip and sing, raising a cloud of dry red dust. The group gets smaller as the children peel off towards their homes. Then there is silence, and nothing moves except the Internal Stability Unit, grinding noisily up the valley in its armoured jeeps.

Table Mountain itself is a remote, reddish cliff a couple of kilometres long, rising up at the back of the valley. The valley is enclosed on four sides, giving the place a mysterious, charmed feeling. The small, scattered homesteads of Table Mountain inhabit the corner of KwaZulu closest to paradise.

The road to Chief Mkhize's domain skirts the hillsides, sinking slowly down to the far side of the valley, away from the mountain. The dirt road is treacherous, with many hairpin bends. It's ideal ambush country, dominated by steep, dense bush. The first *kraals*, or homesteads, lie derelict by the roadside. The roofs are charred, the white walls black with soot. The road winds and winds.

The children's graves are behind a dusty football pitch grazed by goats, in the bottom of the valley. A barbed-wire fence keeps the billies out. As an added precaution each of the six mounds is covered with dead thorn bushes. The stillness is oppressive.

'Before we put the fence up, the goats used to jump on the graves,' says Mrs Mkhize, a plump woman in a faded floral dress. She looks dazed, her eyes listless under the Kangol beret. 'They took the *bakkie* [pick-up truck] to school. It was a quiet day. I didn't expect trouble. Neighbours heard the gunfire,' she says.

A girl taking a short cut back from school saw the ambush from a distance. The girl ran as fast as she could to the nearest house. Mrs Mkhize's neighbours came to fetch her. She started to walk towards the place where the shots were heard, but collapsed on the way. The neighbours took her back to the house. Later, Chief Mkhize, her brother, took her to the doctor.

Six children died in the ambush. Five boys: Tulane, Tutuga, Tulebona, Nce, Wanda. One girl: Nomsa. She was twelve. The youngest boy was nine. Three were Mrs Mkhize's children. Ulundi paid for the funeral.

'As I was pulling out of the bend I saw a man step in front of the car,' says Phigalithetwa dreamily. He was driving the children back from school that afternoon, in 1993. 'He stepped out from the bush and began shooting. I jumped out of the car and ran.'

Besides the driver there were two other passengers in the cab, a young girl and a man from Table Mountain. The girl was grazed on the head by a bullet. She reached over and opened the door on the side of the cab furthest from the gunman. The three of them tumbled out of the *bakkie* and ran into the bush. The girl ran to fetch soldiers from a nearby army camp while the men hid, too frightened to move. The children in the back of the van were screaming. There was more gunfire. Phigalithetwa thought he recognized Qeda Zulu, a local man, amongst the attackers. There were five men altogether. He doesn't know why they did it.

'The accused in the court case said they were looking for Chief Mkhize,' says Mrs Mkhize. 'They used to live over there,' she says, pointing to the neat houses on a hillside across the river. 'Their parents still live there. Qeda Zulu and his nephew Sibusiso. They were Christians, good boys.'

The families of the alleged murderers and their victims are related. Mkhize's grandfather and Zulu's grandmother were brother and sister.

'Their parents are on our side,' says Mrs Mkhize listlessly. 'They don't understand their own children.'

Reverend Zulu's church is at the bottom of his back yard. The walls are of mud, blended with twigs, and the concrete floor has been swept in a regular pattern with a bundle of twigs. A horn lies on the altar, next to a Bible and a diary. There are no pews, and only one window. Reverend Zulu has been building another church, at the bottom of his back garden, but he can't finish it because of the violence. Reverend Zulu is Mrs Mkhize's uncle. The people in the valley believe his son Qeda killed the six children, an allegation which Qeda strongly denies.

'Qeda was a respectful child, well-liked, a good person,' remembers his father. 'He grew up a Christian. He was a good priest. Then he left the church.' The Reverend is a sad man. His homestead looks out over the valley, towards Mkhize's *kraal*. He is building an extension to his house, packing a timber frame with black earth to make the walls.

Qeda was thirty-three, married, with a child. His brother left first, to join Chief Nhlabunzima Mapumulo of the ANC. 'He's on the run,' says Zulu. Qeda followed him in November of '92. He had been a priest in his father's church for one year.

'He went to join the ANC. When he left here he got another education: the gang. Chief Mapumulo told my sons the elders had sold the country to the Boers.'

Chief Mapumulo, the local paramount chief, was a maverick. He came from a line of dissidents, in an area which had never been properly absorbed into the Zulu empire. The local clans had hidden from Shaka's Zulu armies in gorges near Table Mountain and on top of the mountain itself. Mapumulo's grandfather was made a chief by the British in return for loyalty to the crown.

Mapumulo had been a thorn in Buthelezi's side ever since the formation of Inkatha. An ANC stalwart, the president of Contralesa, an ANC-aligned grouping of traditional chiefs, Mapumulo tried to establish an opposition party within the KwaZulu Legislative Assembly. When that failed he made an application to remove his area from KwaZulu Government control and launched a public enquiry to prove that Inkatha was responsible for the violence in the area. Buthelezi became progressively more enraged with Mapumulo.

Mapumulo's area, including Table Mountain, had been a haven of peace in the eighties. Inkatha had not been allowed to conduct its forcible recruitment drives there. People fleeing the conflict in other areas came to find refuge.

Then, in February 1990, as President de Klerk announced the release of Nelson Mandela and the launch of a new South Africa, Mapumulo's *kraal* came under fire. He fled the area, together with several thousand ANC supporters. A year later Mapumulo visited his homestead and was shot dead in the driveway.

Reverend Zulu doesn't understand why the fighting started. 'Too many people from this valley have been killed,' he says simply. He refuses to attend his son's trial. 'He's been killing,' he says with disgust. He shakes his head. 'I blame my sons for leaving me and leaving the Church.' Reverend Zulu pauses, wrestling with something in his mind. 'What is inside one person cannot go to another person,' he says quietly, holding a finger against his heart.

At Mkhize's *kraal* the dogs lie in the sun, listening to the music blaring out from the shebeen into the still valley. The ambushed *bakkie* sits in the yard, with six bullet-holes in the windscreen. Next to it is another burned out car riddled with the familiar neat round punctures. Men in overalls loll on benches around two circular thatched huts. The huts are of the traditional, old-fashioned design, with white walls and thickly matted rush roofs. Inside they are cool, with a large, clear floor space and rolled sleeping mats stowed next to the walls.

'This area belonged to Chief Nhlabunzima Mapumulo,' says Chief Bernard Mkhize, a thin, frightened-looking man who works as an installer in a Pietermaritzburg electronics factory. 'He recruited youngsters from this area to be in charge.' Mkhize's frown conveys his puzzlement. 'As a result children in this area started to hold meetings in the forest. We were surprised by these meetings of the children without the consent of their parents. Then we sent men to the chief to find out whether this was acceptable. His answer was, let the children do as they please. They are free. They will rule in the future.'

Mkhize explains the background:

> Chief Mapumulo was Inkatha to begin with. When he changed to the ANC he forgot to tell us . . . I had heard that your house would be burned if you joined the ANC. Then one day I began to receive threats at work. I was accused of expelling a youngster who used to stay at my place. He was my son's friend. He came one day with an ANC badge. I said to him he had no right to join a political organization. People might burn my house because of him.

The Stability Unit's jeeps labour up the hill from the river crossing. Mkhize ignores them.

> The boy went to stay with Chief Mapumulo . . . This boy and his friends then robbed a liquor store. There was an exchange of gunfire. The boys were armed with *kwatchas* [home-made guns]. One boy was

killed. Thereafter this gang who called themselves the ANC set up roadblocks. They came at four in the morning to burn my van and my house. They said I was stopping people from joining the ANC . . .

They shot my cousin in the leg in 1990. A month later twelve of them came in a Cortina *bakkie*. They killed my brother-in-law. They were looking for me.

A year later, Mkhize became the IFP branch chairman in Table Mountain. Some people say Mkhize is a gangster involved in a car-theft ring, and that the people who murdered his children were disaffected gang members. The rumours are impossible to verify.

Frogs begin to make a din by the river as dusk gathers. Women fetch water up the long slope to the *kraals* on the hillside.

'Since we drove the ANC out of here there is peace,' says Mkhize quietly. In the fading light the shells of burned houses are visible here and there amongst the others on the hillside.

'All the methods of peace have been tried, but they've failed,' says an old woman with a deep, loud sigh.

'It is right that the community should split because of political differences,' says Mrs Mkhize, the chief's sister, angrily. 'Some wanted this area to be an ANC area.' She still doesn't know why her children were shot. Shortly after the killings at Table Mountain there was a revenge attack on a taxi full of ANC supporters, in which nine people were killed.

'We don't understand what is happening in politics,' admits Mkhize. He won't let the ANC back into the valley. 'I don't trust them. This war is forever unless they stop attacking us.'

26 A Normal Policeman

In December 1988 eleven women, children and old men were shot dead during a night-time funeral vigil in the tiny village of Trust Feeds near Pietermaritzburg in the Natal Midlands. The majority of the victims were members of Inkatha. At the time of the massacre, the finger of blame was pointed at the pro-ANC United Democratic Front (UDF), whose supporters had to flee the village. However, after the trial in 1992 of nine men accused of the Trust Feeds massacre, conclusive evidence emerged of a conspiracy by officers of the South African Police to murder the villagers and undermine the UDF.

The small, attractive hamlet of Trust Feeds lies cradled in rolling green hills. The village was established at the turn of the century in a quiet valley, next to a river, on land donated to Black peasants by White farmers. The origin of the name 'Trust Feeds' is unknown, but is possibly a reference to the farmers' charity in donating the land. In 1988 there were perhaps 3000 people in Trust Feeds, working on the local sugarcane farms, living peacefully in their wattle-and-daub houses, and some in houses of cut stone.

In the late 1970s Trust Feeds was scheduled for removal as a 'black spot', a Black freehold settlement in a White Group Area. The villagers resisted, forming a Crisis Committee to campaign for their right to remain on the land. The campaign proved successful, and the Crisis Committee was kept alive. When the river flooded its banks in 1986 the Crisis Committee coordinated relief supplies and assistance from the UDF. A short while later the Crisis Committee decided to join the UDF, and Trust Feeds' problems began.

In 1988 the local joint management centre, part of the state's 'Total Strategy' to combat international communism and Black revolution, received new instructions from Pretoria: political organizations opposed to the government should be suppressed, while those considered pro-government should be supported, or, if none existed in the area, should be created. The instruction was sent to joint management centres nationwide as part of the campaign to defend the White state against the growing menace of Black political mobilization. These facts were revealed when the files of the local joint management centre were examined during the trial.

The perceived security risk in Trust Feeds was the Crisis Committee, which was pro-UDF and therefore considered hostile to the state. The other problem was that no government-friendly political organization existed in Trust Feeds. The commander of the local police station, Captain Brian Mitchell, was given the task of setting up a rival political organization to the Crisis Committee, which he did. A pro-Inkatha landowners' group was established and the violence in Trust Feeds began. Up to this time, in the words of Captain Mitchell himself, Trust Feeds had been 'a peaceful haven'.

Trust Feeds became a town at war with itself. As the violence grew more intense, two local members of Inkatha approached Mitchell for assistance. Mitchell took them to see a Major Terreblanche, the commander of the Pietermaritzburg Riot Unit. Major Terreblanche was, Mitchell claimed at the trial, an influential figure. Mitchell believed that Terreblanche would find ways to assist the two Inkatha men in their struggle against the forces of the UDF.

Major Terreblanche, with Captain Mitchell in tow, took the two men to the KwaZulu government building in Pietermaritzburg, where they allegedly met David Ntombela, the Rothmans-smoking Natal Midlands Chairman of Inkatha. At the meeting it was agreed that special constables (poorly trained Black militiamen, nicknamed *kitskonstabels* – instant constables) of the South African Police should assist Inkatha in fighting the UDF at Trust Feeds. They would be infiltrated into the village by the Pietermaritzburg Riot Unit, without the knowledge of the local police station. The action against the UDF was planned to take place on a Friday night.

Major Terreblanche could not be called to give evidence in the Trust Feeds trial as he was murdered two years after the massacre. He was found slumped over the wheel of his car by the highway. A special constable who had been with him in the car, and whose handgun was ballistically connected to the bullets in Terreblanche's body, was arrested. A few days later the suspect was himself killed by two police detectives when he apparently tried to take a gun from one of them while they were travelling by car.

Having helped to organize the hit squad of special constables for Friday night, Captain Mitchell returned to Trust Feeds. On Friday morning he ordered his men to round up all the local young males on the football pitch at Trust Feeds. Nine were identified as UDF activists and arrested. Mitchell admitted at the trial that the purpose of the arrests was to weaken the UDF's capacity to resist the onslaught planned for that night.

Captain Mitchell then left the rest to the Riot Unit and the special constables. He went out drinking with two White policeman friends. Around midnight, however, his curiosity got the better of him. He suggested to his drinking companions that they drive to Trust Feeds to check what was happening there.

Mitchell and his two colleagues drove to a house where the hit squad of four special constables had allegedly been dropped by the Riot Unit (the Riot Unit's role in delivering the hit squad to Trust Feeds was never actually proven). Mitchell, to his dismay, found two of the special constables asleep. He put the other two in his car, together with his two drinking companions, and drove into Trust Feeds, where one of the local shops was ablaze, after a pre-emptive attack by Inkatha supporters. Mitchell dropped his two by now bewildered White colleagues near the shop. The special constables also alighted and walked away. Mitchell drove off in the police van to collect the remaining two members of the hit squad and their weapons, and brought them back to join the two he had left in the village.

Mitchell and the four special constables then went to the house of a Mr Sithole who had recently died of natural causes. His family were holding a traditional night vigil, singing and praying over the body. Captain Mitchell and his team stood outside the house. One of the special constables claimed at the trial that Mitchell took his shotgun from him, fired several shots through the window of the house and gave the weapon back to him with the words: 'That's how I want it done.' Mitchell denied that he had shot anyone. Eleven mourners were killed. Mitchell's hit squad fired through the windows, then entered the house to finish off the victims with shotgun blasts at close range.

Mitchell then drove two of the special constables back to the safe house and returned to collect his terrified White friends, who enquired about the shots they had heard. Mitchell said he hadn't heard any shooting. The two remaining special constables also denied hearing any shooting. On the way home Mitchell removed a fistful of spent shotgun casings from his pocket and threw them out of the car window. At the trial he justified his part in the massacre with the words: 'I was a soldier fighting a civil war.'

The irony was that Mitchell had targeted the wrong house. Mr Sithole's family were Inkatha supporters. The intended victim, a Mr Mbugwe, lived a few doors further down the road. There was speculation, however, that the attack on the mourners was deliberate, a move calculated to undermine the UDF's support in Trust Feeds. If this was the aim, the operation was extremely successful. When the massacre of Inkatha members at Sithole's house came to light the following morning, the entire leadership of the UDF in Trust Feeds had to run for their lives. Trust Feeds has remained solidly Inkatha to this day.

A preliminary inquest found sufficient evidence, including the testimony of Mitchell's two drinking companions, to issue warrants for the arrests of two of the special constables. Three years passed and no one was arrested. The South African Police claimed they could not locate the suspects.

In the course of investigating a series of ten killings linked to Psychology Ndhlovu, an MP in the KwaZulu Legislative Assembly, Major Frank Dutton of the South African Police Special Investigation Unit in Durban requested access to the Trust Feeds massacre file. The request was blocked. Dutton became suspicious. He obtained a copy of the inquest documents. The file contained the names and addresses of the suspects. After making some enquiries and talking to informers, Dutton was confident that he could locate the men. He informed his superiors that he was in a position to make progress on the Trust Feeds case.

Dutton was then summoned to a meeting in Pretoria, where two South African Police generals handed over the Trust Feeds file to him, encouraging him to get to the bottom of the case. They added, somewhat suspiciously, that Dutton should not oppose bail for the suspects, and that their case should be handled by a single defence counsel. Dutton left Pretoria feeling confused.

The two special constables for whom warrants had been issued were arrested within days. For the previous two years, during which the warrants had been in force, the suspects had been living at their home addresses, which were known to the police. Both men had left the SAP and had joined the KwaZulu Police. The South African Police claimed they had found it impossible to locate the men.

Dutton and his team of plain-clothes detectives discovered that the suspects had received warning one Friday evening from the KwaZulu Police that the case was being re-opened. They had gone into hiding, but were tracked down by Dutton's team after a series of lucky breaks. According to Captain Mitchell's wife, Mitchell had come home that same Friday evening, shortly after Dutton's visit to Pretoria, in a state of turmoil. He had smashed crockery on the floor and shouted, 'I didn't kill anyone!' The warnings were difficult to explain, as Dutton's decision to re-open the Trust Feeds massacre case was only known to a small group of senior officers in the South African Police Force.

In April 1992 Captain Mitchell was sentenced to death eleven times in the Pietermaritzburg Supreme Court. The four special constables who appeared with him got fifteen years apiece. Mitchell is still on death row in Pretoria Central Prison.

'The most horrific thing, watching Mitchell testify,' reflects Major Dutton, 'was that he struck me as a normal policeman.'

27 A Certain Level of Emptiness

Professor Ndhlovu, the chair*person* of the African National Congress in embattled Northern Natal, is a neat, sturdily built man with sparkling, defiant eyes. He communicates in polished, precise sentences.

'Our vision of the region necessitated that we design strategies to facilitate the achievement of that vision. In a time of revolution you have to be militant . . . You can't meet these weapons with a prayer. The most painful thing is going to funeral services . . . To see people crying helplessly,' the Professor muses, 'and to think that maybe there was no need for this life to be lost. I'm not a warlord. I don't engage in war personally. I devise strategies that will bring about security. There is a calculated ruthlessness.' The Professor wipes his chin after a TV dinner at his home on the campus of Zululand University, where he lectures in public administration.

Professor Ndhlovu has managed to entrench the ANC in the heart of IFP

Zululand, not far from Ulundi, the Zulu capital. He is proud of his achievement:

ANC Headquarters had written off this region. This is Gatsha Buthelezi's back yard. In 1990 when we wanted to start political structures, Inkatha vowed we would never have a presence north of the Tugela river. We were weak. We had no defences. Inkatha burned two of my cars and tried to fire-bomb my house in Esikawini. At our first meeting, in July 1990 at the university, there were more South African Police than members of the audience. We're fighting against hit squads trained in Caprivi and Israel . . .

Yet we have not received a single bullet from the ANC. There is ambivalence at ANC Headquarters. They expect us to defend ourselves, then don't provide the hardware. They could not be seen to be supplying guns . . . Certainly people at Shell House (ANC HQ) are very uncomfortable with me. Walter Sisulu told me I am seen as a warlord.

Ndhlovu huffs, but does not seem to be entirely displeased with his warlike reputation. 'When Chris Hani was assassinated I suggested at a meeting of the National Working Committee that we should create our own retaliation squads. Our national intelligence knew who was responsible. We should have retaliated.' The Professor's eyes twinkle gleefully. 'Some people thought that was outrageous. During lunch they expressed surprise that I could even contemplate such a thing. Support came from regions I never expected, not from the so-called hawks.'

The Professor admits that he has already implemented the idea in his area. 'In Northern Natal we targeted the warlords in the forefront of Inkatha , beginning in January 1992 up to now. A number of their leaders have been eliminated,' he says drily.

'We have our own self-defence units, created in terms of a decision taken by the ANC national executive in November 1990 and announced in January 1991. The decision has not yet been amended,' he adds, in his fluid seminar style. 'There is a high level of discipline. Guns are not used for robberies.'

The Professor pauses while his bodyguard goes to investigate why the dogs outside are barking furiously. It's a false alarm and the shotgun returns to its hiding place under the sofa. Ndhlovu embarks on a vigorous dissertation about the new South Africa.

'We have to create a new culture which takes cognisance of diversity, which generates understanding leading to tolerance. The management of diversity recognizes that you can't exclude other cultures,' expounds the Professor. 'It's a concept developed at the University of Georgia, you know, in America.'

Ndhlovu says his contribution to the new South Africa will be to serve on the Commission for Public Service, reporting directly to the new parliament. 'In order to implement political identification by the policy-makers you have to have people who are effective in the implementation phase,' he says, then adds a final cryptic flourish: 'I'm advocating a vertical intervention.'

The topic exhausted, the Professor becomes thoughtful. 'Even when your worst enemy perishes,' he says, gazing at the ceiling, 'there's a certain level of emptiness.'

The ANC's strongholds in the townships of Northern Natal are the workers' hostels, isolated in the midst of IFP-held townships. The Professor's shock troops are the unionized industrial workforce of the Alusaf smelter and Richard's Bay Minerals.

Sinqobile ('we have conquered') hostel at Esikawini consists of four brick dormitories surrounded by a wire fence. Within 20 metres of the hostel gates lies J2 Section of Esikawini, a militant IFP stronghold.

'In November 1991 they tried to force us to join Inkatha, who hate our unions. That's how the clash started,' explains Anthony Mashlangu. The hostel is dark and squalid, but spirits are high. The hostel-dwellers gather to smoke and drink beer in the kitchen, under a naked light bulb. Anthony, a tall, bulky man, who isn't working at the moment, is a Country and Western aficionado and sings in a band.

'We used to have Inkatha members in the band,' he says. 'When Mandela was released Inkatha people were happy too. Some were ready to join the ANC. Then people were told that their land would be taken away. Grandmothers were told by Inkatha that their pensions would be cut off.'

'Inkatha told us the ANC were so terrifying,' laughs a man in blue factory overalls, 'the trees in the forest would run away when they came.'

'Nurses, teachers, factory workers, educated people are all ANC,' says Anthony, 'including many KwaZulu civil servants, but they don't talk about it.'

'When the Xhosa–Zulu war started, Zulus burned their Mandela T-shirts,' remembers another man.

During 1991 refugees from the fighting in the rural areas began to arrive in the hostel. The man in blue overalls had come from Enseleni, after having sought refuge in seven or eight different places.

'When people went home for the holidays,' says Anthony, 'some didn't come back. They were identified as ANC. They turned their faces to heaven.'

In February 1992 there was a shoot-out at Sinqobile between the hostel-dwellers and the KwaZulu police. 'I came back from Country and Western practice,' says Anthony, 'to find the KwaZulu Police and Inkatha and all the grandmothers and kids from Esikawini surrounding the hostel. The policemen were shooting at anyone who came to the windows. Then the sound of the AK became too powerful for them,' he grins. ('We had armed ourselves in preparation,' says Professor Ndhlovu. 'Each AK-47 cost us 1500 rand. There was a hell of a confrontation.')

Sinqobile hostel exists in a state of siege. Hostel-dwellers have brought their fridges from home so they can stock up on food, avoiding the need to go shopping in town. The bus stop has been shifted to a position right outside the hostel gates, minimizing the distance to be walked at night.

'It's not safe to move outside,' says Anthony. 'Alusaf and Richard's Bay Minerals buses have been attacked. If you work at Alusaf or RBM they target you as an ANC member.'

The traditional figures of authority in the hostel, the *indunas*, have been rejected. 'There are no *indunas* here,' says Anthony. 'The traditional system is used by our enemies, who are in the dark ages. We are progressive. We are in the light. They are tools of the state.' But Anthony believes that tradition can be rehabilitated. '*Induna* was good before. If we win we will use it again.'

The men in the hostel are cheerfully fatalistic. 'There is no place which is not hot in KwaZulu,' declares the man in blue overalls. 'So we stay here. It's better to wait to die here.'

'We die together. We stay together and sing one song,' says Anthony, pillaging his Country and Western repertoire.

'I feel sorry for the king, that old man,' comments someone else. 'He's being used by Gatsha.'

All conversations in Natal eventually turn to the Zulu question. 'The problem starts when there is a Zulu,' says Anthony. 'In the hostels in Pretoria there is no fighting because there are no Zulus.'

'Zulus are the best fighters,' opines the man in blue overalls. 'Then the Xhosas. Suthus are humble people.'

Anthony concocts one last incongruous but appropriate C and W lyric: 'We are not here to make a room of hell,' he says, wagging a finger in the air. 'We are here to create the people.'

28 Looking After the Mthetwas

KwaMthetwa, the largest chiefdom in Natal–KwaZulu, lies in the dry northern hills of Zululand, in the heart of Inkatha country. The ruler of KwaMthetwa is Chief Mthetwa. He's an old-fashioned chief, not a politician. Mthetwa is more concerned about his sons. Of all Chief Mthetwa's sons (he has lost count of how many his twelve wives have produced), Bhekabathetwa was the favourite from the minute he was born. Even his name, which means 'the one who looks after the Mthetwas', singled him out for succession to the chieftainship. Chief Mthetwa's eldest son was bypassed, having been born on the wrong side of the harem. The special treatment accorded to Bhekabathetwa made the other brothers resentful.

'The trouble started when I was three months old,' smiles Bhekabathetwa, who has a quiet charm. 'I had to be taken away to my grandmother's *kraal*.' The chief's wives were at loggerheads and Bhekabathetwa's elder brother got jealous. 'I don't want to be the chief,' he says, lighting a cigarette in the office behind his grocery store. Bhekabathetwa, or Bheki, is a tall, bearded, lanky thirty-year-old with a penchant for floral shirts.

'For a long time we were all Inkatha ,' says Bheki. 'We were told that in the rural areas we must join Inkatha or we'd have no chance in business.' When Bheki went to work for Alusaf, a giant aluminium smelter, he joined the union. He was still a paid-up member of Inkatha, however, until he became a shop steward in the union. 'My mind was racing with this union thing. They explained to us about the *bantustans* at COSATU seminars, about how the Whites divided us, the Group Areas Act.' Bheki let his membership of Inkatha lapse, but hung onto the membership card. He led a massive strike at Alusaf in 1982 and was jailed. By the time he finally left the industry to set up his own business he was a senior shop steward.

One Saturday Bheki was sitting in his office when one of his brothers came into the shop and said he'd heard a rumour that Bheki and his cousin Thami had tried to kill Bheki's elder brother with an AK-47. The next day he went to church and found his brother had given the priest a goat, the traditional offering when there is a problem which needs to be solved. Bheki heard his brother tell the priest that Bheki had tried to kill him. When confronted, his brother was evasive.

Bheki began to receive threatening telephone calls. There was another false rumour that he had stabbed his elder brother. People flocked to the hospital, only to find that he wasn't there. 'Those days were bad,' remembers Bheki. 'I was phoned from Joburg. They said I wanted to claim the succession to the chieftainship for the ANC, but if they kill me Inkatha will get the chieftaincy. They said they were coming down and I should expect them at two o'clock in the morning.'

The threats continued, along with rumours that Bheki was targeted for assassination. 'I was warned they would come for me early in the morning or in the evening. So I started opening the shop at eight and going home at four.' He refused to move. 'I'm a chief's son,' he says disarmingly.

In 1991 a purge of ANC sympathizers had begun in the towns and villages of northern Natal and KwaZulu. IFP officials from nearby Empangeni questioned local people and urged them to point out ANC supporters' houses, which were then burned by outsiders. In Enseleni, a prosperous town nearby, one of Bheki's friends came into conflict with Inkatha. Thami, who had a tuck shop in town, was constantly harassed by criminal types demanding money. One night Thami's shop was broken into. Thami caught one of the culprits and killed him. The man was an Inkatha member. A mob came looking for Thami, armed with guns.

Thami had bought some powerful *muti* (protective potion) from a witchdoctor. He had drunk *intelezi* (battle-medicine) and rubbed *muti* over his body in anticipation of a fight. As the mob approached his shop he tore off his shirt to expose his attackers to the power of the *muti* on his body. His attackers tried to shoot him but their guns jammed and they fled in fear. Soon afterwards Thami's tuck shop was burned down and he fled to safety in Bheki's village. 'The guys from Enseleni asked me to chase him away,' says Bheki. 'I couldn't. He's my cousin.'

Then Mathias was killed. Mathias, or 'Mathe' as he was known, was the chairman of the ANC in the KwaMthetwa area, a brave man and a former soldier. He was training ANC militias in the area. Inkatha began to snipe at his house from far away.

The drought in northern Natal was in its second year. A local White farmer had complained that cattle from Mathe's village had broken through the fences and were grazing on his land. Mathe held a meeting to discuss the problem. That morning, as people gathered to wait for the farmer to arrive, the local sub-chief noticed Mathe standing alone. He sent his bodyguard to fetch the IFP youngsters from the village. A mob arrived and Mathe was attacked. As he had drunk *intelezi*, none of the shots could pierce his body. Then someone gave one of the *kwatchas*, the home-made guns, to a fourteen-year-old boy who was still a virgin. Mathe was killed with a single bullet. The others then slit his throat. 'Like a goat,' remembers Bheki ruefully.

As things began to get out of hand in KwaMthetwa, Bheki and a few of his militiamen teamed up with a member of the ANC's guerilla wing, uMkhonto we Sizwe, who had been assigned to their area. He provided them with basic military training, but no hardware.

'You have to get your own gun,' says Bheki, who acquired his first AK-47 from a local KwaZulu policeman, at the bargain price of 400 rand. 'They confiscate them in raids and sell them on,' he says casually. 'A lot of KwaZulu policeman in Esikawini are ANC cardholders. But they hide their membership.'

Meanwhile Bheki's enemies went to Enseleni where they held a meeting with other Inkatha groups. Informers got wind of a plan to attack his village. 'They came in a *kombi* and two *bakkies*,' says Bheki. 'Thami and I waited for them in the bush.' The men opened fire with AK-47s at a range of 1500 metres. The convoy from Enseleni drove away very fast. 'That was the first time they came looking for us,' says Bheki.

Opposite Bheki's general store, across the yard, is his bottle store. The counter doubles as a bar, and there are plain tables and chairs. One evening Bheki was sitting at his bottle store with some ANC men who had been expelled from Chief Dhlamini's village in the purges. Dhlamini was the IFP chairman in one of the nearby valleys. There were reports that he had fetched guns from Ulundi to enable him to drive the ANC out of his ward. Bheki knew Dhlamini well. But the purges had embittered people, and the men were discussing the best way to kill the chief. 'I tried to stop them,' says Bheki feebly, 'saying I would be implicated.'

Bheki's conscience began to prick him, however. 'I went to warn Dhlamini,' he says. 'He got suspicious. He told his wife in front of me that if he was killed, Bheki would know who did it.'

On the last day of April 1993 Dhlamini was gunned down.

The Internal Stability Unit arrived at Bheki's *kraal* in the middle of the night and broke down all the doors. Bheki, anticipating retribution, had slept in his shop that night, leaving his home empty. One of Bheki's brothers, who had fled Dhlamini's area that night, was sleeping in one of the houses in the yard. The Stability burst in and found him in possession of an AK-47. He was arrested, but released on bail shortly afterwards.

The news reached Enseleni and property which Bheki owned in the town was set on fire. Rumours circulated to the effect that Bheki had a lot of AK-47s. Meanwhile Bheki was establishing himself as a successful local businessman, opening two bottle stores and two supermarkets and farming sugarcane on 10 hectares of his father's arable land.

Around this time Bheki's envious elder brother, who drove buses for Empangeni Transport, was caught stealing from the bus company and dismissed. His attitude towards Bheki deteriorated still further. Old Chief Mthetwa, who was going a little blind and relied on Bheki for information, summoned him for an explanation. 'I went to my father and I said, look, my brother wants to kill me,' says Bheki. 'I told my father he should let my elder brother take over the acting chieftainship.'

Bheki's diplomatic move defused the tensions temporarily. But there was petty envy from other quarters, and local shopkeepers arrived at Chief Mthetwa's *kraal* complaining that his favourite son wanted to kill them. And the Mthetwa family was split, with six brothers following Bheki to the ANC. Two of them work in Bheki's businesses.

'I don't employ Inkatha. I couldn't work with them. They could sell me out,' Bheki says, noting that in his ward almost everyone is an ANC cardholder. 'They have Inkatha cards too,' he admits. 'They go to IFP meetings when they are called. We don't take Inkatha as a political organization. It's a cultural thing.'

A plan was hatched by ANC men to assassinate two of Chief Dhlamini's henchmen, Dladla and Mkhize, at the night vigil preceding Chief Dhlamini's funeral. The hit squad consisted of seven men, of whom four were armed with AK-47s, including one trained ANC guerilla. In the early hours of the morning they crept through the bush towards the tent where the Dhlamini family and their friends were holding the traditional wake over the chief's body. They approached stealthily, crawling on their bellies over open ground.

In the darkness the trained man crept up to the tent and peered inside. It was his task to shoot Dladla and Mkhize once they had been identified by the other members of the hit squad. The trained man looked round and noticed with alarm that his accomplices were nowhere to be seen. Their nerves had failed them and they did not have the confidence to crawl right up to the tent. The trained man lay on his stomach cursing and wondering what to do. He waited, thinking one of the men would come to point out the targets. Then he heard the other men in the squad open up with their AK-47s, firing blindly into the tent. The trained man lay hidden, still as a snake, long after the firing had stopped, listening to the weeping and groaning inside the tent. A man came out and pissed inches away from his face, but his training had taught him not to twitch.

Meanwhile the fleeing hit squad had discovered that one of their number was missing. They assumed he was lost and fired a shot in the air to signal their position. There was no response, but the shot was heard by one of the Inkatha militiamen who was combing the scrubland looking for the assassins. He waited till they were a metre away and killed three of them with automatic fire. He was felled in turn with three bullets from an AK. The shooting drew the attention of people in the tent and the trained man was able to escape.

One morning not long afterwards Bheki was sitting at the till of his supermarket when a white Toyota Cressida drove up and parked next to the store after doing a U-turn. Bheki noticed the barrel of a gun sticking out of a window. Bheki recognized the man holding the gun as one of his brothers. He put his hands up to show he was unarmed. 'I walked straight to them,' he remembers. 'I said to my brother on the back seat, "If anyone shoots me, *you* must shoot me." I know him, he's a *skebeng* [a hood],' mutters Bheki angrily. 'I was trying to confuse them,' he continues. 'They said to me, no, no, why do you think we want to shoot you? They said they were so thirsty and asked what I was going to give them. I gave them a dozen Amstels and a bottle of Smirnoff. My brother said, "He gave us this, now let's go." And they left.'

Bheki looks thoughtful. 'The main problem is that Inkatha doesn't want the ANC in the rural areas. But a lot of guys doing the violence are not Inkatha, they are criminals. Inkatha don't know much about politics. They only know that if you are ANC you fall under the Xhosa culture, so they must clear you out.'

Bheki is fortunate enough to have allies and relatives in the KwaZulu police, including a senior officer in charge of hit squads in the area. He also relies heavily on witchcraft for his protection. 'Two weeks ago someone told me that the Inkatha guys from Enseleni were coming for me. I went to Mthandazi – it's always a good idea to go to an *inyanga* from another area – and the spiritual healer there gave me some *intelezi* to spray around my place.'

'A few days later one of my brothers came to me and asked where I had got the *intelezi*. I said "What *intelezi*?" My brother said he had heard that the guys from Enseleni had a row on their way to kill me and never made it to my place.'

Magic and witchcraft are secret weapons deployed by both sides in the civil war to devastating effect. Buses ferrying Inkatha supporters to a recent meeting in Ngwanase were treated with *intelezi* to ensure that they did not reach their destination. Two of the buses overturned and seven IFP members were killed. Battle-medicine is used heavily by both sides. Before an Inkatha gathering someone will go to the venue early and sprinkle *intelezi* on the floor. As the men enter the charmed space they become brave.

'*Inyangas* are getting rich out of this war,' says Bheki disapprovingly. 'They give you bark and leaves which they have gathered in the forest, after dreaming of the ancestors. You put it in a bucket and leave it for a while. Then you rub it on your body.' Bheki has no doubts about the effectiveness of *intelezi*. 'I can walk past you and you won't see me,' he asserts quite matter-of-factly. 'The trouble is, you never know when it runs out. That's when people get shot,' he adds, looking suddenly anxious.

29 The Signoras and New K

On the last day of June 1991 the Signoras had a party at Tulani's place and everybody got drunk. It was a Sunday, and KwaMashu, a large township sprawled on the hills north of Durban, Natal's largest city, was peaceful. The boys were drinking sweetish, rich Castle beer in quart bottles, and mixing brandy with Coke. Fana, Mjozi and Ludick decided to kill Tami, as he was suspected of spying for the ANC-supporting 'comrades'. There was also the small matter of the stolen car which Tami had taken from the gang. They wrapped Tami in a rubber mat which they set on fire. His body was dumped in the ditch in Street Seventeen.

It was the first time the Signoras had burned anybody. They were very unhappy about the fact that Tami had been burned to death, because traditionally it was only the comrades who burned people. The gang members involved were immediately expelled. The KwaZulu police were called in by the gang to arrest the culprits. The killing of Tami marked the decline of the Signoras, who had dominated New K for three years.

The *amaSignoras* started life as a posse of delinquent teenagers in K Section who did not want to join the comrades. The comrades called them *amaSignoras* because they were women, sissies for not joining the struggle. 'We did not like the name at first,' says a former gang member. 'Then we learned that it came from a Terence Hill western. There was a group in the film called the "signoras" who led a carefree life and were good fighters. So we decided to keep the name.'

It all began in late 1987 when Dumisane Zondi called a meeting of the youth in Street Seventeen, K Section. Zondi was an instructor in the South African Defence Force (SADF), where he held the rank of corporal. He was also a gangster who did housebreakings and robberies. Zondi said the comrades were setting up people's courts all over KwaMashu and that he and others from the street had been targeted because comrades knew they were committing crimes in the area. He told some of the gang members that they had also been targeted, and that everyone in the gang should protect the area and stop the comrades from setting up their people's courts.

Meanwhile schoolboys in K Section were being press-ganged by the comrades into joining the Student Representative Councils (SRCs) at the local schools. Younger brothers of Signora members had been attacked and abducted. 'Many of us were not interested in politics or the discipline of the struggle,' remembers a former Signora. 'We wanted to protect our younger brothers, because they did not understand anything about the SRC or why they should be involved.' The non-SRC youngsters in K Section, who were seen as being opposed to the comrades, began to fight against the SRC boys, most of whom were comrades. The criminals in the Signora gang were joined by other local youths who wanted to protect their school-age brothers from harassment by the comrades.

Corporal Zondi became the natural leader of the Signoras because of his age and military experience. He taught the boys how to make guns which could use shotgun, Thirty-Eight Special and 9-millimetre Parabellum bullets, and which kinds of pipe were best to use. He also taught them basic warfare skills, such as how to mount ambushes and the various commands used in combat. Training took place at the creche in Street Seventeen, which had been abandoned because of the violence. Zondi also gave them an R1 automatic rifle he had stolen from the army.

There was another gang in Street Seventeen led by Mlele, a well-known hood, feared all over KwaMashu. The Mlele gang and the Signoras were rivals. In November both the Signoras and Mlele's bunch were summoned by the comrades to a meeting at K Section hall so that disciplinary measures could be taken against them. Mlele thought this was impertinent, so he went and killed a comrade at KwaMashu Station. Just to show he wasn't scared of the Signoras either, he killed a Signora gang member at Mzuvele High School. No one turned up at the disciplinary meeting with the comrades.

The comrades assumed the killing at the station was a joint attack by Mlele and the Signoras. The Thursday after the killing three minibuses packed with comrades drove into Street Seventeen lokking for Mlele and the Signoras. They were waving guns and *pangas* out of the windows as they pulled up. The Signoras were waiting for them with home-made guns. Most of the comrades were killed. It was the first of many clashes between the comrades and the Signoras.

Early the next year the Signoras began to collect protection money from houses in K Section to buy bullets and support Signora members whose houses had been burned down. Corporal Zondi would type the extortion demands on his typewriter. Favourite targets for such demands were families who had evacuated their children from K Section to safety. They were suspected of backing the comrades, and if they did not pay up their houses were pillaged or they were thrown out and the houses taken over by members of the gang. A large area of K Section was purged of all the United Democratic Front (UDF) comrades and renamed 'New K'. Pro-UDF families were easily identified: their children were SRC students or had run away. Either way the family was expelled or made to pay protection under the new regime. Money was collected from approximately 100 houses, from Street Fourteen to Street Nineteen.

Early in 1988 things changed for the Signoras when 'B' appeared on the scene. B was known as B even to his colleagues in the KwaZulu Police. B was a heavy drinker, you could see it in his face. He was in his thirties, tall, clean-shaven and rarely sober. He used to visit the Signoras in his police uniform, driving a blue KwaZulu Police van. B suggested to the Signoras that they should join Inkatha.

There were several advantages. 'He said the KwaZulu Police would be less likely to arrest members of Inkatha,' says a former Signora. 'He said that we would be elevated from the status of gangsters to the status of a political party.' B also said he would put in a good word for them with Inkatha. All they would have to do was keep fighting the comrades and attend meetings now and again in the local branch chairman's yard.

By mid-1988 a number of Signoras had gone to pay their dues to the local Inkatha membership secretary. B began to supply the gang with 'SP' type shotgun cartridges for their home-made guns. How many boxes they got depended on how much action there was against the comrades, but the Signoras never had to pay for the ammunition. B also supplied Tulani, one of the senior gang members, with a 9-millimetre pistol.

During the day they would see B in his van patrolling the area and he would give them a friendly wave. From time to time, in the evenings, he would call a meeting of the gang and praise their defence of K Section against the comrades.

After the Signoras joined Inkatha the KwaZulu Police stopped charging their members when they were caught. 'They just did some of the paperwork, to make it look official, then let us go,' said a former gang member, one of a group who murdered a comrade by the name of Jomo and were still standing round the corpse when the police arrived. They were taken to the station where they denied murdering Jomo, and were promptly released and given a lift back home. 'The KwaZulu Police did not harass us because we were Inkatha and we made war on the comrades.'

The Signoras allegedly began reporting to a local Inkatha official in Street Fourteen. The official was also a councillor, and a chairman of the local burial society. The protection money collected by the gang from the houses in New K was surrendered to him. In return, according to a renegade gang member who 'squealed', the Inkatha official would provide the Signoras with bullets and guns and look after gang members who lost their homes or were arrested by the South African Police. When they asked him where he got the guns from, he told them Mr Shabalala from Lindelani had provided them.

It wasn't long before the Signoras met Thomas 'Forty-Four' Shabalala in person. He was called Forty-Four because he had forty-four tribal scars on his body, including the deep tear-shaped incisions on his cheeks. At their first meeting Forty-Four, who was the Inkatha chairman in the vast Lindelani squatter camp, allegedly gave the gang three shotguns and several boxes of bullets. He told the Signoras they were doing a marvellous job in fighting the comrades and urged them to keep it up, rounding off the pep talk by inviting them round to his house on a hilltop in Lindelani for a barbecue. On other occasions, at meetings in a nearby schoolhouse, Shabalala allegedly gave the Signoras 9-millimetre hand guns and ammunition.

In 1988 Justice, who served in the SADF like Corporal Zondi, started visiting the Signoras with gifts of bullets and a 9-millimetre pistol. He was often to be seen in KwaMashu patrolling with other soldiers in their Buffels. Justice was keen to have Mrs Africa killed. She was a former Inkatha mayoress of KwaMashu who had defected to the ANC. Justice had been her bodyguard at one stage while she was with Inkatha. Mrs Africa's house was attacked and partially burned down, but the Signoras could not find Mrs Africa herself.

Other policemen worked with the gang. There was Mandla, who has since been suspended from the South African Police, and Shange, who is serving life for murdering comrades.

Meanwhile, in mid-1989, Corporal Zondi, the founder of the Signoras, was shot dead by the South African Police, who claimed he was caught raping a woman and attempted to escape. He was found to be in possession of a 9-millimetre hand gun. The Signoras were sceptical about police claims that he was raping the woman as she was the corporal's girlfriend.

After Tami was burned to death by drunken Signoras that Sunday night in June 1991 the gang was never the same. The comrades launched a sustained onslaught against New K, rotating their troops in two-hourly shifts. Section B would fight from eight to ten in the morning, Section C from ten to twelve, and so on. The Signoras were driven underground. Articles appeared in the newspapers exposing the gang. Some joined the A-Team, another IFP-aligned gang in neighbouring Chesterville. At least two gang members joined the South African Police. Others went to fight in the hostels of the Transvaal and never came back.

PART FOUR

The Cape

30 Hard Livings in the Mother City

On the southernmost tip of the African continent, at the foot of the vast flat-topped, green-flanked hulk of Table Mountain, lies the Victoria and Alfred Waterfront shopping and entertainment complex. The Waterfront mall, which is cleverly integrated into one of Cape Town's working dry-docks, is the jewel of South Africa's mother city.

Cape Town has long been the acceptable face of South Africa, a haven of liberalism, a hedonistic lotus-eaters' city in a gorgeous Mediterranean setting. When the conversation at Johannesburg dinner parties falters and dies, and the topics of violence, sex and home security have been exhausted, someone will always say, 'Ah, but have you been to Cape Town?'

Cape Town, on the lush, narrow ledge between Table Mountain and the Atlantic Ocean, is a White city, the first and the last in Africa. Its clubs and beaches, its quiet, steep streets lined with gleaming white-fronted Georgian and Victorian cottages, its hinterland of cool mountains and curly-gabled wine estates offer the sweetest living of any South African city. But Cape Town has a sinister edge. Table Mountain dominates the city; its grey, scrubby cliffs appear close enough to touch, yet distant. Every year several Capetonians freeze to death or fall down crevices, lulled into a false sense of security by the proximity of the city below. Table Mountain is a heavy, brooding presence overlooking this paradise city.

On the vast, sandy plain behind Table Mountain is Cape Town's embarrassing secret. Most Capetonians live here, in gigantic resettlement towns. The Cape Flats, vast, poor and violent, are a purgatory to the mother city's paradise. The Flats are reached via the Hell Run, the stretch of motorway between White Cape Town and the Black squatter megalopolis of Crossroads–Khayelitsha. The army has a permanent presence on the Hell Run, but has failed to prevent youths from stoning the traffic. A wall is being built to isolate the motorway from the shacklands on either side. In the wide buffer zone between the Georgian villas of Cape Town and the sea of tiny Black shanties lie the Coloured housing estates and ganglands of the Cape Flats.

When the Group Areas Act cleared the Coloured people out of District Six, Lansdowne, Sea Point and all the other mixed areas in Cape Town, Rashad and Rashied Staggie found themselves leaving Dieprivier where they had grown up. The whole family, including the twins' father, a head waiter at the smart Mount Nelson Hotel in Cape Town, was uprooted to a new housing estate, Manenberg, which was desolate and stark then, as it is now, built on sand dunes 20 kilometres outside Cape Town.

The gangs were already there, of course. The Globe gang, the Stalags, the Jesters, the Mongrels and the Yakkies were the big ones in District Six days. When Coloured people were moved out of Cape Town by Group Areas all the gangs 'went with'. During the forced removals families and friends became separated and were sent to live in different places. The people you had grown up with in Cape Town were scattered all over those bleak, prison-like estates: Manenberg, Hanover Park, Lavender Hill, Bontheuvel, Elsie's River, Heideveld, Valhalla Park, Belhar and that giant place in the middle of nowhere, Mitchell's Plain. They were lonely, difficult-to-get-to places, so far from Cape Town that Table Mountain became just a sad, far-away blue shape.

Kids on the Flats went wild. There was nothing for them to do, nowhere to go. In Cape Town there was always the city, the sea, the harbour, the shops, the mountain, and everyone was together. Here there was nothing except sand. They called themselves 'sandtrappers' (sand-treaders), because they lived on the Cape Flats where there was nothing but sand. District Six, the heart of Cape Town and the home of the Coloureds, was bulldozed. That's when the gangs really became strong, after the Group Areas removals. The Cape Flats became a gangland, and there wasn't a single estate that didn't have at least a dozen gangs with exotic American-style names.

It was Rashied who had the inspiration for the Hard Livings. The name just came to him out of the blue, even though his English wasn't good in those days. They were a wild bunch of teenagers. Rashied was seventeen at the time. They used to sleep rough on pieces of cardboard in the long grass behind the school, and in abandoned cars. The idea was to rob from the rich and look after your own people. The year was 1971.

When the Hard Livings decided to armour-plate the front of their new pool shed, they first of all did some research. On the soccer field behind the Catholic Church, Rashied and Watson blasted different combinations of wood and metal with shotgun and 9-millimetre ammunition. The shots sent a familiar small-arms echo towards the flat shapes of the hazy blue mountains of the Cape Peninsula. They did not test the materials with assault rifle fire as the heavier crack of an R1 or an AK might have shaken the local police out of their lethargy.

The initiative to armour-plate the front of the pool shed was taken after the Hanover Park Americans turned up in four cars one Saturday morning, just as the shed was receiving the finishing touches. The four pool tables had only just arrived and the Hard Livings were taken by surprise. The Americans cruised by with their guns but Watson and some other lads chased them away with pick-axes and grinders.

The pool shed quickly became the main attraction in the Hard Living section of Manenberg. You could play pool all day and all night, listen to music, drink beer and on Saturdays and Sundays Miles's wife would cook trays of delicious curry *rooties* (fried bread) for the whole crew. The only problem was that when it rained the roof leaked onto the pool tables. Also, it wasn't advisable to stand near the front wall until they put the armour-plating up, just in case the Americans came by.

Manenberg had been quiet for some time, with the odd minor incident. Then two Jesters, Joburg and Ice, were found dead behind the BP garage, and the Hard Livings had a problem. The Jesters would obviously suspect them of the murder. Guys in balaclavas had been robbing cars in Manenberg and stealing bags of *dagga* (cannabis) and 'buttons' (Mandrax tablets) from the drug merchants. People had been getting fed up and the Hard Livings had had to summon the local branch of the Americans to a meeting at Kop's place for a disciplinary talking-to. The Americans denied all knowledge of the robberies but, even so, the leader got a good hiding a couple of days later. And now these two boys had been found, beaten to death, naked, with signs of torture and beach sand on their bodies.

The temperature had been going up anyway, ever since Waleed had pulled a massive heist of several million rand somewhere near Vredenberg, up the coast. He and Wakes and the others, who were not really a gang but a load of upstarts, as far as the Hard Livings were concerned, had spent 100 000 rand on guns and had also got new cars. There was a danger that they would start getting too big for their boots.

Things had got serious back in May when Waleed had sent some of his henchmen to drive past Hard Living valley, about six of them, and just let fly at whoever was on the corner of Aletta or Belinda Courts. The twins spent night after night cruising around looking for Waleed but he had gone to ground. One of the problems was the twins' cars: you could hear them coming for miles, they were so souped up.

Rashad had the maroon 'Bavaria' 735i, with the sun roof open for the hit men, while Rashied drove the trusty Blue Thunder 3½-litre Sierra, which Brendan (the Hard Livings' mechanic) had jacked up to something like 4 litres. The engines were thunderous, and in the dead still streets of Manenberg and Mitchell's Plain the cars' signature roar gave Waleed and his cohorts plenty of warning.

For weeks the Hard Livings hardly slept, hunting Waleed by night, watching the cricket by day. They waited for Waleed to make a false move, to reveal his whereabouts. Rashied played Nintendo video games in his front room for hours on end. Brendan, the young mechanic, would grab a bicycle and pedal off towards the main road, muttering that he couldn't stand just waiting and doing nothing. In the end Rashad was so frustrated with the sleepless nights and the drive-by shootings that he wanted to go and burn Waleed's mother in her house. But somehow the whole business just faded away. There were rumours that Waleed had paid Rashied a 15000 rand ransom so he could be allowed back on the streets of Manenberg. No one really knew.

Part of the problem was that Waleed claimed to have been in the same prison gang as Rashied but he had no respect for Rashied, who had been a four-star general in the gang. The hierarchies and loyalties of prison had to be respected even on the outside, but Waleed insisted on buying guns and selling *buttons* without getting Rashied's permission. So one day the Hard Livings went and tore down his vegetable stall. That was the beginning of the war with Waleed. Then things quietened down but in 1993 Waleed started getting smart again after the massive robbery in Vredenberg. And then there was the small matter of the two Jesters who had been beaten to death and dumped by the filling station.

When Cola came back from a business trip to Johannesburg Rashied went to see him and Sleeps, the other leader of the Jesters, to explain that it was not the Hard Livings who had murdered Joburg and Ice. The explanation was accepted, although there were still some niggling doubts in people's minds. The official version, anyway, was that Marky's cousin from Bontheuvel had done it. Marky drove a blue Mercedes, and came to talk business with Rashad now and again. No one knew exactly what the motive for the killings was, except that it had something to do with those two balaclava men who had been robbing merchants in Manenberg. The word on the street was that they had got the wrong guys, and that Joburg and Ice were not the ones who had done the robberies. But that was too bad.

31 Through the Gates of Sunrise

Rashied and Rashad were in and out of jail: housebreaking, robbery, possession of illegal firearms, assault. After they had been to court once too often the judge decided they were a menace to society. They became long-term *bruingevangene* (brown convicts). Both twins, who were in their mid-twenties, got sentences of fourteen years.

Prison life in South Africa was a hell with its own harsh rules. There were sometimes 100 men to a cell, or more. The warders would come round, beat them hard with their night sticks, throw teargas in the cells if the gangs were fighting, bugger the pretty Coloured boys and generally treat the men like dirt. The prison gangs, on the other hand, gave them dignity and power.

The prison gangs control every South African prison. Some say they began in the African mine compounds, 100 years ago. Others say they were secret societies invented by Zulus who fled into the hills last century after their defeat by the British. Others say Nongolos and the other founders are still alive. But here in the Cape, where Coloureds outnumbered Africans (Whites had their own jails), it was the Coloureds who ran the prison gangs. This was the world which greeted the Hard Living twins, Rashied and Rashad.

After the last bell at night, when the prisoners unrolled their blankets, you would see the Twenty-Sixes bedding down on the right side, in 'London', facing eastwards towards the dawn. They were the men of sun-up, of *Mpumalanga*, meaning sunrise in Zulu. They greeted one another with the words 'Oos, Mpumalanga!'. They were the white calves, *Itole Elimhlope*. Their colours were white and red. Their domain was blood and money.

On the left side, in the 'flower garden', facing west, were the Twenty-Eights, the black calves, *Itole Elimyama*. They were the men of sundown, *uTshonalanga*. Their colour was black, for their job was to have sex with other prisoners in the dark, at night. Their mythical founder was Nongolos, and Twenty-Eights are often referred to as *nongolos*.

In between were the Twenty-Sevens, the Air Force, whose job it was to organize escapes from prison. They believed you must stay fit and healthy, ready for escape at any time. There was a fourth gang, the Big Fives. But the two principal gangs were the Twenty-Sixes and the Twenty-Eights.

Twenty-Sixes identified one another by communicating a particular story, which only the Twenty-Sixes knew. One Twenty-Six could tell another Twenty-Six, just by the way he told the story. The Twenty-Sixes had their rules, set down in *die Wet*, the Law. The Law was unwritten, but it was strictly applied. If a Twenty-Six committed an offence, a court of law was convened, in a *kring*, a circle in one of the cells.

If you were guilty, the sentence was proportionate to the offence. You could get the short knife for less serious offences, or the long knife, which was for capital punishment. Your sentence could range from six minutes to six years. Six minutes, the lightest sentence, meant that you would be stabbed within six minutes of the sentence being passed. A six-year sentence meant that you could be punished at any time within the next six years. Intermediate sentences were six hours, six weeks and six months.

In addition to the unwritten code of the Law, the Twenty-Sixes lived within a strict hierarchy of twelve ranks, from the new recruit to the four-star general. Until the new recruit could prove his worth, by smuggling *dagga* (cannabis) or a knife, by stabbing a designated prisoner or warder, by bringing his own ideas, by showing that he could rob with his mind as well as with violence, he languished in the Stoneyard.

If he proved his 'brilliance' he could enter the Gates of Sunrise ('the Gates of Son-op') and join the ranks of the Twenty-Sixes. Many prisoners never made the grade. They were turned down and (metaphorically) 'buried at the Gates of Son-op'.

Over the years of your prison sentence you could rise up through the ranks, from first sergeant to second to third sergeant, lieutenant, captain, general . . . The Twenty-Sixes had their doctors, their lawyers, magistrates and judges. You wore your gang number with pride: the two crowns of the Twenty-Sixes were tattooed on your body with molten rubber. Some chose to wear the number on their throat, just under the collar, like a dog-tag. The Twenty-Eights also had their rules, embodied in the unwritten Book of Nineveh, *die Boek*. Their tattoo was an open book, next to a sinking sun.

The younger prisoners were taken for 'wives' as soon as they arrived. If you let yourself be taken, and once you were chosen it was usually impossible to resist, you were seen as a youngster and a 'bunny' for the duration of your sentence. Being a *wyvie* had its compensations. Your husband would look after you, put sugar in your porridge, bring you soap, tobacco, *dagga* and sweets. Men who could not afford to provide these luxuries were discouraged from keeping concubines.

Sex in the cells happened after lights out, never in full view. In some prisons the cells were pitch dark, in others the lights were left on all night, and couples had to wait until everyone was snoring. Sex was mostly practised by gang members, with some restrictions. A Twenty-Six could not be a wife, or allow himself to be sodomized. The book of the Twenty-Sevens did not encourage sex, as it might make them unfit, and they might not be ready when the time came to escape. Lasting relationships were forged in prison between men and their wives. It was part of life in prison. In some jails the prison officers acted as marriage counsellors when relationships went wrong. But by no means every prisoner was, or aspired to be, a *nommer*, a member of one of the number gangs. In some prisons there were cells which banned gang activity, concentrating instead on trade and commerce.

Goods were smuggled during the day, and warders bribed to turn a blind eye. Tobacco was bought and sold, sub-divided into smaller 'blades' and sold on by middlemen. Cakes and fried fish came from the kitchen. But *dagga* was the commodity in greatest demand.

In the evening, after the prisoners were locked up, the cells would come alive. The commerce in *dagga* would begin, and small fortunes were made.

Using a long piece of string attached to a cup the *dagga* would be distributed from the dealers to their customers. Large amounts of money changed hands, drawn from a prisoner's personal safe, his rectum, where banknotes were carried, wrapped in clingfilm. Some prisoners were even known to carry loose change.

Prison offered an alternative world, in which some men became rich and powerful and others sank without trace. Men died in gang wars within the prisons, or as a result of feuds. Killings were done in the cells, in front of the other prisoners, who were bound by a code of silence. If you became a *nommer* a long spell in prison could make your career as a gangster outside. For the influence of the prison gangs extended far outside the prison walls, and the secret bonds and alliances forged within prison held good in the ganglands of the Cape Flats.

In his first few months the prisoner was at his most vulnerable. If he did not 'wake up and live' he would become a victim.

Rashied thrived in the Twenty-Sixes, becoming a general, with four stars tattooed on his shoulders. He served his sentence at Brandvlei, although his name became known far and wide in the prisons of the Western Cape. He learned to kill in jail, and was always protected by the rule of silence. The prison authorities decided that he was a danger to the other prisoners. He was certified a psychopath, and kept in the 'tight corner' with the most violent inmates. His body was covered in tattoos. The one across the back of his neck read 'The Chosen Ones'. Next to a rose tattoo on his belly was a fist holding a blazing gun. The flame shooting from the muzzle contained the word 'Rashied'. On his chest were the words: 'Rather Wisdom than Gold'.

Rashad joined the Twenty-Eights and became a well-known figure at Pollsmoor Prison. Like his twin brother he was ruthless and disciplined. Unlike Rashied, he gained the confidence of the prison authorities, to such an extent that he was allowed to walk out of the prison gates at will, and was entrusted with the coveted task of cleaning the prison commander's house. To gain further credibility with the authorities he became a Christian preacher, despite being born into a Muslim family and never having learned to read.

'If you don't drink or smoke,' says Rashad, 'you can survive in prison. Your mind must always be sober. And you mustn't be greedy for food, or people won't respect you. To survive in prison you must also fight dirty. People must say, "Don't mess with him, he'll fight dirty."'

Rashad earned money by providing protection for the wealthier inmates. In return for a regular wage, he would ensure that the man would not be beaten up and that no one would 'make a woman of him'. Rashad's influence was such that he could ensure a man's safety in neighbouring cells as well as his own.

In all the years he spent inside, Rashad did not receive a single visit, a fact which makes him shake his head bitterly to this day. 'No one came. Not even Rashied. When I came out I took him money every month. But I had to survive on my own.'

32 Buttons and 'The Group'

Rashad came out of prison first. He had nothing, and went back to Manenberg to find the Hard Livings. They were a sorry, rag-tag bunch who had almost lost control of Hard Living valley and their headquarters. The fact that they had survived at all was due to Naala, who was a fearless street-fighter, and had taken over the leadership in the twins' absence.

Rashad knew that no one would give him a job, as he had no education to speak of, and having had a high profile in prison he had no intention of joining the ranks of Manenberg's poor. With his entire worldly wealth of 90 rand he bought thirty tablets of Mandrax.

In the seventies Mandrax was the kind of drug White kids would steal from their mothers' bathroom cabinets. The small white tablets were prescribed by doctors for cases of insomnia amongst overwrought urban middle-class women. 'Mandys' were great with booze, youngsters discovered, and they gave you an enormous sex drive. In the United States they were known as Quaaludes, popped as downers by the rich and famous.

In Cape Town someone hit on the idea of smoking Mandrax in a pipe. You crushed the white tablet, mixed it with some *dagga* (cannabis) and put the mixture in the bottom of a broken bottle neck. It was easier to smoke with a partner, who could hold the flame at the mouth of the bottle neck while you took huge lungfuls of the precious, milky smoke. The *witpyp* ('white pipe') is spectacular to watch. The flame from the match grows huge as the mixture burns in the wide end of the bottle neck, with billows of heavy smoke. One lungful can blow your head off. All the blood in your body surges upwards into your brain. Often a youngster smoking in a ring will keel over after a couple of drags, and the next smoker will let him collapse but catch the pipe safely.

Before long the authorities cottoned on and banned Mandrax, creating the biggest clandestine industry in Cape Town. Mandrax tablets, or 'buttons' as they are known in ordinary parlance, were imported from India, Pakistan and Bangladesh, where they were still manufactured legally and were dirt cheap. Illegal laboratories synthesized Mandrax in the Xhosa homeland of Transkei. The tablets were then brought into the Black townships of Cape Town by long-distance minibus taxi before being sold on to mainly Coloured middlemen. Some of the local buttons are junk, the big fat dark grey ones with no stamp. It's easy to tell whether a button is the real thing, you put it on your tongue. When you take the button out, your tongue should be numb.

By the late 1980s Cape Town was consuming a large part of India and Pakistan's output, plus bootleg buttons from Transkei. More than 90 per cent of the world's Mandrax was smoked in Cape Town, most of it by Coloured youths in the Cape Flats.

Rashad knew a good thing when he saw one. He set himself up as a Mandrax dealer. Rashied came out of jail and began to rally the Hard Livings. For a while no one in Manenberg could tell them apart, until Rashied grew a gingery beard. The twins began to work successfully as a team, although they always seemed to be at loggerheads with each other. The Hard Livings grew stronger, more disciplined, more professional. Rashied taught the boys how to do armed robberies and how to shoot. He pioneered a strategy of robbing drug merchants, which established the Hard Livings as the most thrusting, dynamic gang in Cape Town. Rashad, who was prudent and had a feel for money, handled the business side of things. Rashied, who was ruthless and charismatic, took care of moulding the gang, charging it with his own identity, and taking care of what his brother called 'the violence side'.

As the Hard Livings expanded, branches were established in other Coloured townships on the Flats: Elsie's River, Mitchell's Plain, Belhar, Bontheuvel. Each sub-leader came to Rashied for advice, assistance and guns. Meanwhile Rashad set up a prostitution business in Sea Point, Cape Town's upmarket seaside suburb, catering for the Japanese and Samoan sailors who passed through on the container ships. More Mandrax outlets were opened, including several pitches in Cape Town itself, where poorer Whites were acquiring a Mandrax habit.

The Hard Livings also increased their turf within Manenberg which, like every working-class Coloured township in Cape Town, was portioned into zones of gang control. The Hard Livings' logo: HL, or HLK (Hard Living Kids, though this was frowned on by Rashied, who did not like the association with kids) appeared in man-high letters on the ends of the courts which were considered Hard Living territory. The core of the Hard Living jurisdiction in Manenberg is a 100-metre dog-leg of Manenberg Avenue extending from the Hard Livings' headquarters in Aletta Court, opposite the Catholic church, to the Methodist church at the far corner, a territory comprising perhaps twenty courts.

This is the poorest section of Manenberg, a ghetto of two-storey blocks arranged in pairs ('courts'), each containing sixty flats. Access to the upper floors is by means of concrete staircases which zig-zag in rows up the sides of the blocks. The space between the blocks is surfaced with concrete and planted with a row of steel poles which support wire washing lines. The flats are tiny: a living room, a kitchen, two small bedrooms and a bathroom with cold water, for families of ten or twelve people, from grandparents to grandchildren. Between the blocks hang more washing lines, row upon row, with clothes flapping in the stiff Cape Flats breeze. Each 'court' bears a nameplate: Belinda, Beatrix, Aletta, Dorothy, whatever the town planner's whim was on that day.

Manenberg Avenue continues south from the Methodist church towards a series of squalid brick cottages, which mark the beginning of Jester territory. As the Hard Livings expanded in 1990 and 1991 there was friction with the Jesters and the two gangs embarked on a total war. Hostilities lasted one year, until the leaders decided to shake hands on a peace deal at the local mosque. Since then Manenberg itself has been relatively quiet, and the Hard Livings' wars have been fought on foreign turf.

A small, limp Stars and Stripes flag on a wooden base stands on top of the dresser in Rashied's front room, next to the wooden man o'war and the samurai sword. It reminds him never to forget that his life is in peril. 'Some gangsters are stupid,' he says scornfully. 'They don't stay awake. They drink and smoke *dagga*. They don't see the people waiting to shoot them.' His gold rings click faintly as he whips his hand in the universal South African gesture for killing.

The largest and richest gang in the Peninsula, the Americans are well-armed, with a large stake in the Mandrax business. While the Americans and the Hard Livings are not formally at war, a state of hostility has always existed between them. Every few months Rashied's thunderous blue Sierra is accosted at the traffic lights by armed men from the American gang. 'I don't look them in the eyes,' he says. 'Because if they see my eyes they will know that I am going to kill them. Then they might shoot me first.' Usually Rashied's awesome reputation for cruelty, and the knowledge that the Hard Livings are persistent and resourceful once they set out to kill someone, is sufficient to make the gunmen lose their nerve.

'Other gangsters fear Rashied and Rashad,' says Rashad. 'They know Rashied is afraid of no one. Do you know how many times someone pulled a gun on Rashied? Rashied just tells the guy, "Shoot yourself, you *poes*." The big guys don't dare to fight us, they know we will get them. If anyone does something to us we will sleep in his yard until he comes back, and we will kill him.'

The fear of retribution is a powerful deterrent, but there have been times when it has failed. Rashied can't eat strong 'Malay' curries, as he only has one kidney. He also has only one lung, the result of being shot in the chest, then rammed against a lamp-post by a car. A piece of his tongue is missing

Natal, 1990: Inkatha warriors on the warpath against the comrades, near Pietermaritzburg. (*Guy Tillim/ Afrapix/Southlight*)

Natal, 1990: UDF comrades with homemade *'kwatcha'* guns, KwaMashu township, near Durban. (*Guy Tillim/ Afrapix/Southlight*)

RIGHT Mangosuthu 'Gatsha' Buthelezi, founder of Inkatha and Chief Minister of KwaZulu, with followers in traditional garb. (*Guy Adams/ The Weekly Mail*)

LEFT Refugees from the fighting in Mpumalanga, Natal Midlands, 1990. (*Justin Sholk*)

LEFT Inside Pollsmoor prison,
Cape Town. (*Guy Tillim/
Southlight*)

Cape Town, 1993
ABOVE Rashied (second from left)
with several of the Hard Livings
gang, on the corner opposite
Aletta Court, Manenberg, Cape
Flats.
TOP Rashad with one of his
daughters, Manenberg Avenue,
Cape Flats. (*Daniel Reed*)

RIGHT Jurie Potgieter at his terracotta tile factory in Phola Park, 1993. (*Daniel Reed*)

RIGHT Afrikaners pay homage at the Voortrekker Monument, 1950s. (*The Star*)

BELOW AWB (Afrikaner Resistance Movement) march in Schweizer-Reneke, Western Transvaal, after AWB leader Eugene Terreblanche had received the 'freedom of the city', August 1993. (*Henner Frankenfeld/ Southlight*)

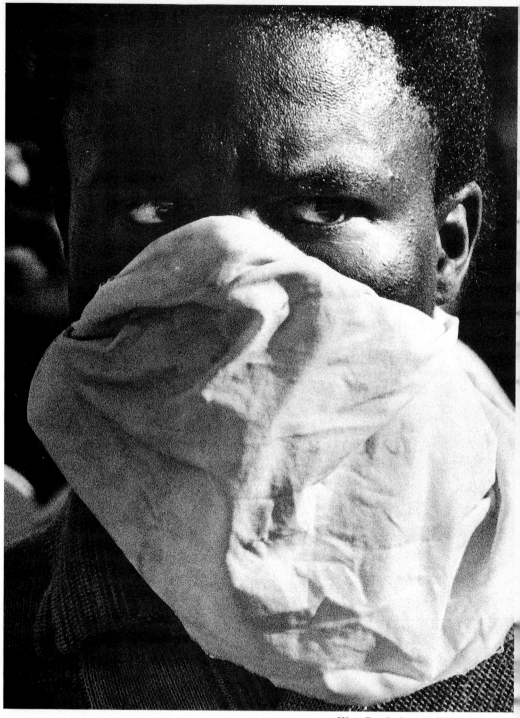

West Rand, August 1990: a comrade
during an attack on the Kagiso hostel
by pro–ANC residents of Kagiso.
(*Ken Oosterbroek/ The Star*)

ever since a bullet smashed through the back of his neck and came out through his mouth. There are seven bullet wounds in his left leg, sustained when a woman shot him in the local police station, after jumping to the (erroneous) conclusion that he had raped her daughter.

Rashied lives in a tiny, turn-of-the-century terraced house in Salt River, just south-east of the harbour, on the edge of metropolitan Cape Town. The front room, where the curtains are always drawn, is small and modestly furnished, with a framed quotation from the Koran in large gilt letters on the wall. Cutie-pie studio photographs of Rashied's daughter Nashiefah adorn the shelves of the dresser, next to a few porcelain trinkets. Two couches and an armchair, upholstered in hard-wearing transparent plastic, take up most of the space. The floors are tiled.

The bedroom is modest, with improvised curtains and a simple dresser. The kitchen is functional. Nashiefah sleeps in a box room, and the back yard has been covered to provide more space. The front is a narrow enclosed veranda at street level, littered with engine parts from the Sierra, with security bars in all the openings and a steel gate, always locked. The house is respectable, unpretentious. Not the home of a man who longs to be rich. 'Rashied is a leader of his people,' says Rashad. 'He could have been a rich man, but he has nothing. He looks after his people instead.'

Rashad owns a more spacious house a few doors down on the opposite side of the street. Creature comforts are more in evidence than at Rashied's. There is a gilt-framed mirror in the lounge where the children watch TV on green plush couches. The lacquered dining room table is covered in a white lace napkin, which Rashad pushes out of the way when he counts the day's takings out of a polythene bag. A Rembrandt reproduction stands on top of the sideboard. Glass display cases contain ornaments in an Islamic style, and a polished brass scales of justice. The kitchen is spacious and there are three bedrooms on the upper floor. The rooms are all carpeted. Rashad has recently swapped his maroon BMW, a fighting gangster's car, for a newish mustard-coloured Mercedes saloon with sports wheels.

The street is usually deserted, except for the trickle of customers who drive up to buy buttons or *dagga* from Rashied's dealers who work out of the burned, gutted house opposite his. Most of the customers are White and drive battered cars. Occasionally the police or the Stability raid the burned house, hoping to catch someone red-handed. Occasionally they succeed. Rashad was caught with a parcel of 1000 buttons. He only had time to toss it away from him onto a piece of waste ground next to the ruined house. To his dismay the Stability, unlike the local police, refused to be bribed. Rashad paid for a good lawyer and the case has been postponed.

Between four o'clock and half-past four the streets of Salt River fill with hundreds of women, the workforce of the local clothing factories, hurrying to catch trains back to the Flats. Rashied and any Hard Livings who happen to be around stand in the doorway and watch the crowd surge past. The textile industry has been Cape Town's biggest employer for decades, though some say that nowadays the buttons trade is bigger.

Devil's Peak, the northern bastion of Table Mountain, dominates the Salt River skyline, its wrinkled crags rising above the dilapidated façades. Wherever you are in Cape Town the mountain is always there, a sinister presence, dimly visible behind a blue veil. At its best Salt River resembles a decaying corner of the former British Empire. The street names evoke little England: Westminster, Portland, Albert, London, Burns, Coleridge, Tennyson, Swift . . . The air smells of the sea when the breeze comes from the north. The main road is lined with low, colonnaded buildings, their Victorian embellishments flaking away. Here and there a building proudly displays a date: 1903, 1906. The shops are small family businesses: junk shops, shoe repair, funerals, *halaal* butchers with an Islamic crescent in the window, take-aways where you can buy samosas and a curry for 5 rand.

Salt River, Observatory and Woodstock, the municipalities on the eastern edge of Cape Town between the freeway, the harbour and the marshy Liesbeeck River, were never completely cleansed by 'the Group'. A few people clung onto their houses, particularly in the area between Victoria Road and the harbour. The rest of Cape Town, however, was purged of anyone with a darker shade of skin.

The Group Areas Act ('the Group' to its victims) was enacted by the National Party in 1948. It was a tool for clearing the inner cities of citizens with dark complexions. Before people could be removed, however, they had to be classified. An army of Afrikaner clerks sorted the entire population of South Africa into different race groups: White ('European'), Black ('Bantu') and Coloured. In Cape Town the task facing the Population Registration Office was particularly arduous. The 'Coloured' category was causing problems.

When the Dutch East India Company established a refuelling station for its ships near the Cape of Good Hope in 1652, it seized land which belonged to the sallow-complexioned San and Khoi-Khoi people. In due course the Khoi-Khoi died out and the San were exterminated. The majority of Cape Town's inhabitants were slaves, who worked for the Dutch. They were shipped over from West Africa, Angola, Mozambique, Zanzibar and Madagascar. Later the company imported slaves from the East. Slaves came to Cape Town from Bengal, Ceylon, Java, Bali, Burma, the Philippines and China. Indonesian slaves included educated Muslims, who brought the word *kaffir*, meaning 'unbeliever', which was their name for the Dutch.

The first official census of the Cape Colony, in 1865, recorded 180 000 'Europeans', 200 000 'Hottentots' and 'Others', and 100 000 'Kaffirs'. The 'Others' later became known as 'Coloured', a word used to describe people of mixed descent. 'Coloured' became one of the race group categories in the new racial classification handbook of apartheid. Legions of Afrikaner clerks now had a label they could attach to anyone who was not obviously 'Bantu' or 'European'.

A Coloured person could have blond hair and blue eyes, or a complexion darker than that of most 'Black' South Africans. A single family could include some members who looked White and others with jet-black complexions. As far as the Population Registration Act was concerned, these members of the same family belonged to different race groups. Therefore they could not live in the same parts of town, go to the same schools, libraries, sports grounds or beaches, or use the same buses. The Coloured part of the family became second-class citizens in terms of the Group Areas Act, the Reservation of Separate Amenities Act, the State-Aided Institutions Act and the other instruments of apartheid. They were dubbed *vensterkykers*, window-lookers, as they would have to ignore their lighter-skinned relatives in the street and pretend to be looking in a shop window. The object was to avoid being seen by informers in the act of greeting a family member of a different race group, for fear of being tainted by association and reclassified.

Once people had been identified as Coloured (part of the broad 'Non-European' group), they were expelled from the cities. An act of parliament was passed to make sure that no more mixed unions could take place. The Immorality Act extended the ban on sex between Blacks and Whites to cover sex between Coloureds and Whites.

The 'ethnic cleansing' of Cape Town literally tore the heart out of the city. District Six, which was a huge, lively slum on the slopes of Table Mountain, home to most of the city's Coloured population, was bulldozed. The people of District Six were resettled in a series of new dormitory townships on the Cape Flats, an area early Dutch settlers described as 'desolate and uninviting'.

Instead of the ancient whitewashed churches and mosques of Cape Town there were corrugated-iron sheds. Replacing the cramped, bustling streets on the mountainside was a hostile wilderness, waterlogged in the winter, parched and bare in the summer.

Meanwhile the Black population of Cape Town was also scheduled for removal to their 'homelands'. Crossroads squatter camp, populated largely by Xhosa migrants, resisted. Vigilantes were recruited to force thousands of squatters to move to a remote settlement called Khayelitsha, 40 kilometres from Cape town.

Khayelitsha ('our lovely home') was a gash in the drift sands where the government had built rows of small houses. Khayelitsha became the largest apartheid city in South Africa, part township, part squatter camp, its shacks stretching far away beside roads clogged with sand. The site for Khayelitsha was selected from the air by President P.W. Botha, who had gone up in a helicopter to find the most suitable spot to dump Cape Town's Blacks. As the chopper swooped over the coldest, wettest and windiest part of the

Cape Flats, Botha pointed and said 'There!'. As for the excess Coloured population in the Cape Town area, they were given their very own 'homeland': Atlantis.

Atlantis. The name had to be a joke. The town planners probably chuckled over beer and *boerewors* sausage at their Saturday afternoon barbecues. Atlantis was a 'deconcentration point'. Like the Black homelands, it was a place far away from the city where surplus people could be dumped and forgotten. To stop people straying back to civilization it was decided to promote the growth of industries at the 'deconcentration points' and on the periphery of the Black homelands.

Atlantis lies in a flat wilderness on the Atlantic coast 50 kilometres from Cape Town. The coast road cuts a straight line between sparsely vegetated dunes towards a featureless horizon. Forty kilometres later the little matchboxes of Atlantis come into view, neat rows in the sand. You pass the section locals call Smarty Town, where the tiny houses were painted bright colours to make them look more appetizing. And Hungry Town, where the houses were so expensive that the residents could only afford to eat porridge.

A programme of subsidies was designed to tempt entrepreneurs to build factories in or near the homelands. The government paid the workers' wages and provided other incentives. All you had to do was collect the subsidies for ten years. After ten years, if your basket-weaving factory wasn't a going concern, you could move to another 'deconcentration point' and build another 'decentralized' factory.

In the mid-seventies Atlantis became a magnet for Coloured families who had been 'cleansed' from Cape Town, Parrow or Belleville, only to become victims of the housing shortage on the Cape Flats. Accommodation could usually be found in Atlantis. Within a few years Atlantis became a boom town. Factories were built, attracted by the gigantic government subsidies. The motor industry employed thousands at Atlantis Diesel Engines and Grapnel Silencers. Then the ten-year subsidy ran out, coinciding with the beginning of the national economic slump. Atlantis died. The gangs ran riot – Americans, Scorpions and Fancy Boys.

Atlantis rose to fame once more, this time as the murder capital of the region. The social hub of Atlantis was Club Memphis, a pale pink Art Deco-style concrete structure with smoked glass windows. White guys came to dance there and the rumour was that they were spreading Satanism amongst the boys and girls of Atlantis. There was also Club Piggles, if you didn't fancy the Memphis. Atlantis didn't have much else to offer. Slowly Atlantis sank into oblivion, half its workforce unemployed, with some Atlanteans literally facing starvation. Sand blew down the sad, still streets of Smarty Town and Hungry Town. Of the boom years of Atlantis, only the cracked pink walls of Club Memphis remained.

33 The Chosen Ones

Sometimes Rashied and his lieutenants sit for days in the semi-darkness of Rashied's front room in Salt River, watching American gangster movies on the video: *Dillinger*, *Mo'Money*, *New Jack City*, *Colours*, *Boyz n' the Hood*. The house is filled with the screech of tyres and the rattle of tommy-guns.

Father Peter Stein, a Catholic priest from Pretoria, visited District Six during the later stages of demolition, in 1979. He told a newspaper reporter that it reminded him of the bombed-out towns of England where he had worked with youth after the war. The children showed all the symptoms of war psychosis. 'When you cut off a society's roots in the past,' said Father Stein, 'it precipitates a frantic search for roots in the present and future. The main problem with the children here,' he added, 'was to get them to face their reality. Because the reality of their situation is so harsh they are constantly escaping into the realms of fantasy.'

Cape Town's street gangs dress 'American', with the latest Nikes or Reeboks, baseball caps, sweatshirts, Ray Ban Aviators and leather jackets. The biggest gang is the Americans, who have a constitution, a president, a cabinet, a White House and count their money in 'dollars'. Their motto is 'In God we trust. In money we believe.' (The Hard Livings' motto counsels the opposite: 'Rather wisdom than gold.')

While their contemporaries in the Black townships worshipped Mandela and nursed AKs for the liberation of South Africa, Cape Town's Coloured youth modelled themselves on the gangsters of the Bronx or South Central LA. Per capita, the number of Coloured South Africans in prison grew to the highest of any population group in the world. 'Coloured people are born in prison and die in prison. They live their whole lives in prison. What difference does it make whether you are inside or outside?' shrugged Rashad one day before going to court for the umpteenth time.

For many Coloured youths gangsterism is little more than a rite of passage, a phase you leave behind if you are lucky enough to get a job. There is a large and prosperous Coloured middle class in Cape Town, boosted by government reforms which aimed to draw Coloureds into an alliance against the rising menace of Black mobilization. Money was poured into

Coloured education and training, into recruiting more Coloureds into the police force and the civil service, in an attempt to beef up the Coloured buffer zone.

To a large extent it worked, creating a large, conservative middle class of 'brown Afrikaners' with a strong vested interest in White rule. The advent of a Black government, far from being welcomed by the Coloured middle class, is seen as the prelude to a disastrous reshuffling of the social order, with Coloureds sinking to the bottom of the pile. 'With apartheid it was Whites on top, then Indians, then us, and Blacks on the bottom. With a Black government it will be Blacks first, then Whites, then Indians, and we will be on the bottom,' says a resident of Manenberg.

You can read the names on the walls of any Coloured township on the Flats: JFK (Junky Funkies), Mongrels, S17 (Stalag Seventeens), Dixie Boys, YuruCats, Y$A (Young Americans), U$A (Ugly Americans), YOK (Young Organization Kids), BFK (Born Free Kids), Naughty Boys, Vietnam Rats, Terrible Schoolboys, Cobra Kids, Sexy Boys, Sicilians, Playboys, Mafias, NTK (Nice Time Kids), Crazy Cats, BSK (Back Street Kids), GTV (Genuine TV Kids), HL (Hard Livings). Each gang has its special rules, its dress code, its own salute and mottoes. 'You've got to belong to something,' says one gang member. 'There's nothing else to do.'

The gangs range from street gangs, a group of youths who have banded together to organize the defence of their block or their street using *pangas* and knives, to powerful syndicate gangs (like the Americans, the Mongrels, the Hard Livings) who have several branches in the Cape Flats townships, and even as far afield as Durban or Johannesburg. These syndicate gangs have a sophisticated economy, usually based on buying and selling buttons. They own quantities of firearms, including automatic weapons, rocket launchers, hand grenades and limpet mines.

In the seventies and eighties disputes between gangs were settled in pitched battles on the local soccer field. Several hundred gang members would gather and march to the field with their weapons, sometimes holding a banner. The Americans flew the Stars and Stripes, whilst their rivals, if they were part of the loose anti-American coalition which fought under the British flag, would carry the Union Jack. In the slang 'british' came to mean ready for action. 'I'm going to british myself,' meant 'I'm going to get a gun.' 'We are british now,' meant 'We are ready to fight.' To the 'british' boys from the back streets of Britain and the Commonwealth, the Americans had no style. They merely lay on the beach all day.

The two armies would then attack each other with knives, *pangas* and shotguns. As the gangs became more sophisticated and more heavily armed, the days of pitched battles became a fond memory. In the early nineties gang warfare evolved into an endless round of Chicago-style drive-by shootings, assassinations and ambushes. Hundreds of innocent bystanders were killed or maimed in the crossfire. Manenberg acquired a reputation for viciousness unmatched on the Cape Flats. The ghetto was nicknamed Murdererberg and Kill Me Quick Town.

'In Hanover Park most of the stab wounds are chest wounds, the idea is to maim,' explained a nurse at the local clinic. 'People in Manenberg stab for the heart or the jugular.'

It's nine o'clock on a winter night in Manenberg, just after rain. There is no one on the streets. Rashied has driven the blue Sierra up onto the concreted area in front of Aletta Court, where the Hard Livings usually sit. The sodium lights glare in the courts, throwing hard zigzag shadows of concrete staircases. Rashied is waiting for Kaffertjie and Watson. They have planned to rob a long-distance truck carrying wine. Kaffertjie is late. Brendan the mechanic leans on the corner, smoking, not saying a word.

Rashied sits in the Sierra. He is in a quiet, melancholic mood. 'Nearly all my friends are dead,' he says. 'Most of the Hard Livings are in jail.' He smooths his beard with gold-ringed fingers. A Krugerrand, a King George gold coin, a gold Twenty-Six ring. 'The younger generation don't understand. They would actually prefer to fight. When there is fighting there is much more money to be made. Protection money.'

Rashied says he would like to resign and let the Hard Livings take another leader. 'But the young ones need a strong person to keep them together,' he sighs, 'to stop them making mistakes. Otherwise they will fight amongst themselves like the other gangs.' The Mongrels have been fighting amongst themselves, says Rashied. Bobby Mongrel's son was shot dead recently. 'Bobby is a fool,' he says scornfully. Then he falls to thinking. 'I am the first leader of the Hard Livings, and the last. After me there will be no more leaders. The Hard Livings don't listen to each other. They only listen to me.'

Although the Hard Livings are involved in gang wars in other townships, and members are dying in Lotus River and Mitchell's Plain, Rashied is keen to see the ceasefire hold in Manenberg itself. 'In past years there was a man with a gun on each corner,' he says. 'We would ride with guns every day.' He thinks of all the people he has killed. 'I feel nothing for them,' he says, perturbed. He only admits to feelings of remorse about two of the men he has murdered. In one case, it was a revenge killing and the man turned out to be innocent. 'I was with a girl this afternoon,' he says thoughtfully. 'She asked me, "Do you have a heart?" And that made me think.'

Kaffertjie arrives in his maroon 5-series, fifteen minutes late, followed by Watson and Ice in the yellow pick-up. Rashied snaps out of his introspective mood and lectures Kaffertjie on keeping time, tapping his gold watch for emphasis. The cars thunder off past the Catholic church at high speed, blotting out the feeble strains of a hymn.

Rashad wanders out of the People's Cafe, his mobile shop, which is always parked across the road from Aletta Court. Business is slack. Rashad watches his twin brother drive off towards the Black township of Nyanga. 'When I see him drive off like that I know he's going to make trouble,' he says. He's worried. He likes to be there, watching from a distance in case something goes wrong.

The fact that there was a ceasefire in 1993 between the syndicate gangs in Manenberg did not mean that individual scores could not still be settled. When Rashied and the others came across Ou'Gat ('Cutie-pie') one Sunday morning in the streets of Mitchell's Plain, they put him in the boot of the Sierra and drove to Aletta Court. The feeling was that he should be tried and sentenced as quickly as possible, but Rashied pointed out that he was a useful hostage, and that he could be bartered.

Ou'Gat was a Mongrel and a Twenty-Six who had shot and crippled Goddeloos ('Godless'), a senior Hard Living. The way it happened, explained Ou'Gat, shaking with fear, is that when Goddeloos was in jail his girlfriend Miena had a thing with Christopher Petersen. When Goddeloos came out, there was a confrontation, a massive shoot-out, and Ou'Gat happened to be there. That's what happened, it wasn't premeditated. After slapping him around a few times the Hard Livings escorted him to Toetie's, where he sat in the corner awaiting interrogation. Meanwhile the Hard Livings sent someone to look for the three guns which Ou'Gat had promised them in exchange for his freedom.

Rashied found it hard to believe that Ou'Gat, who was shaking like a leaf, could be a real Twenty-Six. A Twenty-Six would display more gumption and accept what was coming to him with dignity. Rashied began to quiz Ou'Gat about his prison background, asking him whether, despite the Twenty-Six tattoo on his throat, he was not in fact a *franseman* (Frenchman), a 'civvie'.

Brendan, the Hard Livings' mechanic, stood outside in the court smoking while Ou'Gat was being interrogated. He knew that whatever the man said, it wasn't going to make any difference to the outcome. Ou'Gat would be found the next day in a parking lot or in the river. Although Brendan was one of Rashied's most trusted henchmen, he always liked to keep slightly aloof. Repairing and maintaining the Sierra was his function in life. He was a quiet, good-looking boy with a shy, charming smile, who kept very much to himself. He did not go in for the bravado and the tattoos, although he had the regulation one on the inside of his wrist, as they all did somewhere on their bodies. Brendan was sweet-natured and reserved, although it was not unknown for him to pull the occasional armed robbery, and he knew how to handle a gun.

Brendan was different from the others in that he came from a middle-class home. In fact, if you looked at the Hard Livings, the leading members of the gang mostly had a high school education and came from good homes.

Joining the Hard Livings was the best career move they could make, out of the limited choices available.

Brendan's father was a White security guard, his mother a supermarket manager. His parents had started living together in the days when a White man could be sent to jail for seven years for walking down the street hand in hand with a Coloured woman. They lived together clandestinely for many years, in fear of informers and the knock of the Group Areas inspector or the Vice Squad on the door. But that was all in the past now.

Brendan trained as a mechanic and found a job at a Ford garage in Cape Town. He used to service Rashied's black Cortina, and grew to respect the man. It wasn't long before Rashied recruited him as the Hard Livings' mechanic and his personal driver. Brendan was fed up with working for a boss and wanted his own garage. Rashied offered him a way to make some ready money. The two became inseparable. Brendan's mother didn't really know he was a gangster, or perhaps she preferred not to know. His father understood. Brendan enjoyed the freedom and the excitement of the gangster life.

Now he watched Lientjie take an oven dish full of curry into Toetie's place. It was a Sunday and the fact that there was a hostage in the court was not going to stop the Hard Livings having their regular Sunday lunch.

Ou'Gat sat in the corner of the room, with Watson tenderly, sadistically stroking his hair and giving him the odd slap. Rashied explained to him that they would not shrink from doing what they had to do, because the fact was that he had shot Goddeloos, who was now confined to a wheelchair for the rest of his life. Rashied mentioned that he had shot plenty of people in his time. He had even shot yuppies. He understood that if you shoot people, eventually it catches up with you. So Ou'Gat should understand that if the Hard Livings voted on a certain course of action they might have to do what they had to do. Ou'Gat caught his drift and began to shake all over.

Rashied was aware that the majority of the Hard Livings wanted to sodomize Ou'Gat and then kill him. But Ou'Gat was a Mongrel, and they might seek revenge. Things might get out of hand. Killing, once started, is difficult to stop. Rashied was in favour of some less drastic course of action. Besides, the way this boy was pleading for his life was pathetic to watch. Ou'Gat was definitely small fry and not even worth getting your hands dirty with.

The sun went down and still the guns hadn't arrived. Beers came out and the boys in the court sat outside in the warm night breeze and began to sing old Malay songs, beating out a rhythm on plastic beer crates. Kids came out on the zigzag concrete staircases to watch. Auntie Sue, who was always drunk on a Sunday, did a sinuous dance. Then they sang 'The Young Ones', and some Michael Jackson songs. Ou'Gat sat inside, resigned, awaiting his fate.

What seemed to clinch Ou'Gat's fate was when the police turned up, their yellow vans bristling with shotguns, and Ou'Gat, who was standing outside having a cigarette, made no attempt to escape. The police drove off again almost as soon as the people in the court started cursing them, which wasn't long after they arrived. The fact that Ou'Gat didn't 'pimp' (inform) to the cops counted hugely in his favour. Besides, the hostage drama had lasted all day and people were getting bored. Ou'Gat was given a white pipe to smoke. He barely inhaled at all, as he knew that the white pipe was sometimes the prelude to a bullet in the head. But Rashied gave him a talking-to and reminded him that he owed them one, and when the time came they would call on him to pull the trigger on one of their enemies. Ou'Gat could hardly believe his luck, and thanked Rashied profusely in the secret language of the Twenty-Sixes. Still shaking with fear, he was led out of the court, followed by a dozen laughing children.

34 The People's Cafe

Rashad opened his mobile shop shortly after he was caught in Guguletu with 600 'buttons'. He told the police he was on his way to buy a bottle of brandy for his brother when two Africans stopped his car in the street and started talking to him. He didn't know they were carrying drugs. Why were the police arresting him and not the two African guys? The police arrested him for possession of Mandrax and took him to Mitchell's Plain police station. Rashad now faces two charges of dealing in Mandrax, in addition to a three-year suspended sentence, also for dealing. He looks worried. By day, when the shop is busy, he unwraps cartons of cigarettes to give himself something to do, or stares blankly at the pages of *House and Garden* magazine, perhaps wishing he had learned to read.

The mobile shop was Rashad's stab at going legit. It also gave him a way to account for at least some of his illegal earnings. He bought a huge old Bedford furniture removal truck and put Trust to work fitting out the inside. Trust, who grew up in District Six, had spent eighteen years in jail for blowing off a security guard's head with a shotgun. He was seventeen. The death sentence was commuted to life imprisonment. While serving time in Pollsmoor, Trust qualified as a carpenter. When Mandela came to Pollsmoor, Trust made the bookshelves for his cell.

Trust set to work for Rashad and within days he had created the interior:

rows of wooden shelves along the back wall, a wooden counter with a flip top so you can get in and out, and a space for the fridge and the till. The outside of the truck received a fresh coat of sky-blue paint, and it said 'The People's Cafe' in red letters on the side and the front. 'If the guys in jail hear that I'm running a mobile shop, selling sweets to children, they won't be able to stop laughing,' grins Rashad.

In the first few weeks Rashad manned the People's Cafe twenty-four hours a day. He slept on a mattress in the space above the driver's cab. He would emerge in the morning with a thick growth of stubble, looking bleary in his one good eye. His dynamism was impressive, and he was never short of customers. His prices were low, and there was a ring of truth when he claimed he wanted to give something back to the poor people of Manenberg after so many years of doing business there.

Both twins say they donate generous portions of their illicit earnings to the poor of Manenberg. In the old days, before he had to pay all his money to the lawyers, Rashad used to arrive in Manenberg on a Sunday afternoon and drive his maroon BMW onto the concrete area in front of Aletta Court, honking his horn. The children knew exactly what that meant, and ran headlong towards the car. Rashad would set off through the streets of Manenberg like the Pied Piper, trailing dozens of screeching children. The banknotes would come sailing out, Rashad gleefully pulling handfuls of bills from a fat wad in his hand and tossing them through the sun roof.

By now the whole of Manenberg, with very few exceptions, would be on the street. Some just watched the show; others ran after the money, scrabbling in the road. Some Sundays Rashad would change tactics and stand on top of one of the zigzag concrete staircases in Aletta Court with a plastic carrier bag full of money. The banknotes would came drifting down amongst the lines of washing and the court would fill with shouts and laughter. If he was in a mischievous mood Rashad would take a bucket of water and douse the people who gathered at the foot of the staircase expecting more largesse.

Rashad insists the twins give away at least a third of what they make, after deducting expenses. There are barbecues for the gang and outings to the beach. There are cars and guns to be bought and maintained. There are policemen to be bribed, hot tips to be paid for ('the cops tell us where the money is,' says one armed robber from Manenberg). And when someone gets arrested while on gang business, bail money has to be found. It's an expensive business.

Sometimes the Hard Livings get lucky and bring home several hundred thousand rand or a large haul of buttons, say twenty packets worth, between 13 000 and 15 000 rand each on the street. Then there's a celebration, the cases of beer come out onto the corner, someone is sent to buy bread and fish, and Tinkie or Faisal will put on a show with handbrake turns in the road. Tinkie does terrifying handbrake skids in the Sierra, slewing the car round at high speed, scattering the kids on the corners. Tinkie is a hitman. Smokey is the other hitman. He sat with three guys in a car one day and shot them all dead. Then he just walked away.

Both Tinkie and Smokey are 'button kops' (button heads). They smoke a lot of Mandrax and the palms of their right hands are calloused and stained yellow from cupping the hot mixture in the broken bottle neck. You can also tell by the hoarse voice and the bleary eyes. Smokey is a friendly, good-natured guy with a kind manner. But when he smokes his eyes go stony hard.

Tinkie has been staying out of trouble, minding the Sea Point brothel for Rashad. One day two Whiteys, a boy and a girl came round to buy buttons. They wanted to smoke there as they had walked a long way from where they were staying, in some luxury flat. The girl wore bright orange lycra leggings and a black leather jerkin. She was already stoned, from her first ever white pipe that morning. The guy wore shorts and a cap; he looked nervous but was trying to be cool. When Tinkie gave him a suspicious look he protested. 'Come on, man,' showing his stained yellow palm, 'I'm a user, can't you see?'

So Tinkie sold them some buttons and they were so stoned they couldn't get the money straight. The guy inspected the thick, grey-speckled 'Flowers' (or they may have been 'Germans', with the swastikas on them) but Tinkie told him it was good stuff and took the couple into one of the bedsits. Now Tinkie can smoke anyone under the table and it was pretty obvious what was on his mind. The girl was nice-looking, blonde and very stoned. 'When a girl has had a white pipe, you can do anything to her. Pull her panties down, anything,' observed one of the guys at the flat. Tinkie stripped to the waist, displaying a lean, muscular body. All regular smokers are lean, in fact some people smoke buttons for a week just to lose weight. Tinkie pounded his taut stomach and loosened his belt, feeling good, while someone brought a bucket from the next room.

The Whitey had smoked often, and he puffed energetically while Tinkie held the match for him. He smoked the pipe in two rounds, sucking big lungfuls of the thick, heavy smoke. Tinkie cleaned out the bottle neck and made a new pipe for the girl while the guy began to dribble long, sticky gobs of saliva into the bucket. When it came to the girl's turn she kept on coughing, she just couldn't swallow the smoke. She pulled at the pipe without much enthusiasm, but soon enough her head exploded, her eyes lost focus and she began to sway. As for the guy, he was on his way out. Tinkie made the Whitey another pipe and locked the door. When the other Hard Livings came to check on him half an hour later he was still busy.

Residents of Manenberg have fond memories of the gangsters of District Six: 'You could walk anywhere, any time of day or night,' says Mercia, who lives in one of the flats behind Manenberg Avenue. 'There were gangsters then, but no one would rape you in the street. The police had control. Here there is so much corruption of the police force. Their attitude is "Fuck these people, we're not the fuck worried about them!" The first thing a new government should do is demolish Manenberg police station.'

Like many residents, Mercia complains that the police are hand-in-glove with the gangs. If someone reports a crime, the police inform the gang. 'The gang comes back and smashes your house and rapes your daughter,' fumes Mercia. Her son Joseph was stabbed only millimetres above his heart. The doctor who treated him urged the boy to press charges. But Joseph won't reveal the names of his assailants.

The lack of a credible police force led to the emergence of gangsters' kangaroo tribunals (the equivalent of 'people's courts' in the Black townships). One morning in Manenberg the parents of a teenage boy came to Rashied with a problem. They pointed out their son, tall, good-looking, about sixteen or seventeen. They said he had tried to rape his ten-year-old sister. If they called the police he would get a record, a few days in the cells, a few months in the 'formatory. The parents said the boy must be punished so that he never did it again.

The Hard Livings gathered at Toetie's ('Pussy's') place, their headquarters. Toetie's is the place where they are welcome day or night, and can always sit and talk or drink beer when there's money. It's a small room with a chair and two couches. Twenty Hard Livings crammed inside and the culprit was told to stand and pull his pants down. Rashied, who was sipping Castle from a quart bottle, threw a glass of beer over the boy's genitals. He was told to put his trousers back on. Rashied asked him why he had tried to rape his sister and the youth didn't have a satisfactory answer. Rashied strolled over to where he was sitting and suddenly the beer bottle whipped down with a loud snap on the youth's skull.

The bottle only broke after several blows, and by that time the whole gang had set on him, and the boy was squealing like an animal that realizes it's being slaughtered. While Toetie mopped up the puddle of beer on the floor the culprit was dragged outside next to one of the zigzag concrete staircases and beaten some more. The Hard Livings beat him so hard that beads of sweat were forming on their faces. Rashied held back, or he would have killed the boy.

As they jumped on his head and chest, and tried to break his arm, the boy just shrieked but did not resist. He even held his arm in place so they could jump on it, but no one seemed to be able to break the bone. After a sustained battering the boy got up, steadying himself against the wall. One of the Hard Livings high-kicked his head and he started screaming again. Finally a minibus taxi was hailed and told to take the boy, who was still on his feet, to the nearest clinic.

'Rashied is the power behind the Hard Livings,' says Rashad. 'People know he is a killer. Do you know what a psychopath is? Rashied is a psychopath, a mad dog. He feels nothing for people. All he wants is to be the leader.' There is no love lost between the brothers. Rashied sulks while Rashad winds him up with his buffoonery. But late at night the twins can be found conferring in the front room of Rashied's home.

Rashad likes to keep a token distance from the Hard Livings, although he works closely with Rashied. He will not set foot in Toetie's, the gang's headquarters in Aletta Court, for instance. He is seldom seen hanging out on the corner with the boys, preferring to spend time in his mobile shop.

Rashied leads from the front. He is always to be found on the corner, approachable, malevolent, twitching, laughing, never still. Rashied's presence, or the mere expectation of his arrival, creates a buzz in Aletta Court. He is always there, getting to know the youngsters on the block, sharing a joke, showing off his cruelty. In his more thoughtful moments Rashied claims the Hard Livings are not mere gangsters, but a political brotherhood, united by the creed of Hard Living. He is reluctant to be more precise. 'Everyone in South Africa is a Hard Living,' he says unblinkingly, 'except the Whites and the Indians.'

Rashied's personal authority is absolute. Although he cannot dictate to the gang if the majority spontaneously decide they disagree, only his twin Rashad can openly confront him and get away with it. 'I'm the only one who can argue with him,' he says. 'The others are too afraid. I'm the only one who can say to him you sit there and listen to me, you're wrong, this is what you should do. If I wasn't there Rashied would walk to his death.'

The twins complement each other perfectly. Rashied is charismatic, dynamic, vicious. Rashad, the elder by fifteen minutes, is cunning, practical, the Hard Livings' publicist and financier. 'Rashied and I play a big role. If we were not there many Hard Livings would die. They don't know the skills of warfare. People who fight against the Hard Livings are not fighting against the Hard Livings, they are fighting Rashied and Rashad!' he says proudly. 'Many drug merchants have put a price on Rashied's head. There's a lot of money at stake. When Rashied was shot, the papers reported that he was critically wounded. The drug lords had a party.'

Manenberg residents have mixed feelings about the gangsters. On the one hand, they rarely interfere with the residents, and provide protection and material support for the local community. On the other hand they are resented for their gangster ways and for giving the area a bad name.

'If something happens to Rashied,' says Hettie Bailey, a long-time resident of Aletta Court, 'the whole of Manenberg will go to his funeral. Some will say "It's good that he's gone." Others will say, "Who's going to look after us now?"'

The twins are almost forty years old. Both have flirted with the idea of retirement. 'People know us all over the country. We've got nothing to prove. I don't want power,' protests Rashad, flashing a gap-toothed grin. 'What I like is money, and my children. But Rashied can never retire. People won't leave him alone.' Rashad shrugs expressively. 'We have only a few years left to live. What difference does it make? There's no rest. This fighting will never end until we die.'

PART FIVE

A Painful Transition

35 Back to the Middle of Nowhere

In the middle of nowhere, on the border between Natal and Transvaal, is Charlestown, where the wrongs of South African history are being righted. Charlestown consists of a few houses scattered in long grass by the roadside, the Snowy Biltong store ('the best biltong in the country'), two graveyards, Trumps clothing factory and a drive-in cinema. Most of the White population – about sixty families – recently sold up and left. Then the Indian traders left. Now the Black families who bought their homes are also leaving. Every week Charlestown, a ghost town for the last twenty years, becomes ghostlier still, awaiting the arrival of its past. The first of several thousand Black families are due to return shortly to their rightful homes, in the middle of nowhere.

Charlestown is being generously restored to its former citizens. In 1993 President de Klerk personally sanctioned the return of their land to 8000 former citizens who were forcibly removed twenty years ago. Charlestown will be the second, and by far the largest, restitution of officially stolen land in South Africa.

The most popular show at the drive-in in recent years was an Afrikaans-language movie called *Hard Luck*. Whites flocked to see it from far and wide, creating the first traffic jam in Charlestown since 1896. They had to turn cars away. Now the drive-in is closed. The last show was *Single White Female*.

Behind the derelict screen in the drive-in lot, a green, startlingly empty landscape stretches far away into Northern Natal. Goods trains, laden with iron ore and coal, thunder distantly on the Durban–Joburg line, which skirts the main road on the edge of town. In the gravel streets of Charlestown the stillness is deep.

'This used to be a pensioners' town,' says Con Aveling, a sprightly Afrikaner in his late fifties. 'The old people can't take it any more. A family moved out just last week. They knew the Africans were coming.' Con keeps budgies in a chicken-wire aviary in the yard of his little blue house.

'There used to be 60 000 Blacks in the location,' he says (a vast exaggeration), pointing at the solitary church a few hundred metres from the edge of town. 'In the old days if you drove through Charlestown there was rubbish all over. They lived in shacks and mud huts with grass roofs.

It was a health risk. It was a disgrace.' He becomes suddenly engrossed in the budgies, saying nothing for a while. 'We don't know why they want to come back here. They'll have to travel to work in Newcastle. They say their ancestors lived here.' He raises his eyebrows sceptically. 'There are no jobs here. There are only memories.'

'It's a beautiful place, Charlestown,' recalls Ephraim Zwane, who can still remember his old address. A surveyor's map on the wall of his house in Osizweni, 50 kilometres from Charlestown, shows the several hundred plots which have been restored to their original owners. Each Black Charlestonian family will go back to the very same plot from which they were forcibly removed.

Zwane, the vice-chairman of a committee of former Charlestown landowners, intends to be the first to rebuild his house on one of the acre plots. He dreams of the day when the old community of Charlestown will be reconstituted. 'We were brothers then. That's why we want to go and live together again,' he says earnestly. 'We'll try to get people to build factories nearby. We need jobs. We've told the White people we need them. We can't chase them away.'

'We are down to sixteen White families,' says Con cheerfully. 'Sixty thousand people are moving into an area where there is no work and nothing to eat or drink. They'll steal and slaughter everything in sight.' He pauses, taking a deep breath. 'We've dug another borehole, at a cost of 38 000 rand. There will never be enough water in Charlestown. But we're working on it.'

Six years ago Con retired to Charlestown from his farm in Northern Natal. 'I got up at four thirty every morning for thirty-nine years. That was enough.' After backwatering for five peaceful but dull years he took a job as the manager of the Development Services Board in Charlestown. 'It was sentiment and I needed a job. I grew up with these people. Black people don't worry me. I believe we can all live happily ever after.'

'For ever more!' quips Elsie from the kitchen. Elsie is Con's girlfriend. She works at Snowy Biltong.

Con's job is to prepare Charlestown for the imminent surge of returnees from Osizweni and other KwaZulu townships. He and his 'gang of ten' build new roads, clean the sewers, dig boreholes and cut the grass. 'I suppose we'll give them the same service as everyone else,' he grumbles, suddenly tired and cynical. 'Maybe they'll become human beings one day. I don't know. You can take the *kaffer* out of the bush but you can't take the bush out of the *kaffer*,' he intones. 'It's a challenge,' says Con. 'And I've never said no to a challenge. It will be history once it happens.'

From the hill behind the town you can see the flattish, barren landscape of the Eastern Transvaal, stretching towards Volksrust. In the opposite direction, to the south-east, lie the first swelling, verdant hills of Natal. Balls of bright white cloud blowing in a blue sky trail pools of dark shadow on the bright green slopes. The hilltop is the site of Charlestown's two graveyards.

In the Black graveyard the grass grows knee-high. Every few years relatives of the dead travel the 50 kilometres from the KwaZulu township of Osizweni to clear the weeds. 'We were born in Charlestown, our forefathers' graves are there,' says Ephraim Zwane. 'They are alone without us.'

On Mayday 1991 the former landowners of Charlestown, tired of waiting, put their belongings in trucks and went to reoccupy the land. They were quickly removed by a large contingent of police. 'People want to move right now,' says Zwane. 'People are very emotional.'

'We're trying hard to get the better ones to move back,' explains Con. 'We're giving them the land for free so long as they don't squat. We want to make them into mini-farmers. You get the decent type, taxi-owners etc. Then you get the lower type from the farms and villages. They get drunk on Fridays,' says Con. 'They beat their drums and the dogs bark. You can't sleep. The lower-class Black will shit outside your gate and you'll have to clear it up. And they'll laugh at you,' he adds.

Next to the Black graveyard is the graveyard for Whites, a series of pristine marble headstones with quaintly worded inscriptions. The largest monument is a stone commemorating the six policemen shot dead by Swart in 1916. Swart was a wealthy Afrikaner farmer who had a disagreement with his in-laws one morning, and tried to shoot his mother-in-law. When the local police force arrived he shot them instead. Then he shot his mother-in-law and his horse, before turning the gun on himself. Swart could not be buried in the cemetery. His grave lies in town.

'If God wanted us to mix he would have made us the same colour. We're not allowed to be proud of our heritage. We've got to become one colour,' moans Con. 'They were happy when we ruled and gave them jobs. Now it's give them a nice White palace to live in but no food. In twenty years' time this country of ours is going to be another fucking desert.' In the next room Elsie shakes her head sadly. 'What's going to become of this country I don't know,' says Con. 'Same as the rest of Africa, I would imagine. Charlestown will become a Black town. This will be a Black country and if they don't like you they'll cut your throat and get a medal for it!' Con looks suddenly gaunt and tired, an old man in a deserted town. 'I mustn't talk about these things,' he says quietly, 'because it upsets me.'

Although it's difficult to believe now, Charlestown was once a boom town. In 1890 construction of the Durban–Johannesburg railroad pushed rapidly north and west from Durban Harbour. When the railroad reached the Transvaal border, it stopped. The Transvaal was an Afrikaner republic. Natal was part of the British Cape Colony. President Kruger of the Transvaal said the Colony's railway could not enter the Transvaal until the

Transvaal's own eastern railroad was complete. So the Natal Government Railways line ended abruptly at the Transvaal border. Goods were loaded onto ox carts for the onward journey to the Reef. At the rail head a boom town was born, a town of freight handlers and shipping agents, bars, hotels and brothels. The boom lasted for five years until permission was finally given to extend the line all the way to Johannesburg. Charlestown began to die, although it was still an important railroad town.

The blow which finished Charlestown came after the Boer War in 1910, when the Act of Union merged the two provinces of the Cape Colony with the two Afrikaner republics, to form the Union of South Africa. Natal Government Railways had a workshop for its rolling stock in Charlestown. The Dutch South African Railway Company also had a workshop, 7 kilometres from Charlestown in Volksrust. One of them had to close. Charlestown closed with it. When only fourteen White families were left in Charlestown, the local butcher, a Mr Higgins, took action. If the place became a ghost town, he for one would be ruined. Higgins began to persuade Africans to buy land in Charlestown. More than 100 properties were sold to Black South Africans and the town's fortunes revived.

By 1954, however, Charlestown's Black population was scheduled for removal. Charlestown had been identified as a 'black spot', a place where Blacks owned freehold land outside their allotted 'homeland'. Forced removals began in the 1960s and by 1978 the Black town was empty, ready for the bulldozers. Only the Catholic church remained, a tribute to the piety of apartheid's bureaucrats, who, when breaking the hearts of millions of uprooted people, always took care to leave their churches standing.

'There's one thing I can tell you about the Blacks,' says Con. 'They think it's easy. You buy a house, then your skin's white. But they don't think about all the services you have to pay for. They don't care. The first thing to go is the lights. When the water goes we move them out. Because you can't live without water.'

Black families have already moved into twenty-odd houses in Charlestown, although they were not from amongst the original townspeople expelled to KwaZulu. 'Ninety-four per cent of the Blacks who come to town move out within three years. They can't make the grade,' says Con impatiently. 'They can't live in our type of houses. They're cold and the walls are too high. They prefer a cosy little shack. It's got nothing to do with wealth. It's what they're used to.'

Con elaborates. 'You get the lower-class Black and the lower-class White. The high-class Black is much better than the low-class White.' Not content with this, he adds: 'I believe there are more good Blacks than good Whites. I used to play with them and swim naked in the river. But at night he goes home to his room and you don't mix socially.'

Con remembers the days when South African towns were 'White by night' and no one was allowed in towns after the ten o'clock siren. 'That's all disappeared,' he sighs. 'If they come back properly, it'll be a hell of a boost. They'll put Charlestown back on the map. But will they do it that way?'

The Afrikaner barflies of Volksrust don't think so. Not very much happens in Volksrust, 7 kilometres from Charlestown. Volksrust won the contest against Charlestown to house the region's railway workshops. But as the goods trains became faster it was discovered that the bend in the line at Volksrust was too sharp for the heavy goods trains. So Volksrust was bypassed and became a ghost town like its neighbour.

The social hub of Volksrust is the Transvaal Hotel. The Transvaal Hotel smells of rose air-freshener, an overpoweringly sweet odour which wafts through the creaky corridors, past reception where louche barefoot men buy liquor on Sunday morning, to the empty dining room with its red plastic-upholstered chairs and soiled net curtains.

On a Saturday the Transvaal Hotel is the only place to be in a town where, as someone in the bar so aptly said, they roll up the streets at seven o'clock and turn out the lights. Bulky White men sit round three sides of the bar. The only Black faces to be seen are those of the two barmen.

The return of Black families to Charlestown is one topic which you do not raise in this bar. The drinkers here make Con Aveling sound like a Trotskyite. The merest mention of Charlestown draws drop-dead looks. 'The *kaffers* aren't coming back,' says Vince, ex-Rhodesian, ex-bounty-hunter, ex-hangman. 'End of story. Don't ask about Charlestown or you'll come short, my friend.'

Two hefty German men with slicked-down blond hair, one of them nursing a black eye, sulk over their beers. A beefy middle-aged man in tight shorts walks into the bar carrying a guitar and harmonica, drawing heavy-lidded, sultry looks from the locals. He perches on a bar stool, adjusts his shorts, and strums some *boeremusik*, a series of dismal, schmaltzy Afrikaner folk tunes. A couple of the men start to sing but forget the words.

'You see that *kaffer*?' says Vince to George in his tobacco voice, pointing at the barman. 'I used to shoot *kaffers* like that for a couple of shillings apiece, in my bounty-hunter days.' The barman, his face inches away from Vince's stabbing finger, lights up a cigarette and takes refuge behind a faraway look. The other barman redoubles his smarmy, mockingly obsequious manner which the locals adore. An older man begins to rave like a walrus, steadying himself on the bar.

Saturday night in Volksrust continues at the local *skouterrain*, or showground, where the locals have their disco in a corrugated-iron hangar with concrete floors. The *boeremusik* is loud and distorted. Fluorescent lights high in the roof project a stark white glare over the tables round the edge of the hangar. The revellers of Volksrust devour bright red puffy snacks, drink Coke and tell jokes about *kaffers*. You can feel the bigotry welling up inside them, lifting them out of their misery.

The disco begins, someone switches the bright lights off to get people dancing. Couples take the floor, archly formal, full of quaint olde-worlde etiquette. The hall is almost empty; the dancers are spread out in the semi-darkness, bobbing awkwardly to the distorted sounds. Obese old women gyrate barefoot on the concrete floor, their enlarged, misshapen shadows cavorting on the back wall of the hangar. It's Saturday night in Volksrust, a White town near the middle of nowhere.

36 A Broken People

'White supermarket cashiers are being replaced by Black women,' says Kleintjie Perreira. 'They crochet baby clothes which don't sell. White women are working as maids,' she continues, in the manner of someone describing some awful abuse of human rights.

Kleintjie, a tall, handsome woman with short yellow hair, set up 'Werk en Oorleef' ('Work and Survive') in September 1985. 'Everybody said it would be three months,' she says. 'Now it's eight years.' Kleintjie took over a building in a downmarket eastern suburb of Pretoria, from where she could hand out emergency relief to the growing number of unemployed Whites in the capital. Families turn up in battered cars to collect bags of cracked maize, toothpaste, low-fat spread, and old clothes.

Kleintjie says White poverty started in 1985 with bankruptcies in the building trade. 'Retrenchment', (South African for redundancy) has begun to hit the White working class. 'The retrenched are reticent, out of pride,' explains Kleintjie. 'Your neighbour will have a *braai* [barbecue] and throw the leftover meat to his dog. Your children are hungry and you can see the meat but you won't ask for a piece out of pride.'

On the west side of Pretoria, White down-and-outs shelter in the house of a good Samaritan. They sit in the back garden smoking roll-ups and complaining bitterly. 'There is work available,' says Johann, a former truck driver. 'But who's getting the jobs? The non-Europeans are cheaper labour. You can hire two Black drivers for the cost of one White.' He shakes his head ruefully.

Johnny complains that ten years ago work was easy to get. 'Now it's

impossible,' he says. 'The ads in the newspapers all ask for dynamic people.'
He looks insulted. Johann and Ronnie grunt in sympathy. Significantly,
all three describe themselves as middle class, even though they are
unskilled, uneducated, unmotivated and destitute. In South Africa the idea
of a White person occupying the bottom rung of the social ladder is
unfamiliar.

'Black people have said to me, "You White bastard, now we're taking
the country back!"' says Ronnie.

'The law protects them not us,' says Johnny.

'It all boils down to the new South Africa,' says Ronnie. 'Blacks get more
rights than Whites. Our forefathers fought for this country. De Klerk gave
the country away.'

Johann agrees. 'We Europeans . . . our forefathers built this country, not
the Blacks.'

Says Ronnie: 'Fifty years ago the country was different. Afrikaners
would help each other. Now it's every man for himself.'

Someone else grumbles: 'This whole country is upside down.' The other
men murmur in agreement.

In 1929 researchers sponsored by the Carnegie Corporation in New York
drove round South Africa trying to discover why there were so many poor
Whites in the country. They found that nearly a fifth of Whites were jobless
paupers. The majority of these were Afrikaners. The causes of Afrikaner
poverty included large numbers of farmers leaving the land because of
drought, cattle plagues, competition from commercial farmers and the
British policy of burning farms in the Boer war; a high birth rate; and a
lack of the kind of skills which foreign and English-speaking workers could
offer. There was an additional factor: an unwillingness to do manual labour
('*kaffer* work').

At the turn of the century, after the Boer War, most of the skilled
workers, the businessmen, professionals, entrepreneurs and administrators
in South Africa's towns and cities were of British origin, or English-
speakers. Afrikaners were illiterate *boers* (farmers), strangers to the cities
and factories. They formed a new, disgruntled underclass in the city slums,
rubbing shoulders with the Black poor, who had been their slaves. The poor
Afrikaner, to put it bluntly, was not economically useful: he had no skills,
and would not do manual work cheaply. But unlike Blacks, Afrikaners had
the vote.

Between the two World Wars the Afrikaner was uplifted by the state,
which created unskilled jobs in which he could benefit from an artificially
high wage. Most of these jobs were in nationalized industries: steel,
electricity, railways. To protect White workers from competition, new laws
were made which banned Blacks from applying for skilled jobs. To keep
poor Whites on the land, new laws were made which moved Black peasants

and farmers off the land, and prevented them from competing with White farmers.

When the National Party came to power in 1948 the process continued. Massive new bureaucracies were created to administer apartheid, which was in itself designed to promote the welfare of the Afrikaner. Government officials who did not speak Afrikaans were purged. For Afrikaners, no matter how badly qualified, it was 'jobs for the boys' on a vast scale. Government jobs, whether in the army, the police, or the civil service; and jobs in the nationalized industries and corporations – Eskom, Iscor, Telkom, Spoornet, IDC, Sanlam – were the almost exclusive domain of Afrikaners. With these protected jobs went generous housing subsidies, fringe benefits, cars, pensions, health care, education, a whole system of 'affirmative action' for Afrikaners. By the early 1980s most Afrikaners were white-collar workers. White poverty had been eradicated.

In the mid-eighties economic decline set in, and cracks appeared in the institutions of Pretoria's totalitarian state. Attempts to recruit selected Black South Africans as partners in apartheid sparked a sustained popular rebellion. Black unions grew powerful. It became clear that the White government's days were numbered. Poor Whites appeared once more on the streets of Pretoria and Johannesburg and in the soup queues, like in the 1930s. Despondent civil servants began routinely to pillage the government's coffers. The massive scale of corruption in the civil service was exposed in a series of scandals in the early 1990s. Blue–collar workers took refuge in right-wing politics.

'We're a broken people,' says Dirk, tinkering with his Yamaha in the back yard of his home in Danville, a downmarket suburb of Pretoria. 'The country went down the drain after they let Nelson Mandela out of prison. It doesn't matter who's in power now.'

Dirk, a production manager in a local factory, complains about the high rent on his home. Some Whites, he says, have moved to a Black township outside Pretoria. There you can buy a four-bedroom house for 18 000 rand, five times less than in a White area.

Would Dirk consider moving to a Black township? He chuckles. 'Nie by *kaffers* nie, man! A White man can't live with *kaffers*. I'd wake up in the morning with my throat cut.'

'People said to us, you can't go to Mabopane, they'll kill you!' Susan Daniell's blue eyes fill with tears outside her home in Morula View, a new housing estate in the Black township of Mabopane. 'They've been wonderful to us,' she says over and over again, smiling through her tears. 'The Whites have got to learn, there is no social security. The Blacks are so supportive. They look after each other. Sometimes I wish I was Black,' she says, wiping her eyes.

Susan lives in one of the new matchbox houses on a dusty plot

30 kilometres from Pretoria. Mabopane is one of the many small chunks of the Tswana 'homeland', Bophuthatswana. Susan, who arrived in South Africa from Manchester in England when she was twelve, is a former receptionist, in her early forties with two young daughters, Vanessa and Rona. They are the only White children in the local school. 'The kids in the school were wonderful,' smiles Susan. 'In a White school kids eat their own lunches. Here they put all the food on the table and share it.'

Susan's husband Roy, whose business in Cape Town went bust after he 'made mistakes', works for the Bophuthatswana government. They arrived in Morula View with nothing, and were lent the house by a policeman friend of Roy's. 'Neighbours brought curtains, paid for the children's transport, textbooks. They've helped us so much, even with clothes, these people.' Susan marvels. 'If you think of all the White man has done to them . . . ' she says, at a loss for words. 'They are more . . . forgiving, more adaptable.'

On a bare hill near Pretoria stands a prodigious brown granite bunker. It is reached by way of several flights of broad stone steps, past notices warning that decent clothing must be worn at all times. The interior of the Voortrekker Monument is decked in streaky pinkish-greyish-yellowy South African marble. The decor is very solemn. The space is high and echoey, bare except for a kiosk selling postcards, a Greek-style bas-relief frieze on the walls and a circular hole in the centre of the room. The hole affords a view of a large stone tomb on the level below, bearing the inscription '*Ons vir jou, Suid Afrika*' ('We are for you, South Africa'). On the same day every summer a shaft of sunlight comes through a hole in the roof and illuminates the inscription.

The frieze covers the four walls of the chamber, a heroic narrative in creamy Italian marble, chiselled in the virile, wholesome style shared by unpleasant dictatorial regimes all over the world. This frieze, which has shaped the perceptions of tens of thousands of South African school-children, Black and White, celebrates a series of historic encounters between the different ethnic groups of South Africa.

On the left as you walk in, Africans massacre Boers, then Boers slaughter Africans. On the central panel, Boers are butchered by Africans, who proceed to butcher some more Boers. Then, on the right-hand panels, a young boy and a group of bonneted women play cameo roles, directly or indirectly participating in killing Africans, as a prelude to a really massive liquidation of a large number of Africans. In the last act, Africans slaughter one another with spears. According to the original guidebook to the Voortrekker Monument, the sculpted frieze symbolizes 'the Afrikaner's proprietary right to South Africa'.

Parrow Civic Hall in Cape Town, May 1993. The hall is packed. A small but rowdy group of Coloured 'comrades' wave black, green and gold flags, chanting 'La la la ANC!' The burgers of conservative Parrow, those who have summoned up the courage, the conviction or the curiosity to attend this first ever ANC meeting in a White suburb, huddle together in the corner of the hall, as far away from the chanting, stomping comrades as possible. There is a call for silence from the stage, and the pa system begins to play 'Nkosi Sikelela iAfrika', the haunting anthem of Black South Africa. This time, however, the words are in Afrikaans, and photocopies of an Afrikaans translation of the lyrics are passed round the hall. After one false start, the audience launches into the anthem, although the Whites from Parrow barely move their lips.

As the hymn dies away one of the speakers sitting in a row on the stage wipes a tear from his eye. A tall, dapper man in his thirties with neatly combed fair hair, he looks too fragile to be a politico. Wilhelm Verwoerd is the grandson of Hendrik Verwoerd, the architect of apartheid. He wears in his buttonhole an outsize posy in ANC colours.

When Wilhelm stands to address the audience he is greeted with enthusiastic shouts of 'Viva!' In a voice choked with emotion he begins, in Afrikaans: 'Ladies, gentlemen. Comrades . . . ' He pauses, fighting back the tears. He looks like a choirboy, a grown-up Little Lord Fauntleroy, handsome, intense, neatly dressed in a matching purple shirt and tie. He pleads with the audience to see the right wing not as traitors but as political opponents. His speech is an attempt to explain as well as a confession. 'A healthy form of group identity,' he says, referring to Afrikaner nationalism, 'turned into a collective form of selfishness.' The audience is rapt. Here is the man's grandson in person, saying he is sorry.

'What happened was not a policy experiment that failed. It was an injustice. That imposes a responsibility on those who are in power, especially Afrikaners,' announces Verwoerd. He goes on to talk about his grandfather's evil deeds. 'I get cold shivers,' he admits, 'when people talk about forced removals.' His speech is greeted with a thunderous standing ovation. Verwoerd takes his seat next to Carl Niehaus, the ANC's national spokesman, also an Afrikaner. They exchange warm looks. The Afrikaners of Parrow, herding together for safety at the back of the hall, look sceptical.

37 Them

'In all fairness apartheid was wrong morally. But materially speaking it was lovely,' explains Marianne, slurping the froth on her first cappuccino of the morning. 'It was the ideal situation for a White, let's face it. Never any backchat, the servants did everything for you.'

Marianne and Maura got to Stephanie's early this Saturday, leaving plenty of time for a luxuriating, gossipy breakfast before facing the shops in this fashionable Johannesburg mall. The scrambled egg with smoked salmon at Stephanie's is to die for. And the cappuccino is almost as good as Cafe Brazil's in Rosebank. That's why there is a queue here from ten o'clock onwards, while the other cafés in the mall are still half empty.

Marianne and Maura are in their late thirties – well-heeled, modern professional women. Marianne sells office furniture in Johannesburg. She is an Afrikaner. Her platinum blonde hair is short, her neat lips startlingly red against a pale complexion. She is looking for a husband. This time, she laughs, it's not because she wants children. This time she wants a husband with a foreign passport so she can leave the country. Given the chance she would leave tomorrow. 'All the Northern Suburbs people are leaving. The Jews are leaving, and when the Jews leave you know things are bad,' she says, with one of her knowing looks.

In March 1992, South African Whites were asked in a referendum whether they agreed with President de Klerk's programme of reforms leading to a New South Africa. Marianne consulted her conscience and voted 'yes'. 'They have to be upgraded,' she says. 'But it didn't come from the heart.'

'They' are the Black South Africans. It's curious, but South African Whites refer to their Black compatriots as 'them'. 'Black' or 'African' just doesn't slip off the tongue very easily. The word that comes naturally is '*kaffer*'. But '*kaffer*' is no longer acceptable in public. Especially not at Stephanie's.

Dutch-born Maura, a graphic designer, also voted 'yes' in the referendum. 'From a moral point of view you have to allow them certain things,' she says earnestly. 'But when it affects you personally . . . ' She shrugs.

'Isn't the bottom line our lifestyle?' asks Marianne.

Maura nods, blushing ever so slightly.

At Stephanie's you can sit inside, with the muted jazz and the wall mirrors, or if you want to be seen, there is a neat enclosure with a dozen tables right in the middle of the concourse. Either way you have to queue, but that's part of the enjoyment.

'We have a different way of life. You can build them a house and the first thing they will do is make a fire in the middle of the living room floor. It's a different culture altogether,' muses Maura. 'My mother came from Holland and built her maid a special room. She refused to let her live in that horrible kennel they had out the back. She sent her to sewing and cookery classes. But she's never been able to hang on to a maid. They just want more and more. Now the guy across the road, he used to beat his servants. He treated them like dogs. They stayed for years.'

Marianne nods. 'They understand authority.'

Maura drove into Alexandra township one day with a Canadian friend. Her most vivid impression, as they bounced down the rutted dirt streets, was the piles of smouldering rubbish. 'If you give them a dustbin to put trash in they won't use it. That's how they've been conditioned,' she explains.

'In the townships they don't have gardens,' she reveals. 'There's no greenery. It's so stark. Every South African [i.e. White] family, however poor, has a garden. But they have no interest in gardening, I've noticed that about Blacks in general. They love their music and their singing and their rhythm.'

Marianne shudders. 'No person in their right mind would go to a township.' She admits she is really quite curious, but would only go into a township in an armoured vehicle under police escort.

'They don't understand straight lines,' resumes Maura. 'For instance I showed my maid how to arrange the dining room chairs in straight lines around the table. When I came back they were all skew.' She pauses, searching for something to redeem their shortcomings. She finds it and gushes: 'They have that empathy. When you hurt yourself they say, "Sorry, madam." They will cry and weep with you when somebody dies. They will do that for each other. But then they will kill each other for the slightest thing. Life to them is not worth the same as it is to us.'

'I would actually like to do a study,' ponders Marianne. 'The darker the skin, the more violent the nation . . . '

'The African nation was here first. There's no reason why we can't live in peace,' recites Maura. 'It's going to take a long time, that's all.'

There are no loud clothes at Stephanie's. Instead there are intelligent, well-bred, alert faces. Clothes and behaviour are carefully tuned. You mustn't look like a rich complacent White. Self-assured, sophisticated money – adorned with the merest hint of a social conscience – at ease around the marble-topped tables, feigning lack of interest in one another's new garments and partners. Black waiters move unseen with trays of cappuccino, or Swiss-style muesli for those who ordered the health breakfast.

Maura sighs. 'It started when Mandela was released. Suddenly everybody started marching. You had marches for freedom, then a teachers' march, then an Inkatha march.'

Marianne shakes her head, laughing. 'Mandela came out in February 1990. The joke was: Have you seen the new ANC calendar? January, February, March, March, March . . . '

Maura tells another Northern Suburbs joke: 'Why is Miss South Africa Black, and the two princesses [runners-up] White? In case there's a stayaway.' Guffaw! 'Two more cappuccinos, please, waiter.'

'We used to pay our servants during stayaways. We felt sorry for them. They were being forced, they or their families would be killed if they went to work. But now 50 per cent are taking the day off. In one month we had four stayaways. Now we take a hard line. If you don't come to work, you don't get paid,' says Marianne, tapping the marble table with her fingernail extensions for emphasis.

'Their whole attitude changed when Mandela came out. I remember one of the labourers at work told me his wife would get my job and he would have the boss's job with the Mercedes,' says Maura. 'Then one of my friends who lives in Wendywood said she saw a Black man standing outside staring at her house. She asked him what he wanted. He said, "No, I'm just looking at the house. It has been allocated to me. When we're in power I will live in this house." I mean, how do you explain that it won't work out like that?' Maura rolls her eyes to the ceiling and sips the foam off the top of her second cappuccino of the morning.

'It can only end up in a civil war. We're going to have another Sarajevo,' says Marianne, inspecting the dregs of her third cappuccino. 'Much as the Zulu has been the warrior. Now MK [the ANC's military wing] is coming in.'

'I don't know much about politics,' says Maura wearily.

'Nelson Mandela is a puppet,' Marianne flares up. 'He's being controlled from outside the country. Cuba or Libya. That's where all the terrorism starts from. And when it comes to corruption you can't beat a Black government. Look at the rest of Africa.'

'I think people should respect each other whatever the race, colour or creed,' counters Maura weakly. Then, in a sudden moment of defeat: 'By sheer mass of numbers, we don't stand a chance.'

38 The Brotherhood of Persons

The spectacular failure of community development in Phola Park in 1992 cast a shadow over the bright vistas which community development consultants had foreseen for the new South Africa. At the height of apartheid, a small number of dedicated, highly-qualified White English-speaking liberals turned down lucrative careers and committed themselves to the betterment of the poorest sections of South African society, choosing to undermine apartheid through progressive development. Now the new South Africa confronted them, not with the triumph of reason, but with unpleasant new dilemmas.

'I live in two strange worlds,' says one of South Africa's leading community development consultants, a staunchly liberal White English-speaker who has toiled in the squatter camps around Johannesburg almost daily for the last decade. He knows the shanty towns intimately and speaks fluent Zulu and Xhosa. He prefers not to be named. South Africa does not forgive heretics. He is simply the Disillusioned Liberal:

> I live in the world of Whites who really want to make the new South Africa work, sincerely and genuinely. Full of good will. They are epitomized by the parents at my little son's primary school. Most of them are confronting the new South Africa for the very first time. Up to now they were very comfortable not being interested in politics, which many White South Africans aren't. But now that they have to be they are coming up full of good will.

The Disillusioned Liberal continues wearily. 'There they are with these . . . these wonderful notions that I've had all my life about inherent equality, the perceptions that liberals always have that everybody behaves exactly like them, but they just have a different skin colour.' He looks bewildered. 'And I can't disillusion them, otherwise we'll never get progress. But when you assume a whole lot of things from your own cultural bias and background, and increasingly find out that none of those assumptions are valid, and that all of our core values may not be replicated in any way . . . ' The Disillusioned Liberal pauses, looking a touch startled. 'That is the devastating moment for liberals. It's an absolutely devastating moment. And you can't . . . no one can turn back. I mean, it's the most shattering moment, because you march off on this march, full of good will, full of "brotherhood of persons". Then you suddenly find . . . ' His voice tails off into silence.

The Disillusioned Liberal was raised in a well-to-do Johannesburg household committed to liberal values. His parents had fled Nazi Europe before the Second World War to start a new life in South Africa. Early in life the Disillusioned Liberal devoted himself to bettering the living conditions of Black South Africans. He drove to the townships every day, deep into Soweto, Sebokeng and Alexandra. He was arrested and given a jail sentence for being in the townships without a pass. 'I got into this work to try and bring development. I said, we've got to engage, we've actually got to engage, right now,' he remembers. 'I really believed this. Then I started seeing exactly what it was going to mean.' Almost imperceptibly, disillusionment began to set in.

'It's incremental. It's not a road to Damascus thing,' explains the Disillusioned Liberal. 'It's an accumulation of meetings, of processes, of events. You keep pushing stereotypes out of your head. You say, "I refuse to acknowledge this. You can't generalize from a specific instance." Because you know you can't do that as a liberal. Because that's racist. One thing we learn to do is we learn to lie to ourselves helluva well.' He hesitates. 'But what I do know is that cultural differences come into play very, very profoundly. And the cultural differences are so profound in South Africa that to create a non-racial functioning society would be nothing short of a miracle.'

The end of apartheid, ironically, ushered in changes which threaten the very basis of community development: the freedom of consultants and organizers to move around the townships and talk to people about their needs.

'In the eighties I was involved in protest work about the treatment of squatters,' says the Disillusioned Liberal:

I was arrested and got my criminal record, under the act which says you're not allowed in the townships without a permit. They couldn't keep me out. I refused to get a permit. I was there every morning. I drove round with impunity and never felt threatened. Now I can't go to the townships because people are saying "One Settler, One Bullet!" Before, in the old South Africa, I always used to go to the townships and the worst I faced was three months in jail. Now what you're likely to face is . . .

His voice trails off once more.

He goes on to describe a peace march through one of the townships in the aftermath of a series of racial attacks:

There must have been about thirty Whites and about 1500 Blacks.

Ninety-nine per cent of the township supported us. It was wonderful. They came out with peace signs. But on the corners you could see a couple of youths shaking their heads and giving you the downward peace sign, as if to say "We're not interested." And when push comes to shove the 99 per cent don't come out and help you. They're scared too. They're dead scared.

The Disillusioned Liberal shrugs helplessly, determined to understand, to see things in context:

If you think back to Sharpeville in 1960, when sixty-nine people died, it traumatized the country for ten years. It changed South Africa's ethos, its politics, for ten years. Now it's a weekly occurrence. At least sixty people are killed a week in South Africa. That just shows you where we are . . .

What we don't have in South Africa is any ethos that you get legitimacy and support by what you can deliver, by way of results. In South Africa we still have the idea that you get legitimacy and support by the extent to which you can prevent any others from organizing on your turf. And it's a crucial distinction. There is that tremendous intolerance, even of totally legitimate organizations. It wasn't only the National Party that thought territorially, everyone thinks territorially in SA . . . You want to know what a shock *that* is for a liberal? You wanna know how long it takes you to understand that part of your own country? Because Parktown doesn't work like that. Rosebank doesn't work like that . . .

The Disillusioned Liberal stops, suddenly self-conscious. 'I feel like I'm talking to my therapist.'

39 Baas Potgieter

The Independent Development Trust money was still there – 21 million rand earmarked for Phola Park waiting in a bank account. No one would touch it. To be involved with development in Phola Park was the kiss of death. Prince and other Black community leaders had paid for it with their lives. Legions of English-speaking liberals, overflowing with progressive ideas, had failed to improve squatters' lives, no matter how hard they workshopped. The only man who eventually made an impact in Phola Park was a shrewd Afrikaner entrepreneur.

The Corobrick-Briti factory, which lay between Phola Park and the Old Vereeneging Road, shut down shortly after the war broke out. The management had seen Kalanyoni hostel being demolished brick by brick and figured it was only a matter if time before it happened to them. The factory, which made terracotta mezzanine floor tiles, was abandoned.

Twenty-seven days before the Corobrick-Briti plant was due to be demolished Jurie Potgieter bought the plant, with all the machinery and twenty-five years' supply of clay in the quarry on the factory site. Next to the factory was Phola Park, with 45 000 unemployed people.

Potgieter grew up on a farm in the Western Transvaal. The family was poor and Jurie and his six brothers used to ride the 15 miles to school on a single bicycle. ('It's possible,' he insists. 'You've just got to know how.')

Potgieter's father, who dreamed of getting into big business, quite literally sank all his money into an ambitious venture, building a large industrial park comprising 150 stands. The local (English-speaking) goldmining conglomerate began to feel that its monopoly of business in the area was under threat. 'The mines pumped all their underground water onto our land,' says Jurie grimly. 'We got up the next morning and there was nothing left. The industrial park had sunk into the ground. Our dream to be wealthy was gone. Our father called us together and said, "I can't do any more, the system has beaten us. Go out and practise what I've taught you."'

Potgieter went on to make a fortune marketing peanuts all over Africa. 'I've got my own aeroplane. If I want to go to Zambia I just take my own plane. I've been working in Africa for eighteen years,' says Potgieter. Before buying the factory he went to get the ANC's blessing. 'I went straight to the top leadership,' he remembers. 'I said to them, OK, I will buy the factory, I will retrench all the people, then I will only employ young people from Phola Park, with the idea to train them for the new South Africa, for the future.' The ANC thought it was a nice idea.

The name of the factory was changed to plain 'Briti'. Potgieter decided there was a market for terracotta roof and floor tiles with a hand-made finish. He sacked the Corobrick-Briti workforce, retaining only seven of the most experienced workers, whom he put in charge of recruitment. There were less than 200 vacancies. Nine thousand applicants turned up from Phola Park.

'I went through hell with those guys,' says Potgieter, a corpulent man with a florid complexion and a penchant for paisley ties. 'Some of them had never worked before. I started with time and motion studies, which they knew nothing about. Every month I would have them there when we paid accounts so that they knew exactly what we were paying. They have this perception about businessmen that we make the money and they do the work.'

In his paternalistic way, Potgieter began to educate his workforce about business. Workshops and working groups were not for him. He wasn't interested in what 'the community' thought they wanted. Potgieter talked apples and oranges:

'Look here,' I said to them. 'This electricity bill is 50 000 rand a month.'

Yes, but that's nothing, you just write out a cheque.

I said, 'Fine, let me explain to you. Do you know what is 50 000 rand? You know how much it is?'

Uh, 50 000 rand.

I said, 'No, let me explain to you. You all play soccer?'

Yeeees.

'You know the soccer stadium in Joburg?'

Yeeees.

'If you go to the soccer stadium, is it easy to get in? Is there a lot of people there?'

No, it's very difficult. There is a lot of people there.

'So at the end of the day,' I said to them, 'if we close all the gates and then we open one gate to let them out, how long will it take those people to get out?'

Two days.

'Ok, and if we now get a rand from each and everybody, will we have a lot of money?'

Whew, I will never work in my life again!

I said, 'Right, now if we put a drum there, and everyone gives us 1 rand, after two days that will be enough for us to pay our electricity bill.'

That's the only way they understand it . . . You must tell them over and over. Even if they're educated you must use their language. You have to talk about goats, trees, children. It's the only way they understand.

Potgieter was surprised to find the men busy with a forklift truck in the yard the next day. They were removing stoves from the houses on the factory premises where some of the men stayed. The stoves were usually left on all night to heat the rooms. The men had decided that, since no one in Phola Park had stoves, and the electricity bill was too high, they should not have stoves either. 'That was their contribution,' beams Potgieter. 'Unbelievable!'

Potgieter shrewdly left the day-to-day management of the factory in the hands of the workers themselves. 'It works 100 per cent,' he says:

The one thing they know that's very important is that if you don't have a factory you don't have food. You won't have a house. You won't be able to buy a car or send your children to school. This is what I'm hammering on every day. I say to them, 'There's no need for me to employ White people to look after you, you have to do your own thing. You know exactly what to do. You know how a factory works!' All Blacks know exactly how a factory works because they are there, in the workplace. Whites sit in offices. 'You solve the problem,' I tell my workers. 'I'm not going to tell you.'

The workers from Phola Park were placed in charge of hiring and firing employees. 'They are very strict,' insists Potgieter. 'They come to me and say, "Sorry, this guy didn't turn up." or "Sorry, we had to fire this guy. We have people in the factory who don't give their full support. You will close the factory, then we won't have jobs."'

One Saturday morning Potgieter was summoned to the factory urgently. Three of the night shift workers had been badly beaten up. 'I asked them why' says Potgieter. 'Why they looked like this. I said, "We have to go to the police station and make a case." They said no.'

It transpired that one of the men had worked for three hours at the kilns, then left. One had not turned up. The remaining worker had fallen asleep. When the day shift arrived at the factory on an inspection round during the night they found the kilns unattended. The culprits were found and thrashed. 'I said, "That's not the way you do it!" They said to me, "Yes, but you must remember, *baas* Potgieter, if we lose this factory because of this, then our children are going to die." Now this is the way they operate!' exclaims Potgieter enthusiastically.

Potgieter opened the factory shortly before the Great War, when the men of Phola Park marched with the Xhosa police against Mshayazafe hostel. From the top of the factory chimney he watched Zulu raiders attack the camp:

They used to do it with spears but now they're using the AK. Both sides use these cowskins, about half a metre square. You can't shoot through that. They lie underneath it and they're invisible. You can't see them. They come in very low, very early in the morning. When they start shooting all you see is the smoke. I couldn't believe it! But if you go into history that's the way they used to fight. And if you shoot at them, they are so low that the bullet will just bounce off the cowhide. It's a dry, dry cowhide. I told the police you can forget about it, you can't kill those guys.

The fighting ebbed and flowed round Potgieter's terracotta tile factory. On occasion the factory itself was overrun. 'It was during the daytime,' remembers Potgieter:

Guys were running away through the factory. Then in came the guys with the AKs. Right in front of my office. One of my staff was standing up against the wall. When this guy with the AK saw him he stopped and said, 'Sorry, sorry, sorry, my *baas*, sorry!' He was trying to tell us he was sorry he had to do this. Then he fired a shot and killed one of the guys running away. Shot him right in the back. Killed him outside my office.

Potgieter learned to live with the battles in Phola Park. He bought two trailers to take the dead down to the Transkei. 'Every time it costs me 600 rand in transport.' A bizarre *modus vivendi* evolved, allowing the factory to operate in the middle of a war. 'I saw this one guy on the road next to my factory,' he says. 'He was underneath a cowskin with his AK. You could see the thing firing. He looked at me and he said, "Go through!" Then he started firing again at the guys. That is the way they treat me here.'

Potgieter realized early on that people in Phola Park had taken the law into their own hands:

There's a hell of a criminal element. It got to a stage where people said, "You steal a car, you bring it to Phola Park, you're out. If you steal something and run into Phola Park, and they shoot at you, we throw you out." I think the whole community just turned against those criminals. They killed them. If they can get hold of someone and they know the police are looking for him they kill him there and then. I've seen it with my own eyes. They kill them, I'm telling you now. If it's one of their own guys they will flatten his shack and tell him, "Go!" They don't believe in a system where you have to go through the whole thing, call the police, give evidence. If you're bad, you're out. You're dead. It just happens.

The factory acquired its own defence unit. 'They were very well trained,' says Potgieter. 'Some guys pinched 70 000 rands' worth of copper cable. The defence unit investigated and found those guys. I can't tell you what happened to them,' he adds.

'That road,' he says, pointing to the factory driveway, 'that's my road. There's a moratorium on that road. If anybody touches a car or a truck on that road he will be killed. That's our lifeline. If we can't get transport through, we can't live. It's the safest road on the East Rand. The people of Phola Park have decided this factory must be protected. How they do it is their own business.'

Relations between Potgieter and the White policemen who patrol the shanty town have been tense. 'There were elements in the police that were bad. I was a marked man,' he recalls. 'A policeman put a gun to my head. I always said to them, "You don't burn shacks down. If you kick it down you have to build it up again. You don't call them *kaffers*, that's not the way to do it." The problem was the police called up guys who didn't know how to handle people like this. They thought it was cowboys and indians. But there's been a big change,' he ends with optimism.

Potgieter describes himself as an Afrikaner nationalist. He dissociates himself from the Afrikaner right wing, with a sorrowful shake of the head. 'The AWB [Afrikaner Resistance Movement] drink here in Alberton. I've heard stories that they drink in one of the hotels and say, "Let's go and shoot some *kaffers!*" I saw them with my own eyes. They stop at two o'clock on the old Vereeneging Road and use their revolvers on Phola Park. If there is return fire they just jump into their cars and drive away.'

Potgieter laughs. 'My friends in business say I'm crazy. I tell them that in a few years' time, when they are starting to do what I'm doing now, I can go and relax.' The terracotta tiles are a huge success. Phola Park is the only place in the country which manufactures them. Production costs have been slashed:

> The Corobrick cost was 500 rand per 1000 units. My cost is 168 rand per 1000 units. How did I do that? By explaining to the people what we're doing and why we're doing it. They must know what it's about . . . If you just tell them, 'Take this one and put it there,' at the end of the day, you know, they are so negative they are just doing it. But the moment you get them involved . . . Rejects came down from 54 per cent to 8 per cent . . . And the workers have told me they will only stay away on one day, and that is if Mandela dies.

Phola Park's terracotta hand-finished tiles feature in *Home Owner* interior decorating magazine and the South African Habitat catalogue. Sales are booming. 'We're going from strength to strength. It's not the money for me. Phola Park is something in your blood,' says Potgieter. 'There's something in Phola Park you won't find anywhere else.'

Potgieter is emphatically a new Afrikaner, one who believes that the future lies, not in hiding in the *laager*, within a circle of wagons, but in getting involved. 'I know exactly what's waiting for us,' he says in an evangelistic tone. 'It's going to be tough. It's going to be very, very tough. You will become nothing. But you will still be there. You will have to share. You will learn to share with other people. You will learn that your word is not always the last word. Which we used to think.'

Potgieter is brimming with business ideas for Phola Park. 'I'm trying to give back as an Afrikaner what I received from heaven,' he says earnestly. A pottery business, operated by women from Phola Park, will use the Briti kilns. A huge covered vegetable market is planned. 'My biggest business was always fruit and veg. I know 350 farmers. I will then invite hawkers to join as agents on a market licence. I will then supply to them direct from the farmers,' explains Potgieter, with missionary zeal. 'I've got 25 hectares of land by the road. I'm going to put up small factories where they can do their own thing. I've already given space to guys who want to weld.'

Potgieter has persuaded the Tokoza Town Council to install toilets in Phola Park, which will be placed in the charge of one of the shack-dwellers. People who want to use the toilets will be charged a small monthly fee, enough for the toilet-minder to live on. A security company consisting of men from Phola Park is another project Potgieter is developing. They will provide security for the whole of the Alrode South industrial area, where crime is out of control. 'I'm part of the first world. My destiny is in the third world,' says Potgieter, 'but I don't have to give up my knowledge of the first world. South Africa is going to become a first world country, I can tell you now. If we can create jobs we can stop all the problems. I think Phola Park will become a moral place. This is what we're working for.'

With his evangelizing belief in common sense and business, Potgieter has come closer to the shack-dwellers than any outsider. Unlike the other Whites who set out to help Phola Park, Potgieter, who describes himself as a realist, has embraced the basically violent nature of the shanty town and tacitly acknowledges that without the support of the militias and armed men in the community you cannot get anything done.

Potgieter has indisputably made the greatest contribution to the welfare of Phola Park. He has physically sheltered the residents in times of crisis and single-handedly provided the shanty town with its own economy. What saddens Potgieter most is when people come to him and talk nostalgically about the bad old days: 'People say, "Let's move back to apartheid, because then we had peace and something to eat." A lot of guys who came to look for jobs said to me, "My *baas*, when we still had apartheid, we knew exactly where we were standing. Now we don't know."' Potgieter shakes his head sadly. 'I couldn't believe it.'

Yet miracles do happen. Given a chance, the economic demands of the new South Africa will bring together the most unlikely bedfellows, in ways which political negotiations could never achieve. Every day Jurie, an Afrikaner multi-millionaire, drives his top-of-the-range Mercedes in and out of the most militant ANC shanty town in South Africa. He has never been touched. In a corner of the factory yard lies the compact armoured vehicle which he bought from the army in the early days as a last-ditch means of escape from Phola Park. All four tyres are flat. It has never been used.

40 The New South African

If there is such a thing as a prototype new South African, then Jacob Modise must be one of the rare examples. Jacob is a tall, unassuming twenty-seven-year-old whose soft-spoken charm conceals a driving ambition to make his first million within the next couple of years. He has every chance of succeeding. As the financial director of Teljoy's TV rental division (Teljoy is the world's third-largest TV rental company), Jacob is ultimately responsible for a budget of some 200 million rand (£40 million). His ascent up the rungs of corporate White Johannesburg has been rapid by any standards. For a Black South African it has been little short of meteoric.

Jacob was born into a Tswana-speaking family in Garankuwa, near Pretoria. His parents belonged to the township middle class which established itself in the sixties as the South African economy boomed. Jacob's father Joshua was a school principal. His mother Adelaide was a midwife in the local hospital. Joshua augmented his income by selling household appliances door-to-door on his motorbike. One of the few photographs Jacob has of his father shows a smartly dressed young man in a three-piece suit, overcoat and scarf, perched on the seat of his motorcycle with an uncertain smile. Jacob, his elder brother Simon and their parents lived in a spacious house opposite the school. Before long Joshua was earning enough to exchange his motorbike for a car, a Volkswagen Beetle. Shortly afterwards the family's quietly prosperous life was shattered. In a freak accident Joshua drove the Beetle under a bus and was instantly killed.

Six years later, Jacob's mother perished in another bizarre accident. On her way back from work by train she became trapped in the carriage doors and was dragged along the railway line for a kilometre. It was only after Adelaide's death that the family began to suspect foul play. Various relatives unexpectedly claimed the children's inheritance for themselves. One cousin even changed his surname to Modise and demanded his share of the estate. It became evident that some of Jacob's relatives resented the Modises' success. The strange circumstances of both parents' deaths aroused suspicions that *muti* (witchcraft) was involved. Jacob, and those relatives who took his side in the ensuing family feud, are convinced (without being able to prove anything) that a fatal curse was put on his parents by envious relatives.

'*Muti* is very powerful in the townships,' confirms one of Jacob's cousins. 'The Zulus use *muti* to make women love them, the Xhosas use *muti* to make people work for them. The Tswanas use *muti* to kill people.'

After spending three years at a Catholic boarding school while the family squabbled over the boys' inheritance, Jacob and his elder brother were sent to live with an aunt in a neighbouring township. The aunt in question was part of the hostile faction within the family, and Jacob remembers being left to go hungry so often that a neighbour eventually took pity on him and fed him regular hot meals after school. The inheritance which should have guaranteed the boys a comfortable living and paid for a private education somehow vanished into the pockets of various relatives.

Jacob had always excelled at school, reading widely outside the limited curriculum of the Bantu education system, which afforded Black South Africans the bare minimum of knowledge needed in order to perform menial tasks.

'It wasn't easy. In Pretoria you couldn't just go to a library, pick up a book and study. Blacks weren't allowed to do that,' says Jacob. 'And there were no books in the townships.'

Jacob devoured the small library of books his father had left behind. His teachers lent him reading matter, anxious to cultivate their star pupil. Jacob was soon top of his class in every subject, showing particular aptitude in mathematics.

Jacob's school days, in the years after the Soweto riots of 1976, coincided with the political awakening of Black South African youth. Two of Jacob's cousins were amongst the thousands of angry young men who left the country to join uMkhonto we Sizwe (MK), the ANC's guerilla army. One of them, who worked in MK's intelligence section and infiltrated South Africa after being trained abroad, used to turn up in the township and inspire the boys with stories of guerilla exploits. 'He showed me my first AK-47,' remembers Jacob. 'At the time it was the ambition of every youth in the township to be a member of MK. People had tried every peaceful means and nothing was changing. I wanted to be an MK cadre, to go right to the top.'

The police came looking for Jacob's cousin at night, barging into the house with their rifles and throwing people out of bed. One day Jacob heard that he had been caught by the South African Defence Force while crossing the border, tortured to death and burned.

Far from skipping the country to tote an AK in one of the ANC's boot camps, Jacob found himself entering the inner sanctum of South African capitalism. The Anglo-American Corporation, the largest of the five giant business conglomerates which control most of the shares on the Johannesburg Stock Exchange, had launched a cadet scheme to nurture potential young Black executives. In his final year at school Jacob's headmaster urged him to apply for one of the bursaries. The following year Jacob began his initiation into the world of big business at Johannesburg Consolidated Investments (JCI), one of the large mining houses in Anglo's empire, before going on to take a business degree at the University of the Witwatersrand ('Wits'), one of the leading (White) universities in South Africa.

Up to that time Jacob had had little contact with White South Africans and, like most Black youngsters of his generation, he detested them roundly. His only contact with Whites had been on monthly shopping expeditions to Pretoria. When asked by his tutor at JCI to write an essay on 'the role of the universities in the political arena', Jacob pointed out that the universities were part of the racist establishment and suggested that the only lasting solution to the country's problems would be for Black South Africans to pick up their AK-47s and shoot every Afrikaner in the country. Jacob's essay caused a storm in the upper echelons of the mining house. There were calls for his dismissal.

Jacob, unaware of the furore, was summoned to his tutor's office, high up in the vast steel-and-glass headquarters of JCI. He was accused of writing 'racist stuff' and informed that the essay had been circulated around JCI and that his views had made a lot of people very upset. Jacob blinked in amazement as the essay was torn up and tossed into the wastepaper basket. 'Don't think it's been forgotten,' warned his tutor angrily, producing a photocopy of the offending text from his drawer with a dramatic flourish.

'What I wrote actually got a lot of people upset,' reflects Jacob:

But it was an honest feeling. Back then I didn't mince my words. With hindsight obviously it was an over-generalization, it was wrong. They were youthful views based on my experiences in the township. As I grew up I saw so much violence. I began to believe that the only way to change things was through violence. Later on when I went to varsity I discovered that all Whites were not the same and realized that violence doesn't solve anything. By talking to someone you can change his attitudes. If you shoot him, all that's going to happen is the kids will grow up and perpetuate the whole thing, and hate you because you shot their dad. You can be a guerilla and fight for your people. But you can also be a chartered accountant and interact with people in business and change their attitudes that way. In my own way I am also helping to liberate my people.

After obtaining a business degree, Jacob stayed on at Wits to qualify as a chartered accountant, becoming one of only two dozen Black chartered accountants in South Africa. For the next three years, at the end of a long day's work as a financial planner in JCI's Gold Division, Jacob would spend his nights studying for a Master's Degree in Business Administration from

Wits Business School. After completing the MBA, at the age of twenty-six, Jacob became one of the best-qualified executives of his age in the country.

One summer day Jacob was driving his white sixteen-valve Golf GTI through the streets of Johannesburg with the stereo turned right up, when he spotted two particularly attractive young schoolgirls. They turned and ogled Jacob, his Ray-Ban Aviators and his fast car. Although he was late for an appointment, Jacob couldn't resist stopping to give them a lift. Mary, a slender, strikingly beautiful eighteen-year-old, caught his eye immediately. He found out that she was appearing that night in a beauty contest organized by one of the Soweto football clubs, the Orlando Pirates. Jacob drove back to Soweto that evening and was in the audience to watch her being crowned the Pirates' beauty queen. It wasn't long before the couple were living together in a rented flat in Johannesburg. Two years later they moved to a neat, white-walled modern villa with two garages and a swimming pool, on the edge of the upmarket White suburb of Sandton. Within a few months Mary was pregnant with the couple's first child, a son whom they named Buikanyo ('Trust').

Mary grew up in Soshanguve, a few kilometres from where Jacob spent his youth. Her father was a township businessman who owned several taxis. When Mary was ten years old her father, like Jacob's parents, became a victim of his own success. 'One day my father sold a car to a friend of his,' she remembers:

> When my father went round to ask for the money he kept on postponing the payments. This guy and his friends then planned to kill my father because he kept on coming to collect the money and became a nuisance. They stabbed him all over, but the stab that actually killed him was next to his heart. The blood was all over my father's friend's yard. They tried to clean it up but some of the stains were left. They even took my father to hospital after they stabbed him. Then they sent a person to tell my mother he had been killed. That person was one of the murderers. Can you imagine that? There were six guys who did it. Three of them died immediately after we buried my father. My father's friend also owned taxis, but they all broke down and now he's got nothing. At the time I swore I wouldn't die before killing that man. I prayed that God would take everything they had, because they were jealous of what my father had. It made me realize people are not happy if you succeed. To them it's a threat.

Jacob keeps a Smith and Wesson 0.38 Special pistol loaded with dum-dum bullets in the glove-box of his maroon 3-litre Ford Sapphire. At night the hand gun lies within arm's reach in the bedroom, or, on the frequent occasions when Jacob works late into the night, hidden under a pile of documents on the kitchen table, next to the computer. 'I don't want my son to grow up the way I did, with the same hardships and jealousies,' says Jacob. 'That's why I moved to a White suburb.'

After an association with Johannesburg Consolidated Investments of nearly ten years, Jacob began to feel restless. He had almost completed the company's executive development programme, and there was the prospect of a middle-management post in the coal division at the end of it. But Jacob's career at JCI wasn't moving fast enough. Although he had blended in well and had won the respect of even the hard-boiled Afrikaners on the mines, JCI was too large and slow-moving for Jacob to reach the top in less than a decade. Every week the phone rang with job offers from South African Breweries, BMW or some other blue-chip corporation but Jacob viewed most of the overtures with suspicion.

Rumours had been going round in White business circles that a future ANC-led government would impose quotas for the number of Blacks at management level in the large corporations, in order to redress the imbalances created by apartheid. South African big business was scrambling to recruit from the tiny pool of qualified Black professionals before the supply dried up. In some cases a senior position turned out to offer little more than a luxury car and a fat pay cheque, with no real power or responsibility. Jacob was determined not to fall into the trap of becoming a token Black in a White corporation.

The approach which finally tempted Jacob away from JCI came from Lucia Rose at Executive Resources, a corporate head-hunting agency specializing in both Black and White executives at senior level. Lucia had been impressed by Jacob after being introduced to him at a cocktail party. When Teljoy, the biggest TV rentals company in the country, hired her to track down a young, ambitious executive combining a knowledge of the Black market with strong accounting skills, Jacob was the first name on her shortlist.

After agonizing for six weeks, Jacob finally succumbed to Lucia's persuasion, left JCI and moved into Teljoy's TV-shaped headquarters in downtown Johannesburg. He rapidly mastered the financial nuts and bolts of the TV rentals business and within five months was promoted to financial director of the rentals division. His first boss at Teljoy, John Stoffberg (a man not given to praise), describes taking Jacob on as

the best decision I made in this company. And I say that unalterably . . . Nothing to do with the racial implications. It was just a great decision. He's taken what people have thrown at him. He'll never claim any privilege. He fights by the rules. And his level of productivity is extremely high. If Jacob says he'll have something ready for me at eight o'clock, I can walk into a board meeting with what he's typed. But I think what is phenomenal, given the circumstances of the last few

years, is that a guy like that can come out with no chip on his shoulder
– or no visible chip on his shoulder – and succeed to his level in such
a quick time. I think that's remarkable.

Jacob is probably the closest his country has to a 'new South African',
someone who who can cross the immense gulf between the two South
Africas, Black and White, while retaining the ability to move confidently
in both. Significantly, Jacob belongs to a tiny but vigorous social class of
Black yuppies, flourishing in areas traditionally monopolized by Whites.
Their material ambitions are far greater than those of any previous
generation of Black South Africans, and they have every expectation of
fulfilling those ambitions. It is these self-assured young capitalists, rather
than the huddled masses of Black poor, who will reap the fruits of decades
of struggle by the African National Congress and its allies.

Being a new South African, however, has its drawbacks. In a country
where Black and White have been physically separated for so long there is
no precedent, no ready-made identity available to a person who moves
freely between the two worlds. 'It's confusing at times, you know,' admits
Jacob:

> It's like you put on a different hat all the time. You go into the
> township and you become a completely different person, you become
> Black again. Then you come into the business world, which is basically
> White-dominated, and you have to adapt once more. It's not easy. In
> both worlds you're looked at differently. In the business world you're
> looked at as a Black person, you have to constantly prove that you can
> perform in whatever position you hold. In the township some people
> still see you as a sell-out for going into a White environment. They
> look at your flashy car and think you're either a cop or a traitor, so
> they don't treat you the same as the others. To be rejected by the
> people you grew up with is not easy to accept. It hurts.

When the nostalgia for the buzz of township life and the sheer boredom
of existence in the White suburbs become too great, Jacob takes a trip to
the township with Vusi, another upwardly mobile young executive at
Teljoy. Vusi knows all the best shebeens in Alexandra township ('Alex'),
an area of 4 square kilometres crammed with 400 000 people, the so-called
'dark city' in the middle of the White suburb of Sandton. Vusi was born
in Alex and is reluctant to move from his spacious home on the East Bank,
an upmarket development just across the narrow Jukskei river from one of
Alex's many shanty towns.

Despite the fact that Alex is the car-theft capital of South Africa, Vusi's
gleaming red BMW is off-limits to car-jackers. In Alex, as elsewhere in
South Africa, the moneyed township elites, who drink in the same shebeens
and drive similar luxury cars, include not only yuppies and traders, but the

respectable gangsters in the area as well. Vusi is well-connected and can drive his BMW in Alex with impunity. Only when he and Jacob enter the war-torn streets of Beirut section on their way to the shebeens of Alex, past the acres of rubble and dozens of gutted houses overlooked by the vast, multi-storey Alex hostels, does Vusi touch the accelerator of his BMW with a little more urgency, allowing the shiny red car with its two new South African passengers to glide out of war's desolation and back into the familiar, friendly streets of Alex.

41 Breakfast in Phola Park

It is often said that the first world and the third exist side by side in South Africa. Nowhere else can one enjoy a cappuccino in an air-conditioned mall (indistinguishable – White shoppers, Black cleaners and all – from any upmarket mall in Los Angeles or London) and ten minutes later be in the mud streets of an African shanty town, where warriors brandishing spears and cowhide shields confront children armed with Russian-made assault rifles. Few Whites make the journey, for although only a few metres may separate the township from the city, in the mind of a White South African they are continents apart. Perhaps an excursion to the war-torn townships should be made mandatory for all Whites in the new South Africa, in the same way that impenitent German civilians were herded past the horrors of Auschwitz by the Allied troops who liberated the death camps.

A similar idea was suggested by Peter Mokaba, the outspoken president of the ANC Youth League, famous for his dynamic toyi-toyi and his booming rendition of 'Kill the Boer! Kill the farmer!' at mass meetings. He has proposed (not entirely facetiously) that Phola Park should become a destination for cultural tourism in the new South Africa, a place where Whites seeking to broaden their horizons can learn about life in an African shanty town, while boosting the local economy by bed-and-breakfasting in tourist shacks.

Alternatively South Africa can wait until the much-heralded economic recovery, with its new opportunities for social mobility, gradually erases the legacy of apartheid. There is nothing like prosperity to make people forget the past. As the economy begins (however slowly) to open up, admitting Blacks to better-paid jobs, a class structure will begin to replace the segregated tribal culture of apartheid. Already Black yuppies live in the same suburbs and play golf at the same country clubs as their White counterparts. Their offspring romp freely in each other's back gardens and attend the same private schools. At the other end of the scale, a few poor Whites have moved into the shanty towns of Durban and Cape Town. Perhaps their children will grow up speaking an African language.

If the economy does not perform the necessary miracle, however, South Africa will inevitably slide further into anarchy. The country has been treading water economically since 1990, throwing into reverse the general trend of upward mobility in the Black townships which began in the fifties and ushered millions of rural Blacks into the urban first world. The sons and daughters of these first-generation urbanites have grown up with first-world aspirations, though often without the education to match. Today South Africa can offer them little more than third-world opportunities. Too often the only career path with good prospects in the townships lies in the criminal underworld.

The ANC's Freedom Charter of 1955 called for 'the national wealth of our country, the heritage of all South Africans' to be 'restored to the people'. The redistribution of White South Africa's ill-gotten gains is nowadays no more than a remote possibility, for the ANC's economic advisers are only too aware of the need to keep investors happy. Instead of confiscating capitalists' assets, Mandela is showering them with tax breaks. Millions of South Africans who believe that once an ANC-led government assumes power it will take action to improve their lives materially stand to be disappointed.

The absence of an economic boom will prolong the civil war. The government will then have little choice but to deploy the iron fist of the new National Defence Force. In doing so it may have to assume emergency powers. If, however, the government shrinks from tough and decisive measures, leaving the job of curbing the violence to a police force which is hopelessly undermanned, demoralized and ridden with militant right-wingers, the war will simply drag on, and total war – as seen on the East Rand – may spread to other townships.

The fate of the besieged hostels, at any rate, will have to be decided soon. With the hardening of attitudes amongst township residents, they are unlikely to be left standing for much longer. If the hostels are evacuated under security force protection, Zulu migrant workers in the southern Transvaal will lose their jobs en masse. This would be preferable, however, to the slaughter which would follow the inevitable military defeat of the hostels by the comrades.

The Zulu civil war in Natal will continue to present the biggest single obstacle to peace in South Africa. Buthelezi has threatened to take the Natal-KwaZulu region out of South Africa if his demands for regional autonomy are not met. Should he opt for secession, the new government of national unity would be forced to consider military intervention. The dangers of a so-called 'Savimbi option' have been much debated (Jonas Savimbi's faction in the Angolan civil war refused to accept the results of the 1993 general election and decided to fight it out on the battlefield). Neither Inkatha nor the KwaZulu government, however, has the military capability to challenge the South African Defence Force. Moreover Buthelezi's besieged constituencies are on the verge of capitulating, now that the ANC has gained the upper hand in most of Natal and large parts of KwaZulu. For its part the ANC in Natal is belatedly wooing Zulu traditionalists by promoting itself as an enthusiastic guardian of Zulu culture. Nowadays when Mandela attends a rally in Durban he is preceded by Zulu praise-singers and *inyangas* dressed in skins and makes a point of being blessed by the witchdoctors in full view of the audience.

As for South Africa's five million Whites, should the civil war persist they will doubtless retreat further inside their fortresses, buy yet more guns and wait for better days. Little will change in their lives, in spite of their fears. Whites will effectively retain their pre-eminence in the economy, the professions, the security forces and the civil service. They possess too much wealth and too many skills to be alienated by the powers-that-be in the new South Africa. They will continue to live, much as they do now, in ignorance of the Black world around them. The well-intentioned will be wearing blue ribbons on Peace Day, while the sceptics will be queuing at the shooting ranges. For the truly adventurous, however, there is always bed and breakfast in Phola Park.

Glossary

abaFana   small boys
abungubu   war blankets
amaButhu   Zulu warriors
amaKosi   Zulu chiefs
amaSela   criminal fraternity
assegai   spear
baas   boss
bakkie   pick-up truck
Bantustan   Black reserve or 'homeland'
boerewors   sausage
braai   barbecue
button   Mandrax tablet
comrade   ANC-supporting township youth
dagga   cannabis
iChaka   Zulu (derogatory)
impi   Zulu regiment
impipi   police spies
induna   Zulu headman
intelezi   battle-medicine, said to make men brave
inyanga   medicine man, witchdoctor
kaffer   Afrikaans term for Black (derogatory)
knobkerrie   wooden club
kombi   van
kraal   homestead
kwatcha   home-made gun
muti   magic potion, said to protect against bullets
nommer   member of one of the three most powerful prison gangs
panga   long, sharp machete
shebeen   illegal bar or drinking den
skebeng   hood, gangster
stamp   Xhosa corn porridge
tsotsi   gangster
umKomboti   sorghum beer

List of Abbreviations

ANC   African National Congress
APLA   Azanian People's Liberation Army
AWB   Afrikaner Weerstandsbeweging (Afrikaner Resistance Movement)
COSAS   Congress of South African Students
COSATU   Congress of South African Trade Unions
IDT   Independent Development Trust
IFP   Inkatha Freedom Party
MK   uMkhonto we Sizwe (Spear of the Nation), military wing of the ANC
PAC   Pan-Africanist Congress of Azania
SADF   South African Defence Force
SAP   South African Police
SDU   Self-Defence Unit
SRC   Student Representative Council
UDF   United Democratic Front

Index